The Father, The Son and The and The Ghostly Hole

Rory
McGrath

The Father, The Son and The Ghostly Hole

Growing Up Catholic

(Growing Down Lapsed Catholic)

EBURY
PRESS

1 3 5 7 9 10 8 6 4 2

First published in 2010 by Ebury Press, an imprint of Ebury Publishing
A Random House Group company

The Random House Group Limited Reg. No. 954009

Addresses for companies within the Random House Group can be found at
www.randomhouse.co.uk

A CIP catalogue record for this book is available from the British Library

The Random House Group Limited supports The Forest Stewardship
Council (FSC), the leading international forest certification organisation.
All our titles that are printed on Greenpeace approved FSC certified paper
carry the FSC logo. Our paper procurement policy can be found at
www.rbooks.co.uk/environment

Mixed Sources
Product group from well-managed
forests and other controlled sources
www.fsc.org Cert no. TT-COC-2139
© 1996 Forest Stewardship Council

Designed and set by seagulls.net

Printed and bound in Great Britain by CPI Mackays, Chatham, ME5 8TD

ISBN 9780091924614

To buy books by your favourite authors and register for offers visit
www.rbooks.co.uk

To my parents,
for all their brilliant work in difficult circumstances.

Chapter 1

No Big Bang

Darkness.

No, not darkness; this was before darkness.

Absence of light.

And darkness. Absence of light and darkness.

And everything.

Void.

The universe is compacted into a teeny-weeny ball. No bigger than something non-existent. Then for some reason it explodes, scattering bits of space, mass, energy and time all over the cosmic shop. After this there was a mess of unimaginable dimensions, mainly made of quark-gluon plasma and possibly a supermarket trolley. The expansion slowed down and the temperature fell and things like neutrons, protons and electrons formed alongside their absolutely non-identical twins: anti-neutrons, anti-electrons, etc. Then hydrogen comes along and helium and all sorts of other atoms. These start combining to form molecules and larger structures like proteins and amino acids. These then combine to form complex organisms like nerves, which then join together in a neurotic tangle to produce something called pain. All the pain in the universe. This pain fills up the inside of a spheroid cavity of bone called a cranium. That is, my cranium; part of my head.

My head, which is trapped in a block of concrete. The darkness is solid. Breathing is difficult.

I pass out.

I come round.

My head is now trapped in a block of jelly. The darkness is squishy.

I pass out.

I come round.

Half-light.

Drizzly half-light.

Head, encrusted with scales now; lolling uselessly.

A far-off creaking noise.

A heavy door.

A dungeon door.

Slabs of ancient timber and massive bolts being forced open against centuries of rust and disuse.

A deafening jolt as the buckling ironwork grates to a halt.

A strip of vertical light.

No, not light. A thin column of paler darkness.

Criss-crossed by horizontal bars.

Iron. No, wood.

No, thinner than that.

Almost like eyelashes. Eyelashes.

One of my eyes has opened slightly …

Dry mouth. Needed to lick lips.

Not possible.

No lips.

No lips?

Can't lick my lips because I haven't any.

What happened to my lips?

Wrong. False alarm.

No tongue.

My tongue has gone.

It has been replaced.

By a hedgehog.

At some time in the night, a hedgehog, a seriously wounded hedgehog, crawled into my mouth to die.

The next procedure requires a considerable, concerted effort from both mind and body.

I brace myself, take a deep breath and grit my teeth.

Every muscle in the body is tensed.

Pause.

Here goes.

Three … two … one.

Yes, it worked.

The other eye opens.

I can see. But what is it that I see?

A few feet above my head.

Flat, whitish, square. Almost like a ceiling.

A ceiling, yes, I am in a place with a ceiling! Ceiling is good. Place with ceiling probably has walls.

A building.

I am inside a building.

I'm not asleep between the recycling bins at Sheffield bus station. Again.

Further inspection reveals a neatly furnished bedroom.

Warm. Soft. Feminine. The comfort I feel from this observation is short-lived.

The arm that suddenly appears round my neck, gentle and sleepy, is not feminine. A decidedly hairy, sinewy forearm, pocked with insect-bite scabs, on the end of it a rough hand with nail-bitten fingers.

A man's arm.

I freeze.

I turn a giant mental searchlight up to full power and aim it into the abysmal ocean of last night's memory.

Emptiness.

Nothing but a pitiless blackness; a blackness relieved only by a few strange albino crustaceans, blind white slugs and bizarre jellyfish with eyes on stalks.

I see a pale, boneless sea-slug in combat with a pinkish anemone.

The echo of moaning, groaning, panting, screaming, crying. A benthic world of hints, suggestions and half-formed memories.

Certainly nothing about pub, curry, disco, stripclub, gay bar and back to his.

The arm is limp and clammy. The hair makes it crinkle disgustingly. With some trepidation, I begin tracing its provenance, starting at the hand and working towards the shoulder.

The shoulder.

The shoulder is mine.

It is my arm.

Now tingling unpleasantly, as my remaining blood struggles back up its tubules. The feeling in my limbs returns, along with a disturbing memory.

The dreams.

I had those dreams again.

The alarming tapestry depicting scenes of life-threatening dehydration and bladder-bursting pain.

I get set upon by a bunch of irate ramblers after I've sucked the Lake District dry. The superego subdues the id. Your body craves, your mind represses. I'm in a sort of nightclub and I'm desperate to relieve myself; the urinals are full, the cubicles are locked, or broken, or have no doors. I go to the ladies, but I'm reported to the management, the police come. I'm put in a cell and as part of the punishment I'm not allowed to go to the toilet. My bladder and intestines are knotted with agony. Now I'm on the banks of the River Toilet, which is in full spate. A torrent of piss and shit a mile wide and a million miles long heading to the Sea of Faeces. I eagerly drop my trousers, when two soldiers appear and inform me at gunpoint that there is no pissing or shitting allowed here. And then the worst dream of all. The dream that when I've finally found a place to relieve myself, and struggle to liberate the appropriate instrument, shrivelled and impossible to aim, I let go a torrent of urine and pain which is replaced by freedom and bliss. This lasts for a couple of seconds until I realise it was a dream and my bladder is still solid with fire and fluid.

My arm has stopped tingling and feels as if it has rejoined my body. I put it under the duvet. I feel the sheet. There is a moistness there which can only be described as 'unbedly'.

The superego has let me down badly.

Water.

Yes, water, that's what I need.

The hedgehog was stirring in my mouth and was thirsty.

Two glasses on the bedside table with water in. Perfect. Down in one. Both of them. Although it has the effect of one raindrop landing in the middle of Death Valley, the water was welcome.

I get out of bed. The building is clearly struggling through heavy seas as I stumble around in search of a toilet.

I find it and power-drill grooves into the side of the toilet bowl. Heaven. Steamy, dark yellow heaven with a slight scent of corned beef.

I reel towards the window. I open the curtains an inch.

BANG.

The daylight is merciless. The blow is struck without restraint, vertically downwards like a scimitar splitting me cleanly, but brutally, from the crown of my skull to my scrotum. God's searchlight. No escape. He knows. All night He has waited outside the window while I was sinning. At the moment I stirred and opened the curtains, the blade of accusing light left me in shreds.

I steady myself on the window ledge and look outside for clues. A sports ground. Could be a school. A row of bungalows, one with a 'For Sale' notice. 'For sale'. That's English. At least I was still in England. Or an English-speaking country, anyway. Hills in the distance. Rolling, wooded hills. I'm not in London then. Certainly no part of London that I knew. My head thumps from the Almighty light and I lie back on the bed and give in to the hangover as it punches me with fists of dehydration, hunger, indigestion, guilt, self-loathing, emptiness and loss. A mild erection stirs as if to ridicule me further with its pathetic redundancy.

I get up again to see if the room offers any answers to the questions fizzing around inside my cranium. Where am I? Where have I been? Who was I with? Who am I with? Who am I? How did it all begin? Was there a big bang?

On the wall opposite the window, a mirror. I've always thought mirrors are treacherous and evil. I detest mirrors. Maybe I've got some vampire blood in me.

Mirrors are like cameras; they never lie. I hate cameras, as well. I want something that *does* lie.

I take a long, hard, close-up look at myself. It's not pretty.

Large red areas, pinky-purply blotches, jagged blue-black lines and some sickly, pale green patches I've never noticed before. Not pretty.

Then a horrible realisation dawns.

It's not a mirror at all; it's a political map of pre-War Europe.

It's strange how small details strike you and stay with you, even in a state of extreme dysfunction. I suddenly notice what an interesting collection of tiny countries Yugoslavia used to be. Well, like it is now in fact. It's gone back to being what it was. What an arrogant and punitive imposition the state of Yugoslavia must have been on these proud, distinct and distinctive communities. And what a weird thing to have crossing your mind at that moment.

'Milk and sugar?' comes a shout from downstairs.

Milk and sugar? What does that mean? A girl's voice. But I'm not ready for answering questions; any questions at all. My faculties are certainly not sufficiently warmed up to handle one like 'Milk and sugar?'.

A brain-teaser.

Looking back, I realise that she was making me a cup of tea and was requesting information on my preferred form of said beverage. Now, of course, it's obvious that the answer should have been something along the lines of 'yes', 'just milk', 'just sugar' or 'neither'.

But not, 'Isn't Macedonia tiny!'.

'What did you say?'

'Er … Just milk, thanks.'

I flop back into bed and I hear footsteps on the stairs. The steps get louder. And closer. They stop outside the door. I hear the handle being turned. The door opens slowly. This could prove to be a highly awkward moment. The first things to appear round the door are two very large, steaming mugs of tea. They are painted with bright, childish farm animals. One a black-and-white smiley cow and one a bright pink piggy-wiggy. Then there appears a short, plump totally naked girl with red hair, pale wispy pubes and massive, pendulous breasts.

As far as I know, I've never ever seen her before.

'Nice mugs,' I offer.

'Yeah, I don't get them out that often.'

'Really?'

'Well, I don't have guests for breakfast very often.' She chuckles coyly.

This is definitely one of those times for a tactical 'You are lovely, you know'. It's useful for buying a bit of time in a difficult situation and it wrong-foots the opposition.

'You are lovely, you know!'

'Ah, that's nice.' She goes red. (In an interesting and unexpected variety of places.) 'Do you actually remember anything about last night?'

'Er, last night? … It was dark.'

'Anything else?'

'Let's hazard a guess and say strong drink was taken.'

'You were paralytic. We didn't have sex, you know.'

This would normally be too much information, but in the circumstances it is very useful.

I smile and nod gallantly and say, 'I don't do that sort of thing. Not on the first night anyway. I *am* a gentleman, you know.'

She puts down the mugs and sits on the bed. She is beginning to look less friendly.

'Oh, you *tried* to have sex with me. Almost non-stop.' She pauses and frowns. 'But nothing was, er ... available.'

I breathe in slowly to say something but my mouth and my brain appear to have fallen out and are not speaking to each other. Luckily she carries on talking.

'It never lets you down, apparently, but sometimes you may have to wait up to twenty-four hours, you said.'

The dim image of a pale, boneless sea-slug in combat with a pinkish anemone pops unbidden into my head.

'It's penile dementia,' I explain. 'Sometimes I don't know if I'm coming or going.'

She tuts.

I try again. 'You are lovely, you know.'

This one misses the target by a considerable distance. A silence follows.

'You did suck my breasts for a while, though.'

'I should hope I did. They're lovely.'

That's good. Cheeky but complimentary.

'But you stopped sucking them when the waiter brought your chicken biryani over.'

Not so good.

'Are you sure it was me you were with last night?'

'Well, you're here now, aren't you?'

'Am I though? What is "is" and what is "here"?' I venture, hoping she'll find this enigmatic and engaging.

'Now, you're talking like a twat!'

She doesn't.

Now I am panicking. She leans towards me with unspoken menace.

I take a couple of unseemly glugs of tea. There must be a way of turning this situation round and making today a very good day. I rack the small part of my brain that is still available for racking. I'm sure if I handle this well enough, I could get her back into bed for a few more hours' sleep, wake up, make love, have a full English breakfast, go back to bed for more sex, find out whereabouts in England I am, go home and never see her again. Such a shame my brain's Charm and Ingenuity department is so short-staffed on this morning.

'You don't even remember my name, do you?' she says abruptly.

That is true, but when I drank the two glasses of water, I noticed they were resting on a pile of post.

'That's where you're wrong!' I glance across at the top envelope.

'You are …'

'Yes?'

'Er … the Occupier!'

I feel a good outcome to this situation is rapidly edging out of my reach.

She sits down on the bed and fixes me with a brown-eyed stare. She is waiting for me to say something; she is waiting for an apology for something; something I couldn't remember; something I may not even have done. I would outstare her. I'm not going to cave in with shame and apologise for something non-existent. No! Sod her. A minute passed. It was too much.

'I'm sorry,' I say, riddled with shame.

'What for?' she says.

She is trying to catch me out but I have the perfect, non-specific reply.

'I'm sorry for, er … everything!'

'Don't be daft!' she scoffs.

'Everything in the world that has happened that is evil or unpleasant is my fault. I am solely responsible for the sad state of humanity.' I put my hand over my face and she laughs.

'Are you a Roman Catholic or something?'

Am I a Roman Catholic? Where did that question come from? The last question in the world I expected her to ask.

'You could say that. Lapsed, actually.' I smile, adding, 'Collapsed, more like!'

I sit up on the bed and look out of the window and memories flood instantly back. My parents proudly watching my First Holy Communion, my children being baptised, my first wedding in Holy Joe's, the smell of candles, the excitement of Midnight Mass at Christmas, the purple shrouds on the statues in Holy Week, the beguiling mystery of Latin hymns, the nerves before confession, the guilt of not confessing some sins, the guilt of not going to confession any more, the guilt of sinning and sinning and sinning and sinning and sinning and sinning and sinning. A melancholy hymn comes back to me.

'*Agnus Dei, qui tollis peccata mundi, miserere nobis* – Lamb of God, who takest away the sins of the world, have mercy on us.'

I dryly swallow another mouthful of tea as tears begin to prick my eyes. And then, as if I am being punished further by my angry God, a pair of jays appears on the tree outside the window. Handsome crows, male and female very similar. Birds that mate for life. Devoted to each other. A pair of Js. JJ. I think of JJ, the girl I'd met when I was a student. How cruel of God to bring her back to me at that moment. JJ, the stunning girl who taught me about the birds and the bees. And the birds. But not the bees. The small slender girl whose pretty, sunlit face had touched my body, mind and soul and left its image on me like a birthmark. The best girl ever. The only girl ever. Where is she now? What happened to her? Happily married with lovely children? Locked in my past never to escape? Forbidden to me for ever? Oh, JJ, where are you now? Please come back and get me. Take me home with you and we shall live happily ever after.

A scream of anguish brings me back to the present. My naked hostess is jumping up and down agitatedly, her breasts swaying from side to side.

'Oh my God! My contact lenses!'

What's she on about now?

'I couldn't find a case last night and put them in two glasses of water. Left and right. By my side of the bed!'

I cough. A mysterious dryness in my throat.

The day is beyond recovery.

Well, it is now, as she pulls back the duvet to reveal something that surprises even me.

'Oh my God! That's disgusting.'

If only I'd been on a starship mission on an alien planet in a distant galaxy, I could have said, 'Beam me up, Scottie.'

I say it anyway.

'Beam me up, Scottie.'

Nothing happens.

Nothing except a sensation of pain; the pain generally associated with scalding liquid coming into rapid contact with human male genitalia.

Take me back, God, please, take me back; back to a time of innocence ...

Chapter 2

Introducing the Good Catholic Boy

'… And I baptise thee Patrick Rory, in the name of the Father and of the Son and of the Holy Ghost.'

And everybody says, 'Amen.'

(Except for me.)

I'm not there, you see.

Well, I am sort of.

My part today is being played by a screaming, wriggling splodge; the pink bundle of cuteness having failed to show up.

Everyone is given a candle.

(Except me; I'm too young to play with fire.)

The priest says, 'Shine as a light in the world against sin and the devil.'

Everyone says, 'Amen.'

(Except for me, because I can't say anything, least of all the Hebrew for 'so be it'.)

Amen, indeed.

It's over and I am clean.

Pure. Spotless. Unblemished. Immaculate. The sin of Adam has been washed away. I am stainless. I am stain-free. I am without stain. There is no stain upon me.

'What's that brown stain?' chuckles my father. 'That brown stain; I think he needs his nappy changed.'

But my soul is white, blindingly bright white and full of grace.

'What is my soul, Mummy?' I ask a few years later when I'm old enough to enquire about things like that.

'Well, it's the place in your body where God's grace is kept,' she replies earnestly.

'Is it on the bottom of your foot, Mummy?'

'No, that sounds the same but it's a different thing.'

'Whereabouts in the body is the soul, then?' I ask and from the various answers I glean that your soul is *in* your body but can't be seen. It's like your mind only different. Your mind is something to do with your brain and your soul isn't. Your soul is part of your body but not part of your body; it is all your body but none of your body.

'And what is grace, then?' I ask, knowing that my mother will definitely know the answer. I am at the age when mothers know the answers to everything.

'What's grace?' she repeats. 'Mmm, why don't you go and ask your father?'

'What's grace, Daddy?' I ask and, not looking up from the outspread *Daily Express*, he replies, 'It's a prayer of thanks you say before you have a meal. Or after a meal. Depending on whether it's grace before meals or grace after meals.'

I'm not sure, but I feel that my dad has answered a different question. He goes on, 'Grace before meals: "Bless us, O Lord, and these thy gifts which we are about to receive from thy bounty, Amen."'

I make a mental note to ask one day whether the Bounty is a milk-chocolate, blue-wrapper or a plain-chocolate, red-wrapper, and I persevere with questions about the other sort of grace. And sin.

'What is sin, Daddy?'

'Sin? Ooh, that's one for your mum!'

'Sin is something bad,' she tells me. 'Something wrong. A naughty thing. It's something evil that annoys, upsets or hurts another person or God.'

'Does everybody sin, then?'

'Only bad people.'

'So you and Daddy don't sin then?' I ask.

She replies without hesitation: 'Come on, go and do your teeth!'

The questioning goes on until I am happy with my understanding of the subject, or until I am bored with the subject, or until *Noggin the Nog* starts.

I can't remember when I made the decision, long after this conversation I'm sure, but one thing became clear. I would never have a child of mine baptised in the Catholic Church. My child was going to be blemish-free, with no God to say otherwise. There would be no soul to clean because the soul would be spotless, as only a non-existent soul could be. And my child would not be baptised *just in case* we were wrong about God, life, death, the universe and everything. My child would not be baptised just to impress Catholic friends and relations or to get in with the clergy because they may run the best primary schools in the area. My child would not be baptised. Categorically. Not.

But back in those childhood days, after awkward and frustrating question-and-answer sessions with my parents, I did actually learn something; something fundamental and magical about the nature of holiness; and this is what I learnt: the soul is a small container about the size of a box of Black Magic chocolates, but white. The outside is glowing white velvet. Or possibly corduroy. That's the stripy one. In my mind, *my* soul is corduroy. It is lined with a creamy-coloured satin or silk. Though I probably don't have any idea what satin and silk are or how they differ. Like velvet and corduroy. Four-year-old boys don't really do 'fabrics'. The soul is where God's grace is kept if you have any. Grace is love, protection, excellence or power given by God to those who deserve it; those whose soul is still shiny bright and not darkened or sullied by the soot of sin. I like to think of it as lumps of gold too shiny almost to look at. Or golden dust consisting of tiny particles of light which is impossible to hold because it's so fine. As a baby you start off with a black mark on your soul because of Adam but at baptism this is wiped off and you start with a clean slate.

So, oblivious to the fact that for the first, and only, time in his whole life he is free from sin, the recently baptised Patrick Rory is carried up the dark aisle of the church. The door creaks open; a shaft of light glances across the baby's face. (Blinding, critical light after darkness will become familiar.) This light, which is to illuminate the path of goodness and ward off evil, cuts painfully into the baby's eyes and makes little Rory scream and cry as he leaves the church into the bright spring morning.

Chapter 3

Introducing Danny, Strobo and Jonesy

After the sanctimonious gloom of the church, the daylight made me wince and squeezed a tear from my left eye. I put my sunglasses on and walked the tantalisingly short distance from the side door of the Sacred Heart to the back door of the White Hart. My reflection in the pub window as I approached looked faintly ludicrous, a man in a sharp black suit and shades. A publicity still from the middle-aged remake of *Reservoir Dogs*. I was Mr Ruddy.

Strobo was outside the pub holding a small baby and a large vodka and Coke. His constantly blinking eyes gave him a look of perpetual wonderment, but his pallor was witness to his cyber-geeky life of darkened rooms and computers screens forever blinking back at him. He too was dressed *Reservoir Dogs*.

'Mr Pale,' I said. 'How did you get out so quickly?'

'Screaming kid,' he said, pointing at the now sleeping child. 'A quick pinch on the foot gets her going and you can leave any boring function early.'

I turned back to face the church and I saw Danny, also in a sharp black suit, white shirt and tie, leave the side door, wince and put on his shades. Health and fitness had never been in the top one thousand list of Danny's life choices and his face had a greeny-grey sheen to it. He seemed to be struggling as he walked the few yards from church to pub. He moved stiffly as if unable to bend his elbows and knees. He was disproportionately breathless when he reached me.

'Mr Greeny-Grey, you look knackered,' I said.

'Fuck me, I need a pint!' he wheezed.

'You look as if you're in great pain. Are you OK?'

'It's this giving up smoking. I can hardly walk,' he said, rubbing his limbs.

'That's an odd side-effect,' I suggested.

'No, it's just that I've got thirty-six nicotine patches on. All down my arms and legs. Impedes my motion, don't you know.'

I assumed he was exaggerating and we all went inside to get a drink.

'Good christening,' Danny said after a gulp of his trembling pint.

'Baptism,' I corrected. 'In a Catholic church, it's a baptism not a christening.'

'What's the difference?'

'Nothing.'

'Oh, I see,' said Danny who, out of habit, was walking towards the door to go outside for a snout break.

'You don't need to go outside if you're not smoking,' Strobo pointed out.

'I know,' he said plaintively. 'Allow me a bit of nostalgia. Let me stand in the cold and feel marginalised. It reminds me of happier, life-threatening times.'

We went outside and stood with the smokers in the cold, autumn sunlight.

'Why not "christening"?' asked Strobo.

'The thing about the word "christening", you see,' I explained, 'is that it makes it sound a bit Christian and we don't want that.'

'Aren't Catholics Christians?' was Danny's legitimate reply.

'Well, sort of. A superior sort of Christian though.'

A wave of cigarette smoke wafted over us.

'Ah,' said Danny, inhaling gratefully, 'it's nice to be out here in the foul air.'

'I found the service a bit depressing. Brings it all back to me.'

'Oh, come on,' Danny said. 'You don't remember your own chris-tening, do you?'

'Baptism,' Strobo corrected him.

'No, of course I don't. I remember my children's baptisms, though.'

Danny raised a critical eyebrow and said, 'I thought you atheists didn't do that. Or were you hedging your bets just in case you were wrong about God, life, death, the universe and everything?'

I felt a bit hypocritical but answered honestly. 'No, actually, it was because the best schools in the area were Catholic ones but they were very choosy who they let in.'

'Oh, I see,' Danny went on. 'Practising Catholics only?'

'Yes,' I answered, 'and rich Jews and Muslims.'

Danny patted himself repeatedly on one of the patches on his upper arm. 'I don't normally like going into churches but I liked the christening service.'

'Baptism,' Strobo snapped.

'I find it all totally depressing. A newborn baby coming into the world pre-stained. What a bummer! What a start to life! That sums up being a Catholic; you can't even be born pure. You're born with a shadow hanging over your life. A blot on your soul.'

'But surely you haven't had time to sin if you're a newborn nipper.'

'Exactly,' I agreed. 'It's not even your own sin. It's the sin of Adam.'

This was clearly all new to Danny. 'What sin was that?'

Strobo answered. 'He disobeyed God. He ate the forbidden fruit, the fruit of the tree of knowledge.'

'That's not much of a sin, to be fair, is it?' asked Danny as we watched some forbidden fruit walk past collecting empty glasses and taking them back inside.

I nodded, 'Yeah, a very small sin to condemn mankind for ever.'

'So why did he do it?'

'Why do men often do bad things?' I mused. 'Because a woman told him to.'

'Like you giving up smoking.' Strobo smiled at Danny.

Danny's zeal for a nicotine-free life had been of woman born. It was nothing to do with trying to lead a healthier life but because Rachel, his latest 'girlfriend', was refusing to kiss him, and by extension do anything else with him, until he'd 'kicked the habit'. This was an indication of how seriously he felt about Rachel, as Danny wasn't one to hang around after the first date if things hadn't got a little bit carnal.

'Which woman told him to?' asked Danny.

'Rachel,' said Strobo.

'Eve, of course!'

Danny seemed to recall some bits of his distant RI lessons. 'Oh yes, Eve. But she was naked, though, wasn't she? Hard to turn down a request from a naked woman.'

Danny was warming to this and I felt the conversation was about to veer away from a Bible study discussion. He went on, 'She was probably the first naked woman Adam had ever seen.'

'Er … definitely the first naked woman Adam had ever seen,' I ventured. 'Unless God had created porn mags in between creating man and woman.'

Danny was now smirking irreligiously. 'A beautiful naked woman asks you to eat the forbidden fruit, what can a poor boy do? Mind you, eating the forbidden fruit would have been well low down on my list of sinful things I would have done for her.'

'It was the devil who persuaded her to ask Adam to do it,' Strobo informed us. 'The devil in the form of a serpent said: "You should eat the forbidden fruit because you'll be like Gods and know good and evil."'

'And what did Eve say?' Danny asked.

'Fuck me, a talking snake!' I suggested.

'No, she said, "OK then" and ate the fruit and gave Adam some and as soon as they'd eaten it, they knew they were naked.'

Danny looked perplexed. 'Didn't they know they were naked till then, then?'

'No,' I answered. 'They didn't have the knowledge. That's what happens when you have the knowledge.'

'I thought you became a cabbie.' He smiled.

'You're not taking the story of creation seriously, are you?' I continued. 'There were no taxis in the Garden of Eden. People walked everywhere. Anyway, once they realised they were naked, they immediately covered up their bodies. Adam with a fig leaf and Eve, presumably, with three fig leaves.'

Danny seemed genuinely intrigued and after some thought said, 'You know, a woman wearing three fig leaves is much sexier than a naked woman.'

As we went back inside to get another round, I tried to abridge the story of creation as much as I could for Danny, telling him that the snake for his part in this was condemned to crawl on his belly for ever – which makes one think, what did the snake do before? If it wasn't already crawling on its belly, how did anyone know it was a snake? It might have been a weasel or a naked mole-rat. And, come to think of it, why did God create a talking snake in the first place? A non-talking serpent would have been in no position to beguile Eve into eating the forbidden fruit. And anyway, why did He create the forbidden fruit tree anyway if He didn't want anyone to eat from it? But then there's a case for saying that there's nothing clever in going through Genesis and making fun of it. Its logic is pretty threadbare, but it's only a silly parable written for children and simpletons. I pointed out that silly or not, we Catholics are born with the sin of Adam on our conscience and that's why we need to be cleansed at birth.

Danny looked thoughtful. 'Hang on, though. There's got to be a worry about Adam and Eve having sex with each other, hasn't there?

She was technically of his own flesh, wasn't she? That sounds a little bit Norfolk, if you know what I mean?'

Our dialectic was interrupted by the arrival of more people from the church. The ones who'd bothered to stay till the end of the service and sing all the verses of the last hymn. Included in these was a rather soppy-faced, podgy girl who studied me a little longer than was necessary. Her eyes narrowed and their glance turned into a couple of sly poisoned darts. Then I remembered.

'Ooh dear.' Danny had noticed. 'She doesn't like the look of you.'

'God' – the flashback was getting quite vivid – 'I haven't seen her for about twenty years. Last time I saw her, she was pouring scalding hot tea over my genitals.'

'Ouch.' Danny drew in a pained whistle through pursed lips. 'Was she an alternative sex-therapist or something?'

'No, a one-night stand. Without the stand, as I recall.'

Last out of the church and therefore, bizarrely, last into the pub was Jonesy, who had fallen asleep on the back pew just after the priest had said, 'Welcome to the Church of the Sacred Heart.'

Jonesy was a dishevelled, straggly long-haired fifty-something who, despite wearing a sharp dark suit and aviator glasses, still looked like a tramp. He was Wales's foremost painter and decorator and an occasional bit-part actor.

'Ah, gentlemen,' he intoned theatrically. 'Look at us: we look like the new production of *Reservoir Dogs.*'

'Yes,' I added, 'as performed by the inmates of the asylum of Charenton under the direction of the Marquis de Sade.'

'Whatever,' said Jonesy. 'Pint of Abbot, please.'

'Good sleep?' Danny asked him.

'Yes, very welcome, thank you. I love a good christening.'

'Baptism,' Strobo corrected him.

'I feel sorry for that baby though,' Jonesy continued.

Danny nods. 'Yeah, we were just talking about that. Original sin.

The stain of Adam and all that. Coming into the world with a black mark on your whole life already.'

'No.' The Welshman frowned. 'I was talking about the fucking poncey names posh people give their kids. Kitten Boots. That's child abuse that is.'

We agreed, and I recalled that Woody Allen named his son Satchel because Woody was a fan of Louis Armstrong, whose nickname, Satchmo, was short for 'satchel mouth'. 'But I imagine that when Satchel's mates say, "Hey, why are you called Satchel?" he'll probably say, "Coz my dad's a pretentious dickhead."'

Danny and Jonesy nodded.

'What's your full name then, Jonesy?' asked Danny.

'Well, I've got a normal name, thank Christ: Daffyd Elwyn Hywel Ieuan Jones.'

Strobo tutted. 'Your cruel parents! Makes you sound Welsh.'

'I am fuckin' Welsh!'

Danny sniggered. 'Oh I *am* sorry, I didn't realise.'

Jonesy harrumphed into his beer and sprayed us with froth. When he came up for air he nodded in the direction of the church where people seemed to be busy getting ready for the next service, which by the looks of the flowers and decorations was going to be a wedding.

'How ironic,' grunted Jonesy. 'Just seen someone into this world and now they're seeing someone out of it!'

Chapter 4

Introducing Sinner Boy

I struggled up the platform as far as the station exit, put my luggage down and showed my ticket. The inspector looked at it carefully. Redruth to Cambridge via London.

'You've come a long way!' he said.

'Only from the train!' I smiled eagerly.

He looked through me and muttered to his colleague, 'Another bloody smart-ass student. I hate this time of year.'

I noted the flatness of the local accent. Just like the countryside.

'No hills round there,' my mother had warned me. 'That's why it's so cold. The wind blows straight from the Arctic, across the steppes and into East Anglia. You can't have too many clothes up there.'

It was a sultry late September day and my several layers of warm, sodden clothes clung heavily to me. A mere breath of Siberian wind would be a godsend. I picked up the two suitcases and the guitar, took a deep breath and walked on as far as I could before putting them down again. I was now at the front of the station on the forecourt. Hot and panting. A long queue for non-existent taxis snaked back on itself. Right, that was decided. I'd walk. Taxis were expensive and after an assiduous hour the night before with map, magnifying glass, ruler and piece of string, I'd discovered that Emmanuel College was less than a mile from the station. Nine-tenths of mile, in fact. Easy walking distance. But I'd reckoned without the two cases containing every item of clothing I had in the world, and a catering-size jar of instant coffee, and my guitar. I could manage about twenty yards at a time before the weight and awkwardness of my belongings made me stop for a minute's breather.

This short, two-hour walk gave me plenty of time for reflection. I had left home now. This was it. My struggle from station to college emphasised my loneliness. There were tears and hugs at Redruth station but these had been forgotten by the time I got as far as Truro and the lingering homesickness replaced by a sense of adventure, excitement and danger. A sense of sin. These feelings too had gone by now and as I lumbered round the corner of Station Road into Hills Road, all I could feel was desolation. Leaving home and family now was physical and concrete. I'd left them both, to a lesser extent, when I decided to give up Church. And church.

'How come Rory's allowed to miss church and we're not?' asked my younger brother.

'No one's asking you to go to church if you don't want to,' my mother pointed out with imperceptible menace. 'I just assumed you *do* want to go.'

There was no answer.

'Will you be going to church when you're at university, do you think?' my parents asked. I knew the answer. No. Emphatically no. Categorically no. I won't even know where the Catholic church is. And I certainly won't go out of my way to find out. I'll be far too busy sinning.

'I haven't thought about it, really,' I mumbled.

But despite the minor rebellion back then, I was still at home. I was still in the predictable safety and the safe predictability of a loving family.

'Do you want a hand, mate? You look as if you're struggling,' an elderly man asked as I slumped by the traffic lights.

'No, I'm fine,' I lied. 'That's really kind but I'm only going just up there on the right.'

I'd struggle on my own. I'd accept the suffering. It was my

penance for my sins, those already committed and those yet to be even imagined.

I was the first undergraduate to arrive that year. As a language student, I had to come a few days early to do an oral exam. Because of lifts, train times and cheap tickets, I was there a week before term and was alone in college but for a hundred middle-aged heart specialists up for a conference.

The college buildings had an ancient, eerie coolness. I walked across the grass of Front Court and looked back at Christopher Wren's chapel and the pillars of the cloister. Wonderful; but I felt out of place, that I didn't belong there.

'Oi, get off the grass!' the porter blared. 'You're not a duck or a Don!'

'Sorry,' I said and scrambled onto the path.

'You a fresher?' he went on. I'd never heard the word 'fresher' before, so I was at a loss as to what to say.

'No, I'm not,' I stammered. 'I'm … er, a first year.'

The porter guffawed and walked away shaking his podgy, purple head.

'Oh, excuse me,' I asked after him. 'Do you know where the nearest Catholic church is?'

He turned a quizzical stare at me, then answered, 'Left out of the college, keep going. Can't miss it.'

And miss it you couldn't. Stately and towering over the surrounding streets, a magnificent piece of nineteenth-century Gothic revival. A church, a proper church, so different from the shabby, functional, modern constructions of the churches of my Cornish childhood. This church was, I discovered later, the highest point in the county of Cambridgeshire, no less. (But then, a lot of the county is below sea level.) But it wasn't the architecture that had drawn me there. It was the serenity. The familiar cool stillness. And the smell: the smell of candles, matches, wood polish and flowers; the smell of safety and innocence; the smell of peace. This was the first time in years I'd voluntarily entered a Catholic church. I sat down in a dark recess and felt like crying. As I walked out into the warm evening, I felt better. I made a note of the times of Mass for the following day. The latest was midday. Perfect. Well, just in case. I'd phone my parents as soon as possible and give them the good news; how close the church is to the college; what a lovely building it is; how many Masses there are; even one at midday!

* * *

In the shadowiness of Front Court, the great hall looked resplendent, illuminated from the inside with candlelight. The clanking of cutlery and plates was occasionally drowned out by the raucous merriment of a hundred top cardiologists smoking and pissing it up. I peered in at the hearty scene trying not to feel like a pauper excluded from the banquet.

To keep loneliness at bay, I decided to explore the town, visit a few pubs and chat to a few people, make some friends perhaps. The picturesque riverside city with its varied architectural finery exempted me temporarily from being the loneliest man in the world. As I crossed Magdalene Bridge, I came across a man looking intently over the railings at the river. There was something odd about him. His shoulders heaved oddly. He looked up at my approach. He was crying.

'Are you OK?' I asked. A radiance warmed his face.

'It's heaven sent you are,' he said, in an Irish way but not with an Irish accent, shaking my hand vigorously. 'Call me Slim!'

'Hello, Slim. I'm Rory.' He didn't seem that interested in my name.

'Are you a student?'

'About to be. I've just arrived.'

His smile suggested that this was the best news he'd ever had.

'Have you many friends here?' he asked and before I had time to lie to him he went on, 'This can be a very lonely city.'

'I'm sure it can,' I agreed wisely.

'I'm a philosopher by trade and as such I can make myself very unpopular with some folks.'

I was intrigued by this. I didn't realise you could be a philosopher by trade, and despite my keenness to know, I thought it impolite to ask him what sort of annual salary a philosopher could expect. And what was it in his philosophy that could make this man unpopular?

'I've been robbed by my best friend. All my money! Gone!' He heaved a heavy sigh.

'Oh no! That's terrible,' I said, not really getting a useful handle on the weighty non-sequitur.

'But there's always the river,' he said looking balefully down at the sleepy, black Cam. He looked me in the eyes and gravely pronounced, 'Life and death are the same river. Once you're in it, how can you know which is which?' He grabbed the railings suddenly as if restraining himself then he smiled, nodded and put a friendly hand on my shoulder. 'Do you know who said that?'

I didn't know.

'One of the greatest philosophers of all!' he told me.

'Plato?' I offered.

'Who?' he said, as if completely baffled by my question. 'I need a pound. Can you lend me a pound? Just one pound. Then my future is secure,' he said.

I needed no more persuasion to do this poor fellow a favour. I took out my wallet and removed a pound note.

'You'll get it back,' he said intently.

'No. You have it,' I said magnanimously. 'I know what it's like to feel alone and desperate.'

'You're a saint.' He stopped me returning my wallet to its pocket and asked, 'How much do you have in there?'

I removed all the notes and held them in my hand. There was a ten, a five and four ones. Suddenly I was barged from behind and a thick fist grabbed the money, including the single note Slim was still holding. I dropped my wallet and was just quick enough to stop it slipping through the railings.

'Bastard!' shrieked Slim as the burly thief in a torn, dark brown trench coat bustled past him and started running up Bridge Street.

'Thief! Thief!' Slim shouted in hot pursuit of the stranger. By the time I'd put my wallet away and stood up I saw a surprisingly fleet-footed Slim pounding the pavement round the corner of Trinity Street after the robber and out of sight. I ran after them but by the time I caught up with Slim he was panting uncomfortably and sitting on a litter bin. He looked up at me sadly. 'You're a good person. I'm sorry.'

I'm a good person. And *I'm* sorry. I couldn't afford to lose that money.

'Are you going to be OK?' I asked Slim, realising that he too had not got the money I'd given him.

'I'll survive,' he said, adding again, 'You're a good man.' We shook hands and went our separate ways.

Next morning, feeling richer about being good but feeling poorer about being poorer, I arrived at church at 11.59 a.m. It was packed for the noon service. Perhaps I wasn't the only one who needed built-in hangover time on a Sunday morning. The congregation was unlike any I'd come across in my own church back in Cornwall. They were dressed in what was clearly their Sunday best but they had a relaxed air about them, casual and informal. The women, in particular, radiated a joie de vivre. They were laughing and joking, showing off shoes and skirts to each other. They looked sexy. Deliberately sexy. And there were all ages too. Not the very young and the very decrepit that I was used to back home, but middle-aged people, young couples and teenagers. A sudden silence heralded the arrival of the altarboys and the priest, who in a rich monotone said the words: '*Módlmy, umiłowany bracia ...*'

Wow, brilliant, I thought, a Latin Mass. No, wait a minute, that's not Latin.

I was at the Polish Mass.

I smirked to myself and sat back to enjoy the spectacle, the colour, the music and sounds of the mystery of the Holy Sacrifice; which today would be even more mysterious than usual. It was perfectly lovely but, about ten minutes into the service, as I was just a few rows from the back I decided to make an early getaway. As I headed for the door, something brought me to an abrupt halt. At the end of the very back row sat two men who were giggling and bleary from drink. They were eyeing the congregation and nudging each other obscenely. They were Slim and a fat tramp in a torn, dark brown trench coat.

'Slim,' I said.

They stopped sniggering and looked at me.

There was a pause before Slim said, 'Piss off!' and they collapsed once again in laughter.

I stepped out into the street feeling older and wiser. Sinned against before I'd started sinning. With a mixture of anger and shame, I kicked up a clump of confetti from the previous day's wedding, which flew into the air and fluttered snowily to the ground.

Chapter 5

Introducing Grown-up Boy

'Do you, Rory, take this woman to be your lawful wedded wife ...'
The priest paused. So this was it. Unbelievable. I never thought I'd
ever reach this point in my life. The point in my life when I had a life.
The point when I'd grown up. Marriage is a thing that happens to
other people, surely; to civilised upstanding people; to sane people; to
sensible adults. Yet there I was. Giddy with excitement and happiness,
standing at the altar with my bride, crisply smart in my morning suit,
slim and suntanned.

* * *

Matrimony is a sacrament. For it to be so, both participants (for
Roman Catholic purposes this means a man and a woman) must
be acting under their own free will. The marriage must be by mutual
consent. Yes, I think that's fairly safe. There was no external pressure on us. This wasn't arranged by outside parties, our parents
weren't forcing us. The only pressure was that of age. Or rather
aging. Entropy. The tendency for the world to run itself down and
collapse into chaos. Neither of us was getting younger. We were at
that age when people get married. In those days it was still less
complicated to have children inside 'wedlock'. Though I can't say I
ever liked the word 'wedlock', with its implied coupling of marriage

and things that are difficult to get out of. (The Spanish word for wife is *esposa*, as in 'spouse', but the plural *esposas*, wives, also means 'handcuffs'. Ho ho.)

Between leaving university and this morning, my life had been errant to say the least. Up hill and down dale it had meandered unconvincingly. I was becoming established as a comedy writer for television and radio. I was beginning to appear more on both. There were reasons to be cheerful. There was even talk of me and close friends of mine setting up our own independent production company. 1984 had turned out to be much better than George Orwell had led me to believe. A shining path was appearing before me; the dim and slimy forest, with its dangers and booby traps, was now behind me. And how ironic that the starting day should be in St Joseph's Catholic Church in Highgate, where I'd often sought deliberate and accidental solace.

'I can't believe we're doing this,' I said to my wife-to-be.

'Getting married? I thought you wanted to,' she said, sounding a little perplexed.

'No, this! Running up the steepest hill in London at seven in the morning.' Seven in the morning on our wedding day. We were running up Highgate West Hill. One of the huge changes in my life since meeting her had been taking up running. When I'd first met her we discovered we lived about two miles from each other in north London.

'I run past your house every morning,' she'd said.

'I've never seen you!' I said truthfully.

'About seven thirty,' she'd said.

'I'm usually getting home by then,' I'd said, almost truthfully, with a smile.

'You should join me one morning,' she'd offered.

'I will,' I'd replied. 'I like running. I do it about three or four times a week.'

This had been such a stupid and pointless lie, I realised the following day, as I sat gasping for breath on a bench in Highgate village, coughing up phlegm and spit, while Mary was running effortlessly on the spot saying, 'Come on, let's keep moving, I'm getting cold.' Over the following years, with her help, encouragement and sarcasm, I got to a stage where I could run several half marathons and the London marathon twice in reasonable times. It meant I was fit and healthier than I'd been for years. And not so fat.

My weight on my wedding day was the lowest it would ever be. I had my best suntan ever, as well; a souvenir from two weeks in the Gambia. Our honeymoon. ('We thought we'd do the honeymoon first, just in case!' was our little joke.)

Both participants in the holy sacrament of matrimony must be baptised. (Yes, tick that one.) They must be adults. (OK, this could be quite a long debate, so let's skip that one.) There were no impediments that I knew of. Though when the priest asked, 'Does anyone here know any reason why these two should not be joined in holy matrimony? Let him speak now or forever hold his peace,' some wag did shout out, 'One at a time, please!'

Impotence, strictly speaking, is an impediment. The purpose of marriage is to create more Catholics so this physical requirement is fairly major. Historically, this is a tough one for the Church, with its insistence on virginity and chastity. The early Christian writer Tertullian argued that marriage was licensed fornication. (I'm sure that anyone after several years of marriage could inform him categorically that it is not.) We had no consanguinity to the fourth collateral line. (What a great phrase that is. It boils down to not marrying someone you're related to; as far as first cousin, that is.) We were not related to each other by a previous marriage and neither of us was taking Holy Orders. The service at Holy Joe's, Highgate, could go ahead, unimpeded.

Well, that's not quite true. A delay to the first wedding of the day had had a knock-on effect on subsequent services, meaning ours would be delayed at least an hour. The solution was close at hand in the shape of the Old Crown public house, not thirty seconds across the road from the church. Because of the crotchety, near-senile landlady, this watering hole was known locally as the Old Crow. This turned into a very agreeable pre-wedding reception and there was a growing feeling that it would be quite difficult to get the congregation back across the road for the actual wedding.

It wasn't till much later that I found out how bemused, if not downright annoyed, Mary was when she and her dad arrived at the church in the limo to find a wedding full of strangers in progress and no sign of her family, friends and guests. They eventually returned to the house, despite her father's insistence that they go and sit it out in the Old Crown.

All too soon, one of the ushers returned from the church with the information that the hour was upon us, and we merrily zigzagged across the busy road to the church. I'd been to dozens of my friends' weddings and ironically I'd enjoyed none of them as much as I enjoyed my own. All the people there, I wanted to be there. I didn't have to worry about what I wore or what present to bring. It was a relatively carefree day. My main worry had been that the booze might run out but the enforced hour in the Old Crow meant the wedding guests were well ahead of the game and the reception was all the livelier. The other minor shadow at the back of my mind was, of course, Arsenal. They were playing away at Watford and with the excitement I'd forgotten all about this, until I stood up for the groom's speech to be told by a Northern Irish voice from the back, 'Arsenal's lost two–nil.' Ah, fuck it, who cares. Today my happiness was bullet-proof.

'... To have and to hold,' the priest continued, 'from this day forward, for better or worse, for richer or poorer, in sickness and in health?'

I paused expecting, from my betrothed, a comment like, 'You'll never get a straight answer out of him!'.

It didn't come.

So I said, 'I do'.

And I did.

Chapter 6

Good Catholic Boy Goes to School

'You're the sort of girl who'd be found kissing a boy by the side of a motorway,' said one of the nuns to Mary before making her stand for hours barefoot on the cold tiled floor of the convent.

Mary had an unhappy time with some of the nuns at her convent boarding school in Northern Ireland. She told tales of vindictiveness and spite. I envisaged evil witches who hovered in the eerie black silence of the convent corridors and glided through their punitive world, noiseless as bats and shadows but for the swish of their habits.

I was taught by nuns, too; at primary school.

Nuns, they're just like you and me, I had been told by my mother. They eat, drink and sleep. They do all the things normal people do. Except for the things that normal people do that they don't do; things I was too young to know about or understand. They have dedicated their life to God, which was a wonderful thing to do. I had seen nuns at church and, no matter how they were described to me, there was something faintly disturbing about them. They *were* different. The uniform for a start. Unforgivingly black. Like chain mail and armour, it was there to protect the wearer from the real world, from evil and the devil. But like chain mail and armour, its very existence presupposed conflict. There was a whiff of war and crusade about the nun's habit. And, without fully understanding it, a four-year-old might have sensed it.

The thing about uniforms is they make people uniform. They dehumanise. They de-sex. (I was not in tune with female physiology in those days, but I think I realised that all the nuns who taught me were women.) All you could see of the body was the face, framed starchily in a sweat-lined hood of white cotton and scratchy cardboard.

Around the middle of the body was a rope. Not a cord like a pyjama cord or a dressing-gown cord, but a rope. Now ropes are evil, aren't they? Ropes are for tying. Ropes are for hanging. Evil things. I include bell-ringing.

Then there was a strange bib-like thing of plastic or cardboard that covered the bosom. Not that I knew what a bosom was or indeed whether or not nuns had them. My exploration of planet Bosom was a long way off in the future.

Over these bibs, around the neck, nuns would wear a rosary. A rosary is a string of beads with a collapsible pocket-sized abacus to help you remember how many 'Hail Marys' you'd said on one of those holy occasions when a large number of 'Hail Marys' was required to be said. But nuns didn't wear just any old rosary, not like the fragile tinkly white plastic ones we were given as presents at our First Holy Communion, but a big, chunky 'Don't mess with me' rosary on a chain that looked like something out of the London Dungeon.

Occasionally you'd get a glimpse of the shoes. Boots, not shoes. Big leather boots. The footwear of occupying troops, of the enemy. The whole affair must have been mortifyingly uncomfortable, but maybe that was the point. This too made nuns seem a bit special, a bit different and, dare I say it, a bit strange. And rather terrifying.

And in the bizarre mythology of 'the Faith' they become engaged to, betrothed to or married to God. Like all wives they can therefore change their names if they wish to. Obviously, the tradition of taking your husband's name wouldn't work here because all nuns would end up being called Sister God, so instead they would take saints' names.

This was strange to me as a four-year-old as most of the saints are men. Stranger still that two of the nuns who taught me were called Sister Stephen and Sister Michael, especially as my brothers are called Stephen and Michael.

* * *

My first school was a small Catholic primary school in Camborne in Cornwall. Going to school meant leaving home … and, more frighteningly, Camborne was two and three-quarter miles away. My elder brother had been there for two years already, which was some small comfort to me on the night before my first day.

But my first day must have gone pretty well because all I can remember about it was my disappointment about the letter 'x'. 'A' is for 'apple' and 'b' is for 'bird' and 'c' is for 'cat' and 'd' is for 'dog' and so on but 'x' is 'as in box'.

X is for 'as in box'!?

That just wouldn't do, I'm afraid.

('Xylophone' would come later but, frustratingly, might as well have been spelled with a 'z'.)

Sister Stephen, as opposed to my brother Stephen who was in the big class, wrote lots of four-letter words on the blackboard, a word we can't use now in case it offends boards that actually are black.

There was one word that nobody could recognise except me. The word was 'slot' and I won a gold star for that. It was the first thing I'd ever won and, though I didn't know it then, it was the last thing I'd ever win.

There were three classes. The baby class, the middle class and the big class. Apart from the gold star I got for knowing the word 'slot', the highlight of the baby class was seeing a rat run from one end of the room to the other.

That and going to the lavatory.

In the first year of baby class, if you needed a wee you'd have to be accompanied by an older boy. For me, this was always David 'Gussie' Williams. He always suggested we ran to the toilet block and then back again afterwards. Gussie was well known to be the fastest boy in the school so I never once won this two-part race, but it made going to the lavatory great fun and a bit of exercise and, I suppose, got me used to the enjoyment of taking part and never winning.

The middle class usually had teachers that were lay, that is, not nuns. In my time there we had four separate teachers, all women, of whom one was strict and not very nice, one was quite strict and quite nice, one was very strict and horrendous, and one was not very strict and very nice. The very strict and horrendous one was a wizened old lady with a spiteful tongue and a cruel turn of phrase of whom everyone was scared, even good boys like me who always did their homework and were well behaved in class. She was the first teacher of many whom I hoped would be killed in a car crash on her way to school.

By the time we were in the big class I was nine so I knew everything and was cool and mature. Me and 'Bwaaa' Weeks (don't ask; I honestly can't remember) were given the ultimate accolade: the milk-crate assignment. When the three milk crates were delivered for the playtime's free school milk, it was our job to go and collect them from the school main gate and distribute them to the three classes. This duty was, though unpaid, probably my favourite job ever. It was also an honour I enjoyed much more than being head boy, which came with a lot of responsibility, like showing visitors around the school, doing a reading in church and having to stand up to the school bully when he was transgressing. From that point I decided, subconsciously maybe, to avoid all positions of responsibility. In this I was largely successful, with the exception of husband and father, which I really couldn't avoid.

Whatever class you were in, there was no avoiding midweek Mass. Every Wednesday before school, the entire school would file in a crocodile of pairs the short distance from the school to the church next door. As tedious as this was, it was well worth it as it meant the school day was shorter by about forty minutes.

* * *

The stories I got from my first wife, Mary, about her school life in Northern Irish convents, and my atheistic disdain for Catholicism in the intervening years, often made me forget the truth about the nuns who taught me. Apart from being very good teachers, they were generous, kind, loving and supportive.

I remember years later, when I was coming out of the sea at a local beach after a swim, I passed a woman about to get into the water, just a nondescript middle-aged woman with short hair in an ordinary swimming costume. She beamed at me kindly and said, 'Hello, Rory.' I had no idea who she was and frowned curtly and walked on, but there was something about her.

Something peaceful, warm and friendly.

As the day wore on it suddenly came to me. It was Sister Stephen, one of the most influential people in my life. She looked so different out of her uniform. She was an ordinary person like you and me. Going for a swim.

I was sorry I hadn't recognised her, and when I heard of her death years later, my grief surprised even me.

And the word 'slot' sprang to mind.

Chapter 7

Sinner Boy Sins

It was ten to nine in the morning. The examinees for the Spanish translation final loitered nervously waiting for the doors to lecture block S to open. Translating from Spanish into English and vice versa was one of the few things I could probably manage, so I was feeling more confident than usual. My wacky friend Robin and I decided to have a bit of fun at the expense of some of our duller colleagues.

'Shit,' I exclaimed loudly. 'I've forgotten the Spanish for "saddlebag"!'

'So have I,' said Robin.

'Oh, wait. I've remembered it now,' I said.

'So have I,' Robin added.

A stranger turned to us and said, 'Well, what is it then?'

'None of your business,' I replied.

'Oh come on, you've got to tell. What if it comes up this morning?'

'I'm sure it won't.'

'But it might,' said another student, rounding on us. And then another and another till we were surrounded by nervy and angry students demanding to know the Spanish word for a 'saddlebag'.

Before there was violence, the door to the exam room opened and Robin and I giggled our way in. 'Saddlebag' did not crop up in the English-to-Spanish paper, which was just as well as I didn't really have any idea what it was; I just thought it was appropriately random for the wind-up. It would have been a better anecdote if it *had* cropped up and I hadn't known it. There you have it, sometimes fact is duller than fiction. (Oh, and in case you do want to know what the Spanish for saddlebag is, I've looked it up for you: it's *alforja*.)

It is a fact, though, and a sad one maybe, that that episode was probably the highlight of my academic career at university.

My university life can be summed up in a dozen words: idleness.

I wouldn't say my time was wasted; in my three years at college, I did get enough sleep to keep me going for the six years of late nights that followed. I actively pursued worldly delights, and in an institution where the men outnumber the women six to one, such pursuit has to be very active. There were all the delights of a good healthy student life in the seventies: a lot of drinking, a bit of shagging, a huge amount of three-card brag, a tiny bit of drugs, vast quantities of talking bollocks, a lot of needless violence, quite a bit of necessary violence, a little bit more shagging, some healthy sexism, racism and general victimisation, mainly of Christian groups, some mild dressing up in women's clothes, some intensely passionate discussions about politics, masturbation on a scale unimaginable, a modest amount of poor-quality football, a modicum of comedy writing for some revue groups, a lot more drinking, quite a bit of suicide (well, only one per person), a teensy-weensy bit more shagging, regular vomiting, an outing in a punt now and again, a few demonstrations against some colossal social injustice (the details of which escape me now), more masturbation, half a dozen arrests, some drinking, some more nondescript shagging, vomiting and, apparently, six lectures and the writing of an essay. That was Cambridge in the mid-seventies and among those involved were future cabinet ministers, chiefs of industry, heads of BBC and ITV, leading academics and some homosexuals who are now hugely popular stars on children's television.

To be away from the strictures of parents, teachers and church was too much for an innocent boy like me. Or perhaps I should say immature. In those days, the 'gap year' was not de rigueur, so I didn't benefit, as most children do now, from a life in the real world, either working or travelling, a life that roughens you, toughens you and makes you appreciate more the comparative luxury of academia. I went straight from A levels to Cambridge with only a brief brush with reality in between. This was a job labouring on a road-building project; a relative sinecure which only reinforced my arrogant delusion that being clever meant you didn't have to work. I was sacked after five days of hanging around a civil engineering company's Portakabin.

In my first week at university I was set two essays to be handed in two weeks hence. Two weeks to write two essays! How was I going to fill the time?

'Well, you've got to read the relevant books, go the library and do whatever research you need to do; write them out in rough a few times and then, when you're happy with it, write it up and hand it in,' I was informed by a studious colleague. 'You should easily be able to write two essays in two weeks,' he smirked.

'I should fucking well hope so! Sounds like I've got ten days off!' And so the rot set in. All the diligence and discipline I'd learnt from parents, nuns, priests and teachers were wafting out of the window as I made my way to the Painted Wagon, a pub that was a handy twenty-second walk from the front gate of college.

Though I should point out that I probably didn't say 'I should fucking well hope so', because I didn't swear in those days. I never swore till I got well into my university years. I was taught, and firmly believed, that swearing was something that common people did. Ignorant people. Nasty people. Non-Catholics. (And it was true, in fact, that up till then, the only people I'd heard swear were people who hadn't been to Catholic primary school with me and didn't go to my church.) Good people didn't swear. People with brains or class or breeding didn't swear. It was like being struck by lightning, therefore, when, in my first week at Cambridge, I heard a brainy, posh person swear. His name was Jolyon St.John-Freville, a third-year lawyer.

'Oi, you!' he bellowed. 'You a fucking fresher?'

'I believe so,' I answered eagerly.

'So you don't know that bastard Jellicoe-Smythe then?' he inferred correctly.

'No, sorry.'

'Pity. I need to see him pronto. Cunt owes me a fiver.'

He went off mumbling to himself something like 'fucking hippy tosser'.

I was mortified at his language. But strangely excited. My love affair with the vernacular had begun.

It could be said that Cambridge in my day was packed with fascinating characters, but let's not forget, however, that these were outnumbered, about twenty to one, by some of the most achingly boring wankers the world has known. (And I suppose it's quite possible, of course, that they thought the same of me.) I tried as far as possible to hang around with 'characters', aware all the time that this term is often a euphemism for outrageously pretentious and affected poseurs.

Prof Mick, for one, a delightful physiology student, whose writing was so bad he was called in by the examination board and asked to read out his illegible papers, which earned him a starred first.

'Were you tempted to correct stuff on the spot?' I asked.

'Of course, not.' He smiled archly. 'There were no mistakes.'

He was super-cool and elegant and I remember one idle afternoon calling round to see him at the physiology labs. He came to the door as suave as ever, white silk scarf casually hung round his neck, holding a lighted Gauloise in his blood-soaked hand.

'Look, I'm ever so sorry, I can't talk now,' he said gently. 'I'm in the middle of a pig.'

I learnt that not all Cambridge people were brilliant, but a lot of them could talk the talk. There was Angus McKinnon, whom we knew as Jock MacScot. He had the most cut-glass English upper-class accent I've ever heard and there was something therefore faintly ludicrous about the way he talked about his castle on his very own Scottish island. I had the misfortune of sitting next to him during my first few French supervisions.

'Very important that we clansmen learn Frog, don't you know. Our traditional allies. Got to keep on our toes with you treacherous English about. The Auld Alliance, 1560, and all that clap-trap.'

A girl on the next table pointed out that the Auld Alliance between France and Scotland actually ended in 1560 and was begun in the thirteenth century.

'J'ai une château dans Écosse,' he proudly informed the lecturer, who was quick to point out it's '*un* château' and 'en Écosse'.

'Stupid pointless bloody language,' muttered the red-faced laird.

It was thrilling to know that I, a grammar school boy from the edge of the known universe, was not going to be the thickest person at Cambridge.

* * *

I met three people who were going to have a huge influence on my life.

The first was Griff Rhys Jones. Griff was two years ahead of me, as it were, and was, when I met him, already a highly accomplished actor, director, designer, comedian and writer.

Don't know whatever became of him.

The second was Jimmy Mulville. A fast-talking, viciously witty Scouser with whom I went on to write, and perform in, countless sketches and shows. We were even two of the founder members of a highly successful independent television production company.

The third was Bob Wass. He was an ex-regimental sergeant major from the parachute regiment who ran the best pub in Cambridge at the time: the legendary Baron of Beef on Bridge Street. After my university days I would often stay in the spare room and he would very kindly offer me his barmaids. He sometimes even consulted them on the matter. Two of them were to become very special lovers. Not at the same time, though. Despite Bob's efforts. Having witnessed war, destruction and the death of friends close up, he took no nonsense from anyone. I recall a customer returning to the bar, clearly dissatisfied with his ale, saying, 'Landlord, this beer is disgusting!' To which Bob replied, 'Well, fuck off and drink somewhere else then.'

Since the seventies followed hot on the druggy and sexy heels of the sixties, people assumed that it would be a great time to be at university.

Wrong.

Apart from alcohol (which is just as much a drug as heroin is, you know, kids), I witnessed no drugs, of any class, no drug-taking, no pushing, no possession with intent to supply, no overdoses, no crack whores and no jumping off high buildings thinking you were a pterodactyl.

Well, I tell a lie. One Friday night, Timothy Blaine's girlfriend, Claudia, came up from London. This was pretty heady stuff. Tim Blaine, i.e. someone on MY staircase, had a girlfriend! Not only that, but she was from London. How fucking racy was that!? And she was called Claudia! What a sexy name; I thought I would faint. And this particular night, she'd brought up from sinful London a lump of dope. Word got round and we all gathered in TB's room to look at this yellowy-brown, gritty, Malteser-sized nugget of depravity. Some people held it, some sniffed it and some even put the tip of their tongue to it. I was content just to be in the same room as it and Claudia, who was ludicrously tall and painfully thin, which I assumed was a very London thing, and was oozing sex in that way, which I assumed was a very London way, that I found totally unattractive but strangely irresistible.

Other than avoiding lectures and supervisions, the three years passed uneventfully, apart from the events. These were largely an ongoing feud that my Jewish friend, Karl, and I had with the Christians on our staircase, and the complex efforts I made to evade the attentions of the ponding committee, a bunch of self-appointed rugger-hearties who thought it their duty to strip naked and dump in the duckpond anyone they considered undesirable: swots, hippies, lefties, homosexuals and me.

My inappropriately named love life consisted of a not unimpressive number of girls whom I pursued unsuccessfully, or pursued successfully and caught unsuccessfully, with the notable exception of one.

JJ worked in a bookshop. We fell in love. We were about to devote our lives to each other when she got married to someone else and disappeared. This was a big event in my life; probably worthy of a book in itself.

The day I found out about it I was so distraught that I did something I hadn't done for a long time. I went to the Catholic church and sat alone, in the cool, peaceful gloom, and cried.

One of the saddest postscripts to my three years at Emmanuel College was, I suppose, the fact that no one ever found out the true identity of the 'Phantom Crapper of M Staircase'. Whoever it was had an indisputable and awesome talent, the graphic and brownish details of which are not for this book. Suffice it to say that the college plumber was called an unseemly number of times to the M staircase toilets. The staircase had 13 occupants but it was generally felt that it would have been unlikely that the 'Crapper' was one of their number.

There *was* a question mark, however, over Ricardo Branfield, M4, who was known as 'Pillow' for reasons that remain blurred but began when he inherited a considerable fortune after the untimely death of his great aunt. Pillow didn't talk about this much and kept himself very much to himself, largely because everyone else kept well away from him. It was also generally accepted that Pillow, like the Queen, never actually went to the lavatory.

The offences against the lavatory bowls of M staircase seemed to happen during the day, which ruled out another M resident suspect, Gavin Cockayne. He slept all day and only came out after sunset. His nocturnal habits were, ironically enough, completely unrelated to his surname, which did, however, give him an enviable array of nick-names: Charlie, Chalkie, Snowy, Dusty, el Colombiano, Dangernose and, for some reason that has always escaped me, Princess Margaret.

Cockayne suffered from a condition that meant he needed to avoid exposure to sunlight and he genuinely didn't appear during the day. His condition wasn't infectious, but it's amazing how many of his fellow students seemed soon to be exhibiting the symptoms of Cockayne's condition. Needless to say, there was a vampire rumour surrounding him. This rumour was given added weight by someone who claimed to have been in his room and said that instead of a bed there was a large box of earth, easily big enough for a 'human' to sleep in. Anyway, the 'Phantom Crapper' was not he, it was generally assumed.

Of course, someone mooted that it may not have been an under-graduate at all. It could have been one of the college staff. The obvi-ous contender was Balloon, the grossly gross assistant gardener. He spent most of his time eating; when he wasn't stopping for a sandwich break, he'd be stopping for a sandwich break.

'It's hungry work this gardening,' he'd rail at anyone passing by, though it was a mystery how he knew this. It was also known that Balloon didn't like students. 'Jumped-up little toffs', they were. He was one of those rude and angry people who attempt to dress up their rudeness with frankness and honesty. 'I tell it like it is, me! I speak my mind,' was the sort of thing he'd say. And 'I call a spade a spade!', which must be a plus for a gardener. But it would be quite in keeping for him to 'foul' undergraduate territory.

Then there was the outside chance it could have been Pete Sedgwick. He vehemently denied it, saying he'd never do anything like that, 'on his own doorstep'. But Sedgwick was prone to blackouts. He'd have episodes when for a few minutes he'd forget everything. So he could easily have been the Crapper and forgotten all about it. Like sleep-walking murderers who have no recollection of their actions. It was a worrying thing to witness. More worrying when you consider he was studying to be a brain-surgeon.

I remember once he burst into my room, interrupting a three-card-brag tournament against the Stoners, in his hand a meat-cleaver, screaming, 'Who am I!?'

'You're Pete Sedgwick,' someone said soothingly.

'Where am I?'

'You're in Room twelve on M Staircase in Emmanuel College, Cambridge,' said a Stoner girl, adding, 'and you're with friends.'

He calmed down and asked, 'But WHAT am I?'

I couldn't resist it. I stood up and pointed at him, saying, 'You are the Phantom Crapper of M staircase!'

The Stoners were appalled, and a mite puzzled, but Pete seemed to lighten up and become his old self. He started giggling and whispered , 'The Phantom Crapper, oh yes, I've been hearing about that. No, it's not me. I reckon it's Gary Brigstocke … That Yorkshire bloke in North Court. I'm sure of it.'

Then, as if nothing had happened, he went back to his room to carry on dissecting his brain.

Gary Brigstocke, eh? I began to wonder. His room was in North Court. Of course, it had to be an outsider. Gary Brigstocke from Leeds was studying something called 'Natural Sciences'. 'Nat Science' or 'Nat Sci' is what they called it, and I'd assumed it was the study of gnats.

I was imprudent enough not to check out the veracity of Sedgwick' assertion that Gary Brigstocke was the 'PC', and for the next college magazine I wrote a 'Who-was-the-real-Jack-the-Ripper?'-style article on the subject.

Leeds-born science student Gary Brigstocke somehow decrypted that the 'Leeds-born science student GB' of my article was in fact himself. But GB was not the PC.

One evening two of his rugby mates held me up against a tree in North Court while GB punched me in the stomach. It could have been nasty but I had been in the college bar and was in a pleasant post-Happy-Hour state.

'I … (THUMP) … am … (THUMP) … not … (THUMP) … the … (THUMP) … phantom … (THUMP) … crapper … (THUMP)!'

Thankfully he left out the 'of M staircase' bit.

They left me slumped under the tree in North Court, and as I lay there I looked up and gliding towards me was Gavin Cockayne, his pale face ghastly white in the moonlight. He was wearing a black cape and, I'm convinced … he had fangs.

Chapter 8

Grown-up Boy Leads the DINKY Life

'In the children's series *The Herbs*, what was the name of the police constable?' Richard asked, adding a defiant, 'Aha!'

Ruth, Richard's wife, who was on my team, said, 'Ooh, I know this. Parsley.'

I interrupted instantly to make it clear, as captain of our team, that 'Parsley' was not our official answer. It was a house rule when playing Trivial Pursuit chez moi that husbands and wives were not allowed on the same team. This saved a lot of argument, sex denial and divorce.

'Parsley was the lion,' I informed Ruth, and the rest of my team, Adrian and Carol, agreed. In fact, Adrian went as far as to sing 'I'm a very friendly lion called Parsley', complete with awkward dance, which even after copious Chardonnay was a little embarrassing.

'No more cringeworthy singing and dancing please,' I announced generally.

'So what is your answer, then,' asked my wife from the pink team, suspicious that we were playing for time.

'Basil,' said Adrian.

'That is not our answer either,' I butted in urgently. 'Basil was the king of the herbs,' I insisted, standing up to do the marching song with appropriate movements. 'I am Sir Basil, King of the Herbs.' I sat down sheepishly as the room filled with hoots of derision.

'Basil is the Greek for king,' I pointed out, but this didn't stop the snide comments about my dancing.

'So, what *is* your answer, then,' asked Mary again, determined not to let us off this hook.

'Knapweed,' I said firmly and Richard said 'Correct' before I, or anyone else, stood up to dance and sing, 'I'm Constable Knapweed', etc.

'Hang on; I'm not accepting that,' Helen cut in from another team. 'Knapweed's not a herb.'

'No, but it's the right answer to the question I asked,' Richard pointed out fairly.

'I think you should ask them another question,' Helen persisted.

'Oh, fuck off,' I said, 'we got that fair and square.' Resentment was growing in the yellow team, who were waiting for their go.

'What does …' Helen began. 'Oh, I don't believe this. This is *so* easy. I can't possibly ask that!'

'Come on,' my blue team members said as one. 'We don't want your opinion on the question; we just want you to ask it!'

'What does the acronym "yuppie" stand for?'

'Young urban professional,' Adrian said quickly, and the debate began. How can 'young urban professional' be the answer to that question? What happened to the 'p-i-e'? 'Young upwardly mobile urban professional' surely? That would be 'yumup', acronymically speaking. The discussion broadened out drunkenly, which was a shame, because the blue team (my team) was well in the lead.

The game itself seemed to have been forgotten by the time Ruth announced, 'SINBAD is my favourite; single income no boyfriend and desperate.'

Adrian, who worked as an air-traffic controller at Heathrow, gave us a few airline-related acronyms. 'QANTAS, the national carrier of Australia: queers and nancies travelling as stewards.' This, of course, brought guffaws from most of us, except Benji, who was gay.

'SABENA, the national carrier of Belgium: same awful bloody experience, never again!'

'Remember BOAC,' I asked. 'Before BA.'

'Of course,' said Adrian. 'British Overseas Air Corporation.'

'I've known a few BOACs over the years: bit of a cunt.'

The wives were tutting now. I went on, 'And T-W-A-T, I like that.'

'Transworld Airlines Tea?' asked Adrian.

'No, I just like twat, that's all.'

Richard diverted the subject from its puerile trajectory.

'SITCOM's a good one: single-income two children outrageous mortgage.'

Benji, confident that queers were not going to pop up again, suggested, 'Sara … without an "h": Sexual-activity-related accident.'

Richard and Ruth, whose two-year-old was called Sara, looked less than amused.

Oh dear, is that the time?

Adult games and dinner parties with other married couples. This was our lot now and a very pleasant lot it was for the most part. We were at that age where contemporaries were just married or just getting married and our lives, working and social, were enmeshed with other same-age couples. Conversations often went like this.

'We must have Debbie and Chris round for dinner. We've been round twice to theirs. And we should invite that nice couple George and Andrea, who we met at Richard and Ruth's.'

'But they don't know any of our friends.'

'I know, but Lisa and Phil and Michelle and Ian are very gregarious and get on with anyone. And don't forget it's Nigel and Vicky's wedding next Saturday and we said we'd give a lift to Craig and Lexi.'

'I thought they were going with Simon and Bridget.'

'Simon and Bridget can't go because they're away skiing with Adrian and Teresa.'

'Aren't Adrian and Teresa invited to Nigel and Vicky's do?'

'Vicky's never forgiven Teresa for the episode at Joanna and Derek's murder mystery evening.'

'I don't remember that.'

'We weren't there. Derek doesn't like us round because he's very protective of Joanna. She's a vegan and you always make snide comments about cranks.'

'Like, "So, you're vegan. What do you think of our planet?"'

'Yes, precisely that.'

'She wants to get a big piece of meat inside her!'

'Yes, that sort of comment as well.'

'Why are we driving to a wedding? That means one of us can't drink.'

'Not necessarily. We could share the driving.'

'OK. Fair enough. I'll drive there, you drive back.'

'Ho ho. Oh, by the way, Marie-Helene has got engaged.'

'That's old news. She got engaged about a year ago. To Tom.'

'That all fell through. She found out that Tom was fooling around.'

'Fooling around? What the fuck does that mean? Putting trifle on his head and blowing raspberries?'

'You know what I mean; he was seeing someone else – Suzie Wadham.'

'Suzie Wadham? Lucky bastard, she's ace!'

'They're engaged too; so it could be a double wedding!'

'How depressing.'

But that was how it was. A stable, comfortable life. What could possibly spoil it for everyone? Having an affair, children, getting divorced, or dying maybe?

Divorce and dying didn't feature much in our conversations, but others' misadventures and misdemeanours definitely fuelled late-night chit-chat over the Chardonnay and Trivial Pursuit, as did, needless to say, babies.

'Do you think you'll have children?' was asked with frowning sincerity.

'We're trying for a baby,' was vouchsafed with simpering blushes.

'We're going to wait till Graham gets his promotion and we perhaps move out of London and then we'll think about a family,' was announced with nodding smugness.

'What about you, Rory, are you trying for a baby?'

'No, we're trying for an orgasm and once we've cracked that we may consider children.'

Until that momentous life-changing experience, we had a life that was undeniably dinky.

Double-income-no-kids-yet.

Chapter 9

I Confess

I paced up and down outside the Red Bull to keep warm and to keep Danny company as he puffed desperately on his E-Z Quit artificial cigarette.

'I can't believe you pressed that,' I said, shaking my head.

'Alfred Hitchcock. That's what you shouted,' he countered.

'Alfred Hitchcock was the right answer.' I tutted. 'You pressed Alfred Cockhitch.'

'Well, that's the trouble with these quiz machines,' he said, panting. 'They do things like that deliberately. To confuse you.'

'Yes, it's as if they're trying to get your money off you and not give it back. We were on for a tenner then!'

'Why didn't you press it, then?' was his petulant reply.

'Because I was holding two pints of lager!'

He sighed. 'At least I didn't press Gwen Stefani.'

'No, I don't think she directed any psychological thrillers. Certainly not before she was born anyway.'

'Who's heard of a film called *I Confess* anyway!?'

I had. And I was intrigued by it. It was one of those black-and-white films that used up the roast-beef-filled indolent hours of childhood Sunday afternoons. A film with an inescapably Catholic theme.

A priest employs a couple as caretaker and housekeeper. One night the man asks if the priest will hear his confession, and he confesses to a murder knowing that the priest is bound by the secrecy of the confessional not to tell anyone. What he doesn't confess, though, is that to do the murder he dressed up as a priest and was seen by someone leaving the scene.

As I explained this to Danny I thought he seemed hooked by the storyline but all he said was, 'You Catholics have it easy, don't you? You can get away with murder as long as you confess it to a priest.'

It doesn't quite work like that in real life, I thought, and it doesn't work like that in the film. I was struggling to find a way to explain how it *did* work in real life. I decided instead to say, 'We don't have to stand out here in the cold, you know. That's not a real cigarette.'

'I'll wean myself off smoking first,' he said, shaking his head, 'then I'll wean myself off standing outside the pub every ten minutes.'

'Why don't you chuck that thing down on an artificial floor and stub it out with an artificial heel?'

Ignoring this he pointed an accusing finger at me. 'No, come on, admit it: you Catholics can do what you like, sin your bloody arses off, then go and confess it to a priest and, hey presto, you're back to square one and clean again.'

'Mmm,' I conceded, grudgingly. 'I suppose it does *seem* that way, but you do get punished, you know.'

Danny looked sceptical. 'What sort of punishment do you get?'

I changed the subject. 'Let's get on the quiz machine again, see if we can win some of our money back!'

'We'll never get on now; Strobo's there. He'll be there all night.'

'Not if Jonesy's helping him.'

'What punishment then?' Danny persisted.

'Well, you do have to do penance.'

'Penance? Yeah, but what's that? Just say a prayer or two?'

'Three actually. Often four. I got five once. Three "Hail Marys", a "Hail Holy Queen" and a "Glory Be".'

'Yeah, but that's nothing major,' Danny rightly pointed out. 'You don't have to give up food and drink for a year. Or give a thousand quid to charity.'

'True.' I couldn't argue with that.

'You don't have to go and work in an old people's home for six months.'

'Yeah, OK, alright.'

'You don't have to run ten miles a day.' Danny was beginning to annoy me. 'Or sit through the entire Eurovision song contest. And the results bit.'

'Alright, three "Hail Marys" might not seem like a severe punishment, but think of it this way,' I went on enthusiastically, hoping I might think of something in time. I did. 'It does grind in the feeling, the conviction, if you like, that you are bad, you will be punished, and you will have to serve your punishment.'

'That sounds like psychological abuse.'

That was a possibility I didn't wish to dwell on at this particular time, but I continued. 'Well, I'd say that we RCs are united by a sense of communal wrongdoing. There is definitely something that marks out Catholics from others. I can talk to a stranger and it doesn't usually take me long to work out whether they're a Catholic or not. There's usually something cheerily downtrodden about them; we love life but we're aware that everything comes at an emotional price. The thing is, the sacrament of penance gives you a lifelong awareness that when you do something wrong, you will be punished.'

Danny took a long thoughtful drag of nicotine-free air and said, 'Something wrong or something enjoyable?'

I nodded with resignation. 'Well, sadly the two seem to be inextricably connected. You have fun; something bad happens.'

'Is it scary, this confession thing?'

I cast my mind back a long, long time. 'I think I was scared at my first one but after that it becomes routine and boring.'

'I don't know how you put up with it, mate.'

I didn't any more. It was several decades since my last confession. As you get older the sins disappear. You don't confess them because you don't think of them as being wrong or evil any more. Missing Mass had long ceased to feel like a sin for me. And as for lying, an absolutely essential part of an honourable, civilised adult life.

'Shagging around?' Danny suggested.

'No. What's sinful is how little opportunity I get.'

'What about putting tin cans in your green bin?'

'I consider that my civic duty. A part of the Peasants' Revolt.'

Danny came up with some more putative sins. 'Wanking over the girl in the red swimsuit in the Special K adverts? Deliberately running badgers over?'

'OK, that's enough silly sins,' I said. 'The thing is, the feeling of guilt and self-loathing you feel after breaking God's laws is supposed to stop you doing them again. But it doesn't. It's sin, guilt, sin, guilt, sin, guilt and so on for ever and ever, Amen. I suppose the good thing is it makes you aware of the potential you have for doing something wrong and that awareness makes you realise you have a choice. And the cause of most wrongdoing is the decision in the mind of the wrongdoer to do wrong!'

'You sound like you're defending your old religion. That's weird!' Danny observed.

I was. And it was.

He went on, 'Sounds a bit sick to me!'

I was pleased that the sight of Jonesy emerging from the pub allowed me to change the subject. 'Talking of sickness!'

Wales's foremost painter and decorator stumbled into the cool autumn air, his face glowing like an outdoor heater.

'Who the fuck directed *I Confess*?' boomed his am-dram-trained tenor voice.

'Alfred Hitchcock,' I answered.

'Shit, I pressed Gwen Stefani.'

Chapter 10

Good Catholic Boy Confesses

My mouth is dry. My hands shake. I'm sitting between Jeanette Dalziel, who smells of soap, and Fiona Clement, who smells of stale urine. I am fourth in from the end. Harriet Anderson, Kevin Kinsella, Jeanette Dalziel, then me. I feel sick with nerves. I've never told anyone how bad I am before. I've certainly never told God.

'But if God knows everything, he must know my sins. And if he already knows my sins, why do I have to tell him what they are?'

My mother wasn't standing for this sort of nonsense.

'It's about you confessing to God what you've done, admitting that you've sinned, examining your conscience and taking responsibility for your actions and trying to be better in the future!'

This I had to accept, though I didn't really understand it. Understanding things didn't seem to be high up on the list of importance in Catholicism. Just believe us, accept what we say and don't torture yourself with trying to reason what it's all about.

So now I am about to receive the sacrament of penance. This is the day of my First Confession. I hadn't really thought I was *that* bad or that I had sinned *that* much but as this day approached the number of my sins increased, as did their seriousness. I was beginning to avoid eye contact with friends and family. I couldn't look straight into the mirror; I didn't want to glimpse a flash of evil, let alone stare into the eyes of Satan.

We are in the front row of the church and Father McEvedy turns and looks at us with a knowing smile and a nod, then disappears into the confessional. This is the first blow. We'd hoped the priest would already be in his booth so he wouldn't know who we were when we started confessing. Had he memorised the front row? Would he remember that I was fourth in? I would disguise my voice; obviously, everybody does this a little bit, but he's not going to mistake me for Jeanette Dalziel or Fiona Clement. He would smell the soap, for a start, or the wee. After several minutes the door to the confessional is opened a few inches from the inside. This is the signal that sacrament number two is upon us. Sister Michael ushers Harriet Anderson forward and bundles her into the confessional and slams the door shut. We strain to hear what's happening inside. Not in order to hear Harriet's misdemeanours but to get a sense of how loud we should speak when it's our turn. Just some girly murmurings at first then a disconcerting snap from the priest: 'You'll have to speak up!' There is a communal gulp of fear from the newly penitent. Plague-sized swarms of butterflies go crazy in tummies. We hear Harriet's voice a little louder but mercifully not so loud as to hear the minute details of her indiscretions. And she's out. The whiteness of her soul radiates from her smug smile. She's done it. Her First Confession is over.

We hate her.

We hate her and thereby we immediately gain an extra sin to confess.

Kevin Kinsella is next. He stomps brusquely from pew to confessional, banging into every object between the two. This could take some time. Kinsella sins on an industrial scale, and if his First Confession is to be genuine he could be in there for days. But no, he's out already and returning to his seat and grinning away to himself as he prays out his penance.

Jeanette Dalziel is next and the exact opposite is true of her. Her goodness incandesces through her skin, white and delicate as a communion host. There's hardly any point in her making a First Confession, she surely must be spotless. But in fact she stays in the mysterious booth for what seems like hours. What is she confessing? Is she confessing her lack of things to confess? Does she deem her saintliness some sort of vanity of which she should be ashamed? Perhaps she's haggling about the penance. Perhaps she doesn't think Father McEvedy is being hard enough on her. Only three 'Hail Marys'!? Three hundred, surely? Then suddenly the air around me is suffused with the rosy smell of soap and she is back. And it is my turn.

My First Confession brings back strange feelings. At the time, I didn't feel at all bad or sinful. After confessing non-existent sins, I felt dirtier and more sinful and that feeling has increased to this day. For today one thing is certain. I am a bad person. Very bad. I'm not the worst person in the world. I'm not even in the top twenty worst people in the world. Not even the top hundred. Top thousand? Possibly. Well, probably, come to think of it. But it doesn't matter whether or not I am among the most evil people ever to have walked the Earth, the point is: I think I am. I have been told this repeatedly from day zero. I am a sinner. I was a sinner before I knew what sin was. Not knowing what constitutes a sin and what doesn't in no way makes it less of a sin. Ignorance is no defence. At least I haven't murdered anyone. Well, not knowingly. I have thought about murdering people. Is the sin of thought as bad as the sin of action? No, that can't be right, can it? That is harsh. That makes me a mass murderer, doesn't it? And how many girls have I raped, then? Thousands at least. I am a sinner. What was my first sin? It's unclear, but what is certain is that my first sin, my first proper sin, surely didn't happen till long after my First Confession. Was it losing my temper? Calling my elder brother names? Hiding my little brother's favourite toy? Secretly wanting to stay at home and not go to church one Sunday morning? Chaining 'Clank' Watson's wheelchair to the railings and running away? (No, I actually never did that but me and Kevin McCabe did talk about it and nearly wet ourselves laughing at the idea.) What about sniffing my best friend's mother's dirty knickers? (No, that can't have been my first sin; I was forty when I did that.) I can't remember my first sin. I supposed it has been swamped by the huge number and enormity of those that followed soon after. But I can remember my First Confession, though, in unsettling detail.

Adopting my most solemn face, I move with appropriate decorum through the soapy mist that trailed behind Jeanette Dalziel and I enter the confessional, the spooky venue for the awkward unbosoming of your failings. You and the priest sit on either side of a partition with a veiled window. This and the conventional low lighting means the whole affair is private. I adopt the same volume of voice as Harriet Anderson, audible to the priest but inaudible to my friends outside, straining to hear what my sins are. The priest breathes heavily. I didn't expect he'd be so close to me on the other side of the screen. I can feel the warmth of his breath. That's far too intimate, far too intrusive, surely? He mumbles a few words somewhere between inaudible and incomprehensible and I start my confession.

'Pray, Father. Give me your blessing. This is my first confession.'

More inaccessible burblings from the dark side of the grille and I go into the list of sins that my mother has carefully prepared for me in case I couldn't actually remember what they are.

'I have told lies,' I say, down to a faint whisper for this bit. Sanctimonious mutterings and more heavy breathing from beyond.

'I have been jealous, I have disobeyed my parents, I have fought with my brothers and sisters, I have used wicked language, I have had improper thoughts, I missed some prayers out of my rosary, I spent my threepence Lenten Alms money on sweets.'

My heart pounds during the ensuing few seconds of silence. The priest, I assume, is totting up the wickedness of my behaviour and weighing out the appropriate punishment.

'For your penance, say three "Hail Marys".'

I sigh with relief. I don't know what I was expecting but I feel that three 'Hail Marys' is not too arduous a punishment.

It didn't take too many visits to the confessional to learn that three 'Hail Marys' was Father McEvedy's standard punishment. Occasionally we'd get an 'Our Father', which was a bit dull. The 'Our Father' was considered the prayer's prayer. The basic unit of prayer. Dull but solid. Much more fun to get a 'Glory Be', which was very short, or a 'Hail Holy Queen', which had a poetic charm. My brothers and I used to fantasise about confessing a really bad sin just to see if Father McEvedy would up the retribution from three 'Hail Marys'.

'Forgive me, Father. I broke into the church and stole all the charity money.' Or 'I set fire to the orphanage, killing all its occupants'. But I suppose we knew, deep down, that you could own up to assassinating Pope Paul VI and you'd still get three 'Hail Marys' because the priest wasn't actually listening to what you were saying.

It should also be borne in mind that all Catholics learn very quickly that you can say the 'Hail Mary' in roughly four seconds. It goes like this: 'Hail Mrflgray slordwcc blesdartmongwim n blessfroo ywoom JESUS ho mer murrago prtsner nowr nat nowr death AH MEN.' (Remembering the hugely exaggerated bowing of the head at the mention of the name of Jesus.)

But the oddest thing about penance is that I always actually did it. There and then. I don't think there was ever a time when I didn't do the penance. How's that for effective brainwashing? But what if the priest had asked you to do something genuinely painful or difficult? Don't watch *The Man from Uncle*, or don't look at the underwear section in your mother's mail-order catalogue? Then there would have been a problem. There again, I could rely heftily on the assumption that my penance was between me and the priest, or rather me and God, and that Father Mack would not have the time, energy or inclination to check up on whether or not I'd fulfilled my duties. To anyone who asked, I could just say, 'Penance? Oh, only three "Hail Marys" today. It's been a quiet week on the sin front.'

But despite all that, it was true to say that after the twelve seconds of penance you'd feel positively elated and full of a renewed zeal to start sinning energetically once again.

And at my First Confession, I can recall nothing but genuine relief that I'd got all those weighty sins off my shoulders and could now look my friends, family, teachers, priest and God squarely in the eye again. I couldn't wait to leave the confessional for the real world, aglow with holiness.

'And we now ask the Lord God Almighty to cleanse your soul …' Father McEvedy continues, before his voice dwindles off into the muffled gibberish of liturgy that he's said a billion times. The meaning eventually re-emerges as he says, 'And bless you in the Name of the Father and of the Son and of the Holy Ghost, Amen.'

'Amen,' I say, chiming in with the reflex that all Catholics have, and it is over.

I'm so happy. 'Thank you, Father,' I say and get up to leave. Then a shock of pain shoots through me. The priest appears from behind the screen and says, 'Are there any more kids out there for confession, Rory?' The shame. He knew it was me all along. He knows I tell lies. He knows I treat my parents with disrespect. He knows I have improper thoughts, even though as far as I knew I'd never had any.

And so I emerge from my First Confession feeling more unclean than when I went in.

Chapter 11

Sinner Boy Looks Forward to Sin City

'The River Thames is not an artery pumping oxygen-rich lifeblood to the thriving vigorous organism of London. It is the cloaca of the city. While it meanders through London it is a sinuous, twenty-mile-long open sewer charged with every putrescent gobbet of detritus that is exuded, excreted, ejaculated or defecated from man, dog, cat, rat and flea. But unlike a sewer, it does not take this effluent away. Instead it takes it as far as Greenwich where the incoming sea will have nothing to do with it other than merely to agitate it, so that every stinking atom enters the atmosphere. Here it mingles with the sooty smoke of a million coal stoves to form a suffocating cloud of stench with which it enshrouds the streets. This fetid blanket hatches the seeds of evil that prosper in the shadows. Robbers, murderers, drunkards and prostitutes shuffle raucously in the squalid dimness of back alleys, fearless of retribution or punishment and protected by the rank fog itself. Neither decent folk nor agents of the Law dare set foot in the knee-deep slime of London's East End.'

'Wow, it sounds wonderful. Can't wait to get there,' I said as Karl read from *An Introduction to Victorian History*.

'Listen to this,' he went on. '"Here Jack the Ripper was able to murder, rape and disembowel his victim in the streets where even daylight feared to tread. Whores in the doorways of taverns were so disease-ridden, bescabbed and bepoxed at their front, their clients would enter them from behind; this was considered less of a danger for both. This fact contributed to the difficulty of identifying the ripper as the victims probably never saw him. This minuscule yet repugnant detail declaims eloquently the state of our modern capital.'"

'They sound like Homerton girls,' I sniggered. In the seventies Homerton was an all-girl teacher-training college and in that zeitgeist it was considered fair game for offensive puerility. (Especially for people like me and Karl, who had never got near a girl for two years, let alone the good-looking, worldly, sexy Homertonians.)

In a few months' time, I would be living and working in London. Fifty-six miles from Cambridge in distance; a million light years away in most other respects.

'I think you'll find London has changed since 1888,' muttered Karl superciliously. 'I can't believe you've never been before.'

'I've changed trains at Paddington and King's Cross and been on the tube between them.'

'That's pathetic,' Karl continued. 'You haven't lived until you've lived in London. Everyone should be forced to live there for at least a year. It should be the new National Service. It's an education in itself just being in London; it's a force for civilisation.'

Karl's pompousness annoyed me and I reminded him that he too had never been to London or certainly hadn't stayed there for more than twelve hours.

'Hang on a minute, you've only been to London once and that was a day trip.'

'I did a lot in those few hours.'

'Did you see the Queen?'

'I couldn't fit her in. Ran out of time.'

'I bet she was livid.'

'She hasn't spoken to me since,' Karl said, shaking his head.

'So why am I being lectured by you about London, you Son of Hull? You know about as much as I do about it.'

'Ah,' he said, wagging a finger. 'I was school *Monopoly* champion four years in a row.'

'Then I think you might have the wrong idea about London as well. There's no place called Go, you know.'

'Well, there's definitely no Free Parking,' he replied.

So this was it. I was on another of Life's thresholds. Four years in Cambridge was nearly over: three years at university and one year doing unskilled labouring jobs for TJ Brown, small works of Girton. A time to look back and make a little inventory of what I'd learnt.

I'd learnt lots of Spanish words (though not saddlebag) and not quite so many French words, a bit of German, a bit of Russian and a bit of Esperanto through my studies, and quite a lot of Hebrew through having a Jewish best friend. I'd learnt the fascinating basics of phonetics and the tedious basics of linguistics. I'd inadvertently learnt the scientific names for most British birds (but not for the glaucous gull, for some reason). I'd learnt what my capacity for alcohol was but I hadn't learnt to put this information to good use. I'd met some great people who were going to be lifelong friends and a few who would stab me in the back unexpectedly – though I didn't know that then.

I had started writing comedy when at school, which necessarily had improved from 'schoolboy rubbish' to 'undergraduate rubbish', and I'd started to appear on stage despite the violent sickness it caused me (and still does). In common with the entire male student popu-lation of Britain, I'd learnt to play the intro to 'Stairway to Heaven' by Led Zeppelin on the guitar. I'd learnt the difference between chicken tikka jalfrezi and lamb korma. I'd learnt to play the pennywhistle and to work a cement mixer.

Towards the end of my time there, I'd also met a beautiful girl called JJ. I'd fallen in love, I'd had sex. In one day of ecstasy, I had lost my virginity, my heart and my grip on reality. I had no idea whether I'd ever get any of them back.

'At least moving to London means you'll be able to get JJ out of your system,' Karl was saying.

'That's true,' I lied, 'loads of girls in London.'

I wasn't quite sure that I did want to get JJ out of my system, and I was fairly convinced it wasn't up to me anyway. She was always there, somewhere in my bloodstream, lying dormant until some chance memory or dream made her flare up, a bitter-sweet relapse of an incurable disease that left me helpless and sobbing on my bed.

My life for a long time was separated into three distinct phases:

Phase one: before I met JJ.

Phase two: time spent with JJ.

Phase three: the time since JJ left me at the altar (though, strictly speaking, it was not me at the altar; she was at the altar with another man not long after she had left me, but that's a story for another time).

The long-lasting pain from that experience had left an indelible mark visible only to me. I used it lazily to explain my fear of getting involved, my reluctance to embark on a serious relationship and my hatred for any emotional commitment. And some self-protective mechanism in my mind seemed to have found a way for my feelings to bypass the Catholic guilt that was lurking, gurgling and splashing lethally like a pool of lava, somewhere in my psychology.

Karl clapped his hands and made me jump. 'You've got that look on your face, McGrath, that mopey JJ look! This is a time to look forwards, not backwards.'

Yes, indeed, forwards! I was on the move again. London. The big one. I reflected briefly on how a simple geographical move could have such on impact on your life: the move from our council house to our own new bungalow, barely two miles away, when I was eight, had changed my life so much. Cornwall to Cambridge had left the inside of my head unrecognisable. And now from university to real life. And, I'd been constantly informed, life didn't get much more real than in London.

I would at last be earning money and living alone. This was freedom like I'd never known it. And London sounded like the place to be. A place of fun and a place of sin. Apart from missing Mass and having sex before marriage, I had been quite well behaved. Things might well be different in the capital.

*   *   *

Sinning has always been a confusing business to a Catholic. The attractive, black-and-white simplicity of Right and Wrong is far too vague. Those of us instructed in the small print of the catechism knew of original sin, super-mortal sins, mortal sins, venial sins, sub-venial sins, reserved sins, sins against the Holy Spirit and capital sins.

Capital sins (sins you could do in London?) excited most interest, both serious and prurient, because of their alternative name: The Seven Deadly Sins. What an attractive, almost showbiz title that is! You can't help but think of other racy numerical groupings: The Magnificent Seven, The Seven Stars, The Seven Wonders of the World, Seven against Thebes, The Seven Hills of Rome, The Seven Medieval Champions, Seven Brides for Seven Brothers, Snow White and The Seven Dwarfs and, of course, The Seven Musketeers (yes, really: I read an obscure early draft of the tale. Dumas cut a lot of it out before the final version).

Sadly, the lethal epithet of these sins belies their status. There are, in fact, more serious sins than these; many that, in the eyes of the Church, deserve far greater punishment.

There's also some confusion as to how they are described. Pride, Covetousness, Lust, Anger, Gluttony, Envy and Sloth, says one source. Another lists Pride, Avarice, Lust, Wrath, Gluttony, Envy and Sloth. Some put in Greed to replace Avarice or Covetousness.

OK, wrath and anger we can assume *are* the same thing. Wrath sounds grander, more Biblical, more frightening, more akin, perhaps, to what you'd hear in horror or sci-fi films. 'You miserable wretch! Your puny attempt at rebellion has kindled the wrath of Emperor Zabulox. For this you will be sent to the cavern of the Dripping Cockroach where you will ...' Etc, etc. (This quotation, from my next book, *The Rude Marbles of Dribblegowl*, appears by kind permission of the author.)

Whichever word you use, the concept of anger is fairly straightforward, as are the concepts of lust, gluttony and pride. But there is a thousand-hectare grey area surrounding the others.

Where does covetousness begin and envy end? Is avarice different or somewhere on the same spectrum? And greed to some would only mean greed for food, thereby making gluttony redundant.

The blur that is greed, avarice, covetousness and envy makes them all seem rather dull. But if you're talking red-blooded, beefy transgressions then lust, gluttony and anger will do nicely. Sloth is included in the list, but there is something almost harmless, fluffy and comical about sloth. An image not mitigated by the actual animal of that name: that sleepy-eyed, lackadaisical mammal of South American rainforests. It moves so slowly that algae grows in its fur. Far from conjuring up any notion of sinfulness, it presents an altogether attractive picture of enviable indolence.

I think I can safely say – without immodesty I hope – that envy, pride and avarice have largely passed me by. I've never been big on money and possessions. I'm fairly happy with what I've got and am equally happy for others who may have far more than me. I'm not a proud person. I wouldn't go as far as to say I was humble, however, but I am at least realistic when appraising my own abilities, skills or talents; i.e. not very significant.

As for lust, gluttony, sloth and anger, well, they're different. And London awaited me.

Chapter 12

Grown-up Boy Is Going to Be a Daddy

The world is over-populated by half. There are about seven billion people living on the planet. 6,782,536,522 according to the United Nations population survey, but I would call it 6,782,536,521 because I probably wouldn't include Victor the Vulcan. Victor is an ex-postman who drinks in our local but claims not to be living on our planet, just waiting for the Mother Ship to collect him. (I wonder why he lost his job with the Royal Mail.)

Apparently planet Earth would be well happy with half this number of people. The human race would be happier as well, I dare say, and healthier. But which three and a half billion should we get rid of? It's a difficult one ethically. Off the top of my head, I can only think of 1,817 people the world, my world anyway, could do without. And that's just people out of the people I know. And mainly people who work in television. I haven't even included Victor the Vulcan, who actually is quite a benign bloke, even though he claims that his copper-based blood is the reason he can never quite manage to buy a round.

Most politicians would have to go and obviously all lawyers; most estate agents and about two-thirds of the advertising industry; Manchester United supporters account for a largely unpleasant excess in world population.

I'd happily say goodbye to most vegans, especially that fat, pasty girl with the nose-ring who works in Granny's Granary in Camden

Town; the one who deliberately tried to empty a cup of scalding carrot and coriander soup over me when I suggested an alternative use for her butternut squash. A lot of dog-owners would have to go too. Not all, just those ones who are convinced, erroneously, that everyone else is as mind-boggling besotted with their stinking mutts as they are.

The dustman who shouts, 'Oi, fat boy!' when he sees me out jogging – I'd happily see him dumped into the back of his lorry to be squashed and pummelled.

All people who work in the Health and Safety industry would certainly not be missed. Indeed their absence would surely make the world an infinitely more joyous place, not to say safer and healthier. All the male presenters on Sky Sports (except Jeff and Rhodri). Michael Jackson (oops, too late). Al Gore and anyone who believes his climate change claptrap. I suppose terrorists, criminals and military dictators wouldn't be a sad loss to humanity and neither would anyone who's appeared on *The Jeremy Kyle Show*. We could all probably come up with our own personal blacklist (oh, what about people who think the word 'blacklist' is racist?), but this is all missing the point, isn't it? It's not about getting rid of people, it's more about stopping people from breeding so much. Millions of us the world over accomplish it effortlessly.

Insert. Squirt. Wait nine months. Plop. Next!

But it's not always straightforward. One night after a successful session on the quiz machine, Strobo, our cyber-nerd friend, described the difficulties he'd had with the process. Strobo's parenthood was always a surprise to us. As a pony-tailed twenty-five-year-old who spent most of his time in darkened rooms fiddling with his joystick, we assumed the intimacy required to father a child was beyond him. However, he'd taken to it with relish and was amusing about his and his partner, Paula's, attempts at conception.

'So she was lying back screaming, "Stick it in! Just stick it in. It's really straightforward!" Trouble was,' he went on, 'at the time it wasn't straight or forward!'

Danny, Jonesy and I laughed.

'Anyway, I go on and say, "Are you sure you want it put in there?" and she says, "Where else could you possibly put it?" and I say, "Well, you normally put it in your mouth." Well, it was a bleeding thermometer!'

'You stuck her knob in your mouth, did you?' chuckled Jonesy, who wasn't long back from finishing a crafty spliff in the car park and hadn't quite caught up.

'Anyway,' Strobo continued, 'the thermometer was duly inserted vaginally and we waited the official three minutes then removed it. Then Paula says to me, "What does it say?"'

'It says, "I'm not going back in there again. It's like the Tardis!"' spluttered Danny mirthfully.

'Well, let's put it this way, the time wasn't right to conceive. It was a bit of a blow.'

'Well, you'd have to make do with a bit of a blow, if you weren't shagging,' Danny cut in, mainly to Jonesy's amusement.

'Blow job,' he said with a red-eyed giggle.

'Worst thing was,' Strobo continued, 'we hadn't had a drink for three weeks. Paula had got this woman, Jenny Krantz or something, an alternative marital, sex and fertility therapist.'

'Oh, I know the sort,' I said, casting my mind back to mine own conceiving days. 'We knew one like that. She had clients who were mainly the affluent, the bored and the gullible. But someone tipped us off that she made you give up drink for months till you conceived so we avoided her.'

'You did well,' Strobo said. 'They tell you can only shag on three nights in twenty-eight, provided it coincides with a new moon, a neap tide, a vaginal temperature of two over normal and an "r" in the month.'

'And don't they say you should refrain from wanking?' I asked.

Strobo tutted and shook his head at the memory. 'Oh yes. No target practice. No dummy runs. Everything must be saved for the real thing.'

I thought back twenty years and was pretty sure that Mary and I had not experienced the same problems as Strobo, but I struggled to imagine how the conversation would have gone if I'd been interrogated about refraining from masturbation.

'You have been "continent", haven't you?' asks Partner pointedly. 'You have kept it in your trousers?'

'Well, you know I have,' say I unconvincingly. 'Knobby has been a very good boy.'

Partner looks at me suspiciously. 'Well, I know you haven't had sex with me.'

'Well, I haven't had sex with another woman,' say I immediately.

'I should hope not. What about you-know-what?' Partner continues.

'Another man, you mean?' I say facetiously, playing for time.

'You're being facetious now, which probably means you're playing for time,' says unimpressed Partner. 'I meant masturbation.'

Whenever I think about masturbation, my mind always goes back to a Catholic retreat I once attended as a boy in Torquay. There were strange night-time fumblings in the communal dorm and pointed smirks and nudges the following day. I had no idea what was going on but felt I was missing out on something excitingly secret and grown-up. After this memory came the image into my mind of a friend's budgie. When it was just a young, lively ball of fluffy green and yellow feathers, the bird regularly spilled his seed on the ground. Because of this he decided to call the budgie Onan.

Onan was, of course, the famous biblical masturbator. The second son of Judah, Onan was asked by his father to impregnate the widow of his late brother, who, incidentally, was called Er.

Er, surprisingly, given his name, was not shy and hesitant, far from it, in fact. He was downright wicked and evil and God took Er to one side and … er, killed him.

Judah was keen for Er to have an heir, even though Er's heir would be Onan's, not Er's. Er's wife Tamar seems to have had no say in the matter, though, technically, Er's heir would be hers if not Er's.

Onan had sex with Tamar repeatedly but each time he withdrew his member and spilled his seed on the ground. Onanism is now the erudite word for 'bashing the bishop', though, to my mind, it was clearly 'coitus interruptus' and not masturbation. Whatever you call it, it brought the wrath of God down on Onan and he was killed. Early proof indeed that wanking's bad for you.

'Well?' insists Partner.

'Sorry, I was thinking about a friend's budgie,' say I truthfully.

'Stop talking bollocks and answer the question: have you had a wank in the last three weeks?' Partner asks emphatically.

I have to think deeply about this question. Or at least look as if I am. I toy briefly with telling the truth but decide a lie is what is really needed here and now.

'No,' say I.

'Liar!' says Partner.

'No,' I repeat. 'Categorically and emphatically, no.'

'I don't believe you,' says Partner, adding, 'You once told me that all men wank at least once a day and if they say they don't they're lying!'

'Did I say that?' Me and my big, pompous, generalising mouth; once a day, really!

She is adamant. 'Yes. Now, answer me honestly. Have you had a wank in the last twenty-one days?'

'OK,' I admit. 'Once.'

'Once?'

'A day!'

'I don't believe you!' snaps Partner.

'Well, make up your mind. Do you believe me or not?' say I, trying to sound resolute.

'I believe you but I think it's disgusting. I mean, where do you find the time?'

I think the question is a bit naïve. 'Why, how long do you think it takes?' I ask, though I do not find the subject appetising enough to want to pursue much further.

But Partner is clearly on a fact-finding mission. 'Well, where do you do it? In bed? In the toilet? In the bath? In the shower? In front of the telly? In the office? In the swimming pool? On the bus? On the tube? On the train?'

'Keep going, I'll tell you if you get one wrong,' I answer.

'That's gross. I thought we were trying to conceive. You're supposed to be conserving your seed. Not spraying it indiscriminately over the London Borough of Camden.'

I suggest that a daily tribute to Onan makes very little difference to a man's sperm count as the sperm, or gametes, are constantly being manufactured in the twin sperm-factories, the gonads, or testes, which dangle outside the body in the scrotal sack, right in harm's way.

'But you're wasting millions of potential babies,' Partner insists.

'I didn't realise you wanted such a big family!' is my fatuous reply.

No, fortunately I never had to have that conversation in real life. Though it occurred to me that it might have been fun to talk about masturbation and have a laugh. It hadn't always been this way. How many nights, weeks, months, years of shame and fear and filth did I endure with that particular sickness? I don't remember ever being told it was a sin. Or that it was bad for your health. Or that it was disgusting. Or that it was a crime against God and humanity because it meant babies were being murdered. All I knew was that it felt good and was concerned with things genital, therefore it must be evil. Did I just intuit that it was one of the most vicious activities in the world?

One that would inevitably mean I would end up in prison, or, worse, in front of that nice Catholic doctor, Dr Fahey?

Mary and I had managed to have a normal life without too many excesses and conceived our two stunning (of course) children fairly straightforwardly. Not so Strobo.

'I suggested to Paula,' he recounted to us, 'that we forgot all the mumbo-jumbo and the science and just got slaughtered and had a shag on the kitchen floor!'

'Shag on the kitchen floor,' echoed Jonesy, waking up.

'So, that's what we did and we had a baby and Bob's your uncle!'

'No, he's not,' mumbled Jonesy. 'My uncle's called Robert. Uncle Bob, we call him.'

Strobo and I exchanged dewy-eyed fatherhood reminiscences and I zoomed in on the moment that Mary told me, 'We're going to have a baby.'

I recall the joy and trepidation I felt at the thought that I was now to be connected finally to humanity, to history, to life. Soon I would cease to be the most important person in my world.

Chapter 13

Good Catholic Boy Considers Becoming a Priest

It was just a matter of time before Sister Stephen would try to beguile us with the wonders of the priesthood. It's hard to imagine any other career that is force-fed to a boy so early in his life. From the age of four onwards we were told how wonderful it would be to dedicate your life to serving God. The girls could of course become nuns but this seemed somehow secondary and inferior to the opportunity of becoming a priest, which could lead on to becoming a bishop or even an archbishop or even a cardinal or even, dare I even say it, the Pope.

Pope Rory the First, Bishop of Rome, Vicar of Jesus Christ, Successor of the Prince of the Apostles, Supreme Pontiff of the Universal Church, Primate of Italy, Archbishop and Metropolitan of the Roman Province, Sovereign of the State of the Vatican City, Servant of the Servants of God.

No, I still wanted to be a bus driver. Like my Uncle Jimmy.

Or one of the Beatles.

Or maybe one day I could drive Thunderbird 2. When Virgil retires.

When I was a bit older, it was promised, I would go on a retreat (whatever that was) to reflect seriously on whether or not I wanted to be a priest.

In the meantime, all I could do was observe the priests I came across.

For a start, they all seemed to be Irish, which I was beginning to learn was something significant.

Father O'Connell. 'A great man; a wonderful priest. From Donegal, you know!' parents, grandparents, aunts and uncles would tell us.

'Where's Donegal?'

'Well, it's in Ireland, of course.'

Father O'Connell had been a missionary (whatever that was) in Mauritania (wherever that was) when he'd tried to address local problems. One of these was over-population and venereal disease. I recall a story he told one day in church, which caused an outburst of laughter and many other emotions. In demonstrating the condom, he put one over the end of a spear while he talked the men through the process of what now would be called 'safe sex'. A year later he found there was no fall in the birth rate or the cases of disease but all the men in the village had condoms on their spears. The issues raised by this inappropriate story were an incomprehensible mixture of VD (whatever that was), contraception (no idea), and the church's teaching on contraception (still, no idea).

But it was concluded that, however controversial, he was a good man, a good priest and Irish.

Then Father O'Gorman. 'A good, good priest. He's a Cork man, you know.'

'I thought he was real,' joked Stephen, my elder brother.

'Lovely town, Cork. Good people,' we were assured by relatives, even though we knew that no one in our family had ever been to Cork, or indeed Ireland.

'Father O'Gorman worked with the poor of Guatemala, you know.'

'Where's Guatemala?' I asked.

'In Ireland, of course,' said Stephen.

'Father Lynch was a good priest,' it was said when he turned up as a locum for a summer month. 'But quite traditional,' it was added in hushed tones.

This clearly meant what we could call 'zero tolerance' of anyone not a Catholic. In one sermon he inveighed against the horror of the 'mixed marriage'. (Now I was under the impression that a 'mixed marriage' was one that involved a man and a woman. So the 'horror' of this left me a little confused.)

In the congregation that night was a recently married couple, the husband of which was Church of England (yes, that's right, a Protestant!). Father Lynch was in full lambast against this particular evil when the young Catholic wife could stand it no more and left the church in tears. Her polite and bemused husband followed her.

This was, apparently, a disgraceful episode, but it didn't stop Father Lynch being a good priest, if a little traditional.

And then, of course, Father McEvedy. He was the padre we all grew up with, our formative parish priest.

His sermons were masterpieces of language; which language, was a matter for debate. He was champion of the monotone, unbridled master of the platitude and unashamed abuser of grammar. Main verbs would crop up in unexpected places or not at all; clauses would be repeated several times in a sermon with little or no regard for things such as sense or comprehensibility; words would appear as if by magic on his lips, untouched by thought or reason, and flutter into the air dancing in an excitable blur, each with its own life, darting to and fro, soaring and tumbling in a haphazard cloud of gibberish.

Despite years of self-restraint, the ascetic tastes of a cleric and only a humble stipend and charity to support him, he was absurdly fat. His bright cherry-pink head was completely chinless despite its three chins. His fingers, which we were to see regularly and in close-up at the wine, water, bread rituals of Mass, were stumpy, uncooked sausages. And he was a short-tempered oaf, too, and being confident, in his infallibility, of the worship of the good womenfolk of the parish, he was able to be mercilessly patronising to them. But he was *Irish*, so that was alright.

'Oh yes, he's from Tipperary,' said Mum.

'Where's that?' I asked.

'It's in Ireland,' she replied.

'Is it a long way?' Stephen asked.

The neighbouring parish was under the beady stewardship of the gaunt and lanky Father Cullen, who was not only from Ireland but actually from Dublin, which is the *capital* of Ireland in anyone's book. He was the priest of the church next door to the primary school so we saw him every Wednesday before lessons without fail. He was a shy man, it appeared, though we all liked him because we associated him with missing a bit of school time. He would come and talk to the nuns and children after Mass and he seemed to have an aura about him. A strange sort of cloud. A scent of something that was alien to us children. Perhaps it was the odour of sanctity, of holiness, of saintliness. No, it was cigarettes and whisky, we found out years later after the coroner's report.

Truro was looked after by Father Mulvanney, Falmouth by Father Kelly and St Austell by the squat, purple-faced and grumpy Father Lennox, who was from Linlithgow.

Now, Linlithgow, being between Glasgow and Edinburgh, was technically in Scotland. The Scots, as anyone who's done even the most rudimentary history will tell you, were from Ireland; they went over to Scotland to join up with the Picts who were already there, to form 'the Picts and the Scots', who gave the Romans so much grief that they built Hadrian's Wall. (Though when they were building it, they probably didn't call it Hadrian's Wall; they probably just called it 'the wall'.) The point being that the Scots, including Father Lennox, were therefore even more Irish than the Irish, being the aboriginal form of the race.

Summers meant visiting priests, when Father McEvedy was back in Tipperary visiting family. One year the locum was a charming, sophisticated young priest called Father Silvano. He was from Viareggio in Italy. This is, of course, in the very far south of Ireland. Italian priests, despite the strange words they'd use and the ludicrous accent, were even more Irish than Irish priests in the sense that they were, geographically at least, closer to Rome and therefore closer to the Pope and therefore closer to God. The Popes of my childhood were John the Twenty-third and Paul the Sixth; respectively, Angelo Giuseppe Roncalli and Giovanni Battista Montini – a couple of Paddies, if ever there were!

The pluses of being a priest seemed as abstract as the minuses to the mind of a young boy. 'You can't get married if you're a priest', we were informed, but it was never explained whether this was a good thing or not.

(As far as I can tell, this question remains unanswered.)

'Can you sin if you're a priest?' I asked.

'No!' I was told firmly. 'Well, yes, I suppose you can. But if you're a priest, you just don't sin.'

Good thing or bad thing, I wondered. Could there be a good sin? Perhaps, unless I became a priest, one day I would find out.

Chapter 14

Sinner Boy Commits a Deadly Sin: Sloth

The alarm clock went off.

I'd left it at the far side of the bed-sit, by the lavatory door, to make sure that when it went off I wouldn't just stay in bed all day pressing the snooze button every six minutes.

I got up and hurried to the annoying little clock with its nagging high-pitched whine.

I picked it up and threw it down the lavatory and pulled the chain.

And went back to bed.

Chapter 15

Grown-up Boy Dreams about School

All my dreams are bad. All my dreams are sunny. Mutilation or death to loved ones, invasion and torture by Nazis, standing at the top of gigantic crumbling cliffs, being on a beach as the tsunami approaches, being buried alive in a coffin, being on the top floor of a blazing tower block, being on *I'm a Celebrity Get Me Out of Here!* – whatever the nightmare, it's always sunny. Bright unequivocal sunshine. That's why I don't like sunshine; especially not first thing in the morning. If I wake from the inevitable scary or unsettling dream to find a damp dismal morning awaiting me, I dance for joy. Sun, never.

I can't remember which panicky dream I was in that particular morning but the alarm went off and I sat up with a start and blinked in the sun-drenched bedroom. Sunny; damn, this was going to be a bad day. I collected my thoughts. This didn't take long; there were only two of them. It was Sunday morning. I had a hangover. Then I remembered. Mass. High Mass at St Joseph's. It starts at eleven. We were going to be late.

'Wake up! It's half eleven!' Together Mary and I struggled free of the bonds of sleep and got dressed in the closest we had to Sunday best, which was somewhere between smart-casual and 'you're not going out like that, are you?'.

We struggled up the hill to the imperious Gothic monstrosity that was our local church and slipped invisibly into the back row as Father Aidan was declaiming, 'The Mass is ended, go forth in peace.'

'You're naked!' Mary told me in a deafening whisper.

I looked down at myself. Oh no, my clothes had fallen off on the way up the hill and my skin was inexplicably covered in dried mud, with scabs at the knees and elbows and huge blue-black bruises blossoming all over. The people in the back row were beginning to turn round. A bright shaft of light assaulted my eyes. I blinked.

The alarm went off. Another sunny day. This was depressing. Why doesn't it ever rain in this country?

'Hurry, we're going to be late,' shouted Mary. We had to be in church before the Mass ended and the congregation and celebrant filed out. We took a taxi, which was a preposterous expense since the church was less than a mile away. The taxi broke down and we had to leg the last two hundred steep yards to the church and just made it in time despite losing our shoes.

'The Mass is ended, go forth in peace,' Father Aidan was declaiming as we slipped invisibly into the back row.

'Thanks be to God,' we responded with the energy of people who had not been enervated by the previous sixty minutes of boredom.

We were first to file out and stood just outside on the porch, but close enough to the doorway to be an absolute nuisance to the rest of the congregation as they exited.

But the point was that everybody had to go past us, if not bump into us, including the celebrants, Fathers Aidan and Hubert, when they eventually emerged from the vestry.

'Well, good morning to you both,' said Father Aidan. 'I didn't see you during the Mass!'

'Only just made it in time for the start, Father; ended up right on the back row!'

'Behind the tallest family in the word,' added my wife, a little unnecessarily I felt. 'No wonder you couldn't see us till just now.'

I gave her a firm but surreptitious nudge.

Father Hubert smiled at her then turned archly in my direction. 'It's always the people who live nearest turn up last!'

'Indeed, Father.' I laughed. 'It is uphill all the way, though.'

'And a very, very steep one,' added my wife.

At this point, our attention was diverted by several large bulls stampeding wildly up the aisle of the church. Ahead of them, running with vein-bursting speed, were several Spanish youths, dressed all in white but for a red bandana and a black beret. The bulls were gaining on them and the young man at the back stumbled. It was Michael! It was my younger brother who lives in Pamplona! He fell just as the leading bull lowered its head and aimed its horns.

The alarm went off. A sunny day. This meant bad news.

I was nervous talking to the priest. Did he know we rushed up to church every Sunday so that we could get in just before the end and pretend we'd been there throughout the service? So he'd think we were regular church-goers and when our child was born and of an age he could go to the local Catholic school, the best in the area, with the minimum of fuss and questions asked?

I sweated as I spoke to the priest. I think he knew.

'Well, now,' said the priest in a private whisper. 'You'll have to come a little bit earlier next week, won't you?'

'Will we?' I asked, now literally standing in a pool of my perspiration.

'Yes,' he said with an avuncular hand on my shoulder, 'because I want you both to read the epistles.'

'We can't,' I said panicking. 'My feet are soaked with sweat. I need to change my shoes.'

'Come down to the sacristy ten minutes before Mass and we'll go through the texts. Do you have a favourite epistle?'

This was certainly one question I wasn't expecting to be asked that morning. But I said, in a silly gruff Irish voice which he must have realised was an impression of him, 'St Paul's epistle to the Corinthians.'

'He's pissed, Father, I do apologise,' Mary said.

I went on: '*Stikete en ti pisti; andrizesthe!*'

'You see, Father,' Mary insisted, 'he's cunted.'

The priest raised his eyebrows approvingly. 'St Paul. One Corinthians 16; 13!'

'Of course,' I nodded.

'Guard the faith and act like a man,' the priest added.

'Indeed,' I nodded. Mary punched me hard on the arm. She punched me again. And again. I woke up. The room was sunny.

Oh no, I hate sunny days. Something bad's going to happen.

'We're late. We need to get to church in ten minutes,' Mary said.

It was hard work running up the steep hill, especially as the pavement was moving downhill towards us. Exhausted, we were scarcely able to stand as we reached the top. We lay there breathless and saw another couple, roughly the same age as us, panting hurriedly towards the church door.

'Damn,' said the man, 'we're too late. It's finished.'

I grabbed him and threw him to the ground and started punching him and screaming, 'You're too late to grovel to the priests and pretend you're regular church-goers so you can put your children down for the good Catholic school, you fucking charlatans!'

He punched me back.

Somebody else grabbed my shoulders and shook me.

'Wake up, wake up!' It was Mary. 'You must have been having a terrible dream; you were kicking and twitching all over the bed.'

As my eyes got used to the light, I realised it was a bleak, rainy day.

'Ah lovely,' I sighed. 'What day is it?'

'Monday.'

'Fab.' I love Mondays. Unless it's Christmas Day.

Chapter 16

'Tis the Season to Be Jolly

The pub door was highly sprung. I let it go and it slammed shut behind me, turning the laughter and music into a dull throb and wafting a wave of warm, boozy air over me.

The first person I saw was Strobo, pacing up and down the pavement talking to Paula on his mobile, negotiating an extra half-hour's seasonal drinking before going back for baby bedtime.

'You must wish you had a boy-child when Christmas comes round,' I suggested. 'All those nerdy games for boys on Xbox and PlayStation and Wee-wee or whatever it's called. You must feel you're missing out.'

'No,' Strobo said blinking. 'There's some great stuff for girls. Hannah Montana, Lego Rock Band, Persona 2: Eternal Punishment. I'm up to the highest level on that already!' Not giving me time to express my huge respect for this achievement, he went on, 'And talking of eternal punishment ...'

He nodded in the direction of the pub door, whence Danny was emerging with his now familiar rubbing of the upper arm where the nicotine patch was.

'Still off the tabs, then?' I asked.

'Got an extra patch on today ... as it's Christmas.'

'Has it got a holly leaf on it?'

'It's doing my head in, I know that.'

'So, you must have kissed her now? Three months off the cigs,' enquired Strobo.

'Yes, not much further than that, though,' confessed Danny. 'She wants to make sure I'm completely off it before, well, you know. Anyway, Happy Christmas, guv'nor.'

We clinked glasses and I mused about the season-to-be-jolly. Christmas for me had been through so many incarnations, good and bad, that I thought I was immune to its charms and its evils, though looking at our drab local pub in the winter evening gloom, decorated with spray-on snow, tinsel, holly and fairy lights, I was quite moved. 'Wow, even the Royal Oak looks nice tonight. Almost looks pretty,' I said to the boys, 'all sort of tingly and magical.'

'I fucking hate Christmas.' The spell was broken by the familiar voice and Jonesy, Wales's foremost painter and decorator and occasional bit-part actor, slammed open the pub door, the crazy foam and party-popper streamers straggling from his head making him seem more of an alien baddie from *Doctor Who* than ever. He was dressed in his usual collection of second-hand clothes, but as it was Christmas he had chosen a set without any paint stains on it. There was something in his buttonhole that could have once been a sprig of holly or possibly the remains of a spare-rib.

'It's a good look, Jonesy,' I said pointing to his outfit. 'What's it called? Homeless chic?'

'Fuck you,' he boomed.

'All that money your parents spent on sending you to finishing school wasn't wasted, eh?'

As he joined me, Danny and Strobo on the pavement, he began the complex and sacred rituals of the 'roll-up'.

'This'll be my last Christmas,' he declared.

'Are you turning Muslim?' Strobo asked.

'Nobby's dancing away in there like a teenager,' he went on, ignoring Strobo and crumbling some shreds of tobacco onto a paper. 'He's the same age as me and he's got all sorts of bits of totty canoodling with him. I tried dancing with this girl and I lasted about thirty seconds till I pulled a muscle.'

'At least you pulled,' said Strobo.

'You're bloody good at that, Jonesy,' said Danny, admiring the Welshman's cigarette-rolling technique.

'It's an art and I'm a master at it. Watch and learn. Mind you, I must have done it a few thousand times in my day,' he replied, then went on to say, as he folded the paper around the ready-rub, 'I invited Nobby to my funeral and told him to bring a couple of those birds along.'

'They'll be no good to you at your funeral,' Danny pointed out.

'You never know; he'll be stiff for the first time in ages!' Strobo smirked, his constantly blinking eyes giving an innocence to his edgy remarks.

'Piss off,' said Jonesy as he ran his tongue along the gummed edge of the paper.

'When exactly is your funeral, Jonesy?' I asked. 'I'll get it in the diary.'

'Very soon. The day after I snuff it,' he answered. 'And that'll be when I hear the man on the telly say, "And now the Christmas special of *Strictly Come Dancing*."'

'You should go to church, Jonesy,' I suggested. 'It gives Christmas meaning and depth. It'll help you think of those less fortunate than you.'

'There isn't anybody less fortunate than me!' he replied.

'That's true,' said Strobo and Danny, nodding.

'I only go to church for funerals,' the Welshman went on, 'and, as I said, the next one will be mine.'

'That's not true,' I corrected him. 'Last time you were in church was for Kitten Boots's christening, remember?'

'Baptism,' Danny corrected me.

Jonesy gave his home-made cigarette a last few rolls in his fingers and put it between his lips. He clicked his lighter and held it to his work-of-art, which immediately unrolled, fell to pieces and fluttered to the ground. 'Fuck it. I hate Christmas.'

'Oh, come on, Taff,' Strobo said encouragingly, 'it's only an excuse for a piss-up!'

This observation was wasted on Jonesy, who had never needed even the most microscopic excuse for a piss-up.

'Now, listen, here,' Jonesy began, 'the shops are full of crap, the television is even more feeble-minded than usual and, worst of all, the pubs are packed with amateur drinkers, the once-a-year pissheads, the office snoggers, the botty-photocopiers, the leery blokey-blokes with mistletoe hanging over their flies and fat girls who puke up and sob their hearts out sitting on the stairs blocking the way to the gents. And another thing, never ever fuckin' well call me Taff!'

'I wish there was something you could do to avoid Christmas,' Danny thought out loud. 'A place you could go where Christmas is banned and all mention of Christmas is removed.'

'Even Jews and Muslims have festivals which roughly coincide with Christmas,' Strobo pointed out.

'Maybe there's money to be made in setting up a hotel where the Christmas break is advertised as being a Christmas-free zone,' Danny said.

'Yes,' I said, 'but doesn't that acknowledge Christmas straight away? The very fact you're setting something up as being a non-Christmas Christmas just reinforces the fact that it's Christmas. What are you going to have? A non-Christmas dinner? A chicken tikka biryani? That makes it special, immediately.' I began to warm to the idea. 'How about a holiday package that is seven days of asceticism. Only water to drink. No television or radio. No mobile phones or computers. And no big blow-outs. A slice of bread for breakfast, some raw vegetables for lunch and maybe a teaspoon of cottage cheese for dinner. Lights out by ten o'clock and you have to be up at seven in the morning to do a five-mile walk. It's heaven. I bet thousands of people would sign up for that!'

I looked at my friends and waited for their comments.

'I think it would be a fantastic Christmas for some,' Strobo said, 'but my little girl would want presents and treats and pampering and all that. And we'd have to have television and—'

'Pathetic,' I interrupted, and Jonesy interrupted me with, 'You've got to have alcohol.'

'And turkey and the works,' added Danny.

'Why?'

'Well … it's Christmas.'

'I thought the point was to avoid Christmas,' I said, thinking suddenly of something else we could do. 'Hey, what about this? What about spending Christmas Day down at St Andrews church hall?'

'That's where all the alkies, dossers and tramps go for their free soup and sarnies,' said Jonesy.

'You probably know most of them,' Strobo broke in.

'Very droll,' said the Welshman, getting out his tobacco pouch for a second attempt at the roll-up.

'Seven o'clock in the morning till seven at night. Twelve hours of Christian charity; it'd be a laugh!' I urged.

There was a pause while my companions gave it serious thought. Three smiles eventually appeared. 'It's not a fucking bad idea, guv'nor, as it goes,' said Danny.

Strobo agreed. 'Could be a hoot. Are you sure they'll let us join in? They're quite earnest and goody-goody, that crowd.'

'They're not going to turn away volunteers who want to help dole out food to the destitute, are they?' I argued. 'At Christmas?'

'True,' Strobo conceded.

'And the best thing about it,' Jonesy said, chuckling uncharacter-istically, 'is that we'll miss stingy Steve's two-hours-only Christmas-Day lunchtime opening.'

That was a tiny plus, I suppose, compared to the good-deed-ness of the good deed we were planning to do. I was genuinely looking forward to a different 'Christmas', and duly the four of us cleared it with family and friends. We would be finished by seven in the evening, time enough to have normal convivial festivities.

'Stingy Steve *will* think you have snuffed it, Jonesy,' I pointed out, 'if you're not banging on the side door of the Oak at five seconds to twelve on Christmas Day, screaming, "Open up, you miserable Jock, it's Christmas!"'

'And he has the nerve to send a hat round for our' – Jonesy does his nearly-Scottish accent – 'seasonal contributions to the bar and kitchen staff who've worked so hard all year. He should pay them more, the tight cunt.'

'Ah, truly the angel of Christian charity has blessed you this day, Mr Jones.'

* * *

… And so it came to pass that at five seconds to twelve on that very Christmas morn of which we speak, Jonesy was banging on the side door of the Oak, screaming, 'Open up, you miserable Jock, it's Christmas!' And duly, the tight cunt did open up the side door of the Oak and accord admission to Mr Jones, myself, Danny and Strobo.

'Those holier-than-thou wankers. I can't believe it. How dare they?' Jonesy was incensed.

'Well,' Strobo started judiciously, 'you do look a little bit like a tramp dressed like that, Jonesy.'

'OK, I admit I dress on the casual side, but do I look destitute? Do I look like a dosser? An alkie?'

The answer to these questions didn't seem to be forthcoming and Danny tried to smooth things over.

'We did try. We did our best. We turned up in good faith. We shouldn't beat ourselves up. We did good deeds for at least an hour.'

'"Get in the queue and wait your turn like all the rest," that sanctimonious cow said to me.' Jonesy wasn't letting it lie. 'To me! What wrong have I ever done her?'

'Have you ever painted her kitchen?' I offered.

'Fuck off.'

'Perhaps it was a mistake asking my little girl to come along and help,' Strobo said ruefully.

'It wasn't her fault. She's only three,' said Danny. 'And anyway, if she hadn't been standing where she was it could have been much worse.'

'That's true,' I agreed. 'Two gallons of simmering minestrone is not to be messed with.'

'Do you think he'll be alright, that bloke?' asked Strobo.

'Yeah, that sort of thing is an occupational hazard for a wino,' I said. 'He'll be in hospital now, being well looked after. Probably having the best Christmas of his life.'

Drinks had been ordered and served so we were feeling a little cheerier, but Jonesy still wasn't letting go.

'I was once in a film with Marlon Brando,' he was saying. 'That's what I should have said! That would have shut her up!'

'She probably wouldn't recognise you from that film, Jones boy,' Danny said, 'especially as your bit was cut out.'

Strobo handed him a pint to shut him up.

'I don't think it was just the way you looked, the way you dressed. Those churchy types don't always like their helpers to turn up smoking a huge spliff, as a rule,' I said.

'Well, you and Danny turn up with a litre of vodka and a litre of whisky!' Jonesy said, indignantly spitting beery froth at us.

'Yes, well, that's why *we* got asked to leave.' I accepted the point. 'Perhaps it just wasn't meant to be. Perhaps we were always meant to be here in the Oak having a swifty or two before going back to the warmth of homes, friends and families.'

I lifted my glass and we all clinked. 'Merry Christmases' were wished all round as Aimee the pretty barmaid came up to us holding out a beer-mug with various notes and coins in it.

'Tip for the bar staff, gentlemen?'

'I've got a tip for the bar staff,' Jonesy snapped. 'Get a job somewhere else.'

Chapter 17

Good Catholic Boy Celebrates the Birth of Jesus

'You should have been Second Wise Man,' my mother had said comfortingly. 'That poor Pascoe boy couldn't say "frankincense". Oh, my heart did go out to him.'

'Should have been Joseph, you mean!' chimed in my father with exuberant loyalty.

At least the ordeal was over and we were on our way home. I had been sick with nerves throughout the play, dreading the entrance of the Magi. As Third Wise Man with the line 'And I bring myrrh', it shouldn't have been such torture, but I loathed appearing on stage, appearing in front of the public. How could anyone do that for fun? Or for a career? Hell, I think I'll be a bus driver, like my Uncle Jimmy.

The nativity play seemed to have gone down well with everyone, though a lot of the parents were crying.

'Look, here come more people to worship the baby Jesus,' mumbled Frank Tresidder as an exceedingly monotonous Joseph.

'We are three wise men who have followed the Orient from a star,' said Gianni Toldo incomprehensibly, though the crowd was firmly on the side of this diminutive Italian boy manfully playing chief Magus in his second language. 'And I bring this baby for some gold … I bring this baby gold. I bring this baby some gold for this baby.'

Then it was the Pascoe boy's turn. 'And I bring francing, er …
frankishness … fracksinense, er …'

He eventually plumped for 'frankinshness'.

Me next.

I felt I couldn't go wrong with 'myrrh'. It was similar to the way
Cornish people say 'tomorrow'. 'I'll see you tomorrow' would come
out as 'I'll see 'ee myrrh'. This was a useful guide and I stuck to it.

'And I bring myrrh,' I declaimed perfectly; though I say it myself.

We were a happy family as we drove back home from the church
hall. The nativity play was over, school was over, and it was the Christmas holidays.

'He was a scream, that little Italian boy playing the gold king. I
did laugh.'

'He can't help having an Italian accent,' said Stephen wisely.

'Why did you do your line in a Cornish accent, as a matter of
interest?' asked my cheeky younger brother.

* * *

It all started long, long ago. There was a census in the Holy Land.
(This is what we were taught.) The Romans, you see, occasionally
cheered themselves up by totting up just exactly how many people
they'd managed to conquer. (This is what we weren't taught.) Everyone had to go back to their home town to be counted. Mary and
Joseph had to make the long and arduous journey by donkey from
Nazareth to Bethlehem, despite the fact that Mary was heavily pregnant with child. It was always 'with child' in those days. Not with her
child, not with Joseph's child, just with child. We learn later that it
was the Holy Ghost's child and we remained none the wiser, if not
even more perplexed.

There was no room at the inn and the expectant couple were
accommodated in the stable round the back. There was this manger

in a lowly cowshed and it was in this very trough of animal feed that the Son of God (sometimes, confusingly, known as the Son of Man) was born. An angel appeared to shepherds who were seated on the ground, watching their flocks and glory shone around. The three mysterious Magi, one of them a small Italian, brought mysterious gifts that they had been traversing about the place.

Despite its fantastical events, it was a wonderful story and the keystone to a Catholic Christmas. It's great for children and we pondered it with awe and didn't trouble ourselves with questions like: What's a census? What's an inn? What does 'lowing' mean? Is it anything to do with lowly? Did the baby Jesus have a halo inside his mother's tummy and, if so, did it cause complications at birth? Of all the people in the world, why was the miracle in the stable in Bethlehem only made known to a handful of shepherds and Three Wise Men who came from afar (wherever that is)? Why did they bring such useless gifts: gold (OK, could be handy, I suppose), frankincense (we had no idea what that was) and myrrh (a complete mystery, right down to its slippery spelling)?

In addition, there was a bloody coda to the story when Herod, intent on getting rid of the newly born so-called 'King of the Jews', decides to slaughter all the babes in the kingdom, causing Mary and Joseph to flee with their halo-topped, mankind-saving nipper.

… And so to trees, decorations, cards, feasts, stockings, presents, and Father Christmas with sleigh and reindeer. We didn't know or care that our Yuletide was a clumsy mixture of Christian, Roman, Celtic, Pagan, Nordic and Victorian culture, folklore and traditions. It was just our very own joyous, sugary, magical, tinsel-strewn celebration.

Feasts were always preceded by fasts, so Advent was a period of abstinence. Not as full on as Lent, the lead-up to Easter, but there was definitely a sense of deferred gratification.

'If you don't eat any chocolates for four weeks, you can stuff your face at Christmas and enjoy them all the more.'

'And remember to start saving your pocket money so you can buy presents for the family.'

Yes, that is something that has definitely stayed with me.

I can do deferred gratification; 'def-grat'.

I can be patient.

I can endure suffering; I'm a Catholic. I can do pain, especially if I know there are lots of goodies at the end.

Maybe this is my total legacy from Roman Catholicism? Not a bad one: tolerating bad times; enduring anguish; putting up with hardship knowing that I will one day be rewarded with eternal life or a Cadbury's selection box.

* * *

The rituals of our domestic Christmas Day were rigid. There was no questioning the order of the day. There was no questioning of any orders, come to think of it.

Get up; open stockings.

'Yes, Father Christmas has been,' we'd cheer, having got up several times in the night to check and find out he hadn't been.

Breakfast.

Open presents.

Play with presents.

Friends may come round or (boring!) neighbours, and grown-up drinks with strange chemical smells would be offered around.

Christmas dinner was always turkey, always just the family and always at home.

When we were old enough we could go to Midnight Mass on Christmas Eve, which was doubly exciting because it meant we could stay up till about 1.30 a.m. and not have to go to church in the morning. We'd have late-night sandwiches after Midnight Mass as we opened our presents. This meant the gift business was all done by bedtime and we could have a lengthy lie-in on Christmas morn. But we never did. We were children, we didn't do lie-ins. I wish I'd saved some for now.

I suppose for me Christmas can be divided neatly into sections:

1) Until you find out there is no Father Christmas.
2) Until you find out there is no God.
3) After you discover alcohol.
4) When you have your own children.
5) When you get divorced and separated from your children.
6) When you and your children are too old, bored or knackered to care about Christmas.

As a time of magic and wonder, Christmas was destroyed for me at the age of seven. It was Jack Menzies who did it. One day, the last school day before the Christmas break, he told me that Father Christmas did not exist.

I was devastated.

But still not convinced; so I thought I'd stump him with the obvious follow-up question.

'So who puts the presents under the tree, then?'

'Your dad,' said Jack.

'Oh, I see.' I nodded glumly. 'So, hang on, you're saying that my dad is Father Christmas?'

'Yes,' said Jack pityingly.

I was dumbfounded, but secretly knocked out that my dad was Santa Claus and spent Christmas Eve visiting all the houses in the world and leaving presents.

In one night!

* * *

When the reality dawned, part of the magic had gone.

By the time we were in our teens, Father Christmas had gone. God had gone and he'd taken Jesus with him. There was still the story of the baby born in a stable at Bethlehem who shall be the Son of God and shall deliver us from evil. For us 'Papes', this is powerful stuff. Christmas was God's incarnation. Of course, none of us had known what this meant when we were younger. The word 'incarnation' was one of those Catholic words that we all knew without knowing; various theories involving evaporated milk were put forward unconvincingly.

Teenagers we were, but still nominally Catholic, so we persevered with the now empty rituals and enjoyed the giving and receiving. Though financial reality had crept in. I had already started being crap with money. Stephen, my older brother, was organised and more sensible than me.

'Can you lend me some money so I can buy you a Christmas present?' I asked him.

'Sure. How much do you want?'

'Depends. What do you want for Christmas?'

'More than you can afford,' he said.

'Well, I haven't got any money so everything's more than I can afford,' I pointed out.

'How much were you thinking of spending?'

'A fiver?' I suggested.

'A fiver? Where are you going to get a fiver from?'

'You?' I pleaded.

'I'll think about it.'

Then I added, 'Or if you'd rather have the money instead of a present, then why don't you just keep the fiver you were going to lend me.'

He looked pensive. 'OK, here,' he said, handing me the note.

And that is, of course, what's nice. The giving and receiving. The thought. The effort and time spent choosing an appropriate item, of personal significance to the receiver. He was paying for it (until I paid him back), but on Christmas morn he'd get a beautifully wrapped gift (if I could persuade my sister, Catherine, to do the wrapping) and experience the excitement of not knowing what it was and unwrapping it.

'What do you want for Christmas?' my younger brother asked me soon after.

'I don't want any presents this year. I want the money instead,' I said firmly.

'How much?'

'A fiver?'

'OK,' he said, perfectly happy with that.

I added, 'You will wrap it, though, won't you. I like a surprise!'

"Course,' he said. 'Well, I'll see if Cath'll do my wrapping for me.'

A significant difference in this teenage incarnation of Christmas is that alcohol had now been invented. Furtive sipping of Cinzano before midnight Mass. Giggling during the singing as we stuck silly words in the carols.

'God came down to Earth from Sheffield ...'

'Oh Little Town of Birmingham ...'

'Once in Royal David's lavvy ...'

(You get the idea.)

One year a member of the congregation, a gentleman of a certain age who had clearly had a little too much pre-Mass sherry, came up to the lectern to do an Epistle. He bumbled through his reading with only a few slurs, he did read the word 'immortality' as 'immorality', causing distress to some and delight to others as he boomed: 'We must strive for immorality. God has promised us the gift of immorality and we must take it!'

And, when slightly tipsy, Father McEvedy's sermons seemed more surreal and errant than usual.

'The people who have walked in light have seen a great darkness,' he began. 'Words from the prophet Isaiah. I mean light, of course.

Have seen a great light, those dark people. And what better time to think of light, to look at light, to enjoy the light, than midnight on Christmas. Yes, Christmas. The Mass of Christ. Commemorating the day when Jesus was born. So unlike Easter, when he wasn't born at all but died. But died so we could be born again, but not on Christmas Day, of course. Unless, December the twenty-fifth happens to be your birthday, as it very much was Christ's. And remember that when he was first born, he was no bigger than a little baby; a small child in the manger, with his mother Mary, and Joseph and all the humble creatures of stable, horses and cows and sheep and chickens and camels. For Jesus Christ, even though he was a little baby, not even a year old when he was born, was still the Son of Man, the King of all Creation, but so humble he was that he chose to be born in a manger, a little crib full of hay, surrounded by the beasts of the stall, the cows, the oxes and the oxen. And the shepherds came to visit him and worship him and they gave him a lamb. The Lamb of God, though it wasn't the Lamb of God until they actually gave it to him; before that, it was the lamb of the shepherds. Though Jesus would, of course, grow up to be a big shepherd, with the biggest flock in the world, but not sheeps, but humans, like you and me; humans grazing happily on the hillside under the watchful eye of Jesus, a humble shepherd. And Jesus himself was humble even though he was king of everything, but he didn't live like a king and wasn't born in a castle, or a palace or a private hospital but a cowshed in Bethlehem; in a manger full of hay; a baby in a manger; not like a dog in the manger, not at all stopping the other animals from eating the hay and not wanting to eat the hay himself but a baby in the manger; in Bethlehem; the middle of nowhere, or more like the outskirts of nowhere; the back of beyond, behind the back of beyond even, miles from the comforts of the home. No central heating for him, or television or a roast turkey or a bottle of inexpensive but very welcome Cyprus cream sherry [WINKS AT CONGREGATION], but the humbleness and humility of the stable round the back of the inn which was full. And how appropriate that the baby Jesus should have been born a child. And at Christmas of all times, which is a time for children, a time we think of children and give them presents just as the three wise men, the Maggies, we three kings from Orientar, as the popular carol tells us, gave presents to the baby, Jesus, wrapped in swaddles, not the three wise men, but Jesus, the little baby Jesus. An innocent baby, a baby without sin who would die for our sins at the age of thirty years. And what presents they gave; gold because he was king, King of the Jews; frankincense because he was er … king. Yes, how fitting that a king should be given frankincense for all those little jobs around the palace that a king needs frankincense for. Not that Jesus had a palace but a little manger in a little cowshed. And myrrh. Myrrh, fit for a king, as Jesus surely was. Myrrh; yes, the very name makes you think of … . that unknown thing, which nobody knew about except the baby, Jesus, and he wasn't saying because he couldn't speak but, then again, who could, in the excitement of Christmas with shepherds and wise men all over the shop, to say nothing of the beasts of the stall, who was Lord and maker of all. And because of King Herod, who wanted to kill all the babas in the land, Jesus has to leave the stable with its cows and horses and goats and chickens and spiders and fleas. And flees. Flees to safety. He wasn't ready to die yet; Jesus couldn't die yet, because he had to save mankind first. And it was still three months to Easter. So, my dear brethren, I ask you to give generously to tonight's second collection which is your personal gift to me this night, this Christmas night, this special night, when we must remember the children, the poor and the priests. Amen.'

Chapter 18

Sinner Boy Commits Another Deadly Sin: Anger

Michelle was too good to be true. Beautiful face, gorgeous figure, husky voice. She was a sophisticated, well-brought-up and disturbingly well-read eighties girl. She had a healthy but not doctrinaire interest in outdoor pursuits. She loved the Lake District, the Peak District and the coast. She adored horses. She swam, she cycled and she had a motorbike; she looked life-threateningly sexy in her biker's leathers. She loved the theatre, the cinema, good food and wine. She possessed a wicked sense of humour, and her worldliness and maturity belied her twenty-two years. She conversed effortlessly on a huge range of subjects and could talk to anyone from any walk of life with neither false humility nor haughty self-satisfaction.

She was wonderful. We had absolutely nothing in common.

She worked in a pub, so I suppose we had that in common. She was a part-time barmaid and I used to work at the table in the corner gazing into the distance, frowning with the weight of serious musings and filling a small notepad with incoherent jottings. I hoped I looked like a writer, struggling with the climax of some future classic. I hoped.

I was a writer, literally speaking. I was writing links for BBC Radio 2 shows; jokes of the sort that came between sentences like:

'Next on the show, ladies and gentleman, we have a top group from Ireland; now, talking of Ireland ...' and, 'And so, a big hand for the Nolan Sisters!' It could be hard work, it could be demanding, it might even necessitate some sort of talent, but it wasn't cool. It wasn't 'chat-up'. If I could pass myself off as a novelist, I thought, I might make some in-roads.

I knew deep down, though, that I could never write a novel. Or even a book. Even a mediocre one, at that. All that discipline. All those words. All that correction fluid. I was deluding myself. So how could I hope to delude this stunning creature?

'What are you scribbling in your notebook?' she asked me one night when the pub was quiet. 'You look very furtive.'

'I'm writing a novel,' I confided.

'Oh, I'm sorry,' she said, putting a blissful hand on my shoulder.

'Don't be. I know it's pathetic, but—'

'No, I meant I'm sorry for saying you were scribbling furtively. I'm impressed. What's it about?'

I glanced furtively over each shoulder and seized my chance. I whispered, 'It's about you.'

'Oh, you sweetie. Can I read it?'

'When you're older!'

She laughed and caught me off-guard by asking, 'Why, is it full of explicit sex?'

I wondered if, in the gloom of the bar, she noticed how red my face had gone. 'Is it full of explicit sex? Well, it might be. I haven't read it yet.'

She laughed again.

'I'll finish writing it first and then I'll read it and if it's any good I'll let you look at it.'

'You'll have to give me a signed copy. With a personal message.'

'OK. I'll need to know your name, then.'

'I thought you'd know it. You come in here often enough.'

'I keep myself to myself. I don't like to pry.'

'Michelle.'

'Michelle. That's nice. Perfect.'

'I'm glad you didn't say, "Michelle, ma belle", like the Beatles song. Everyone else does.'

'Didn't cross my mind.'

'Michelle Seymour,' she went on.

'Oh, really? Interesting name. Well, Michelle Seymour, if the personal message is to be really personal, I'll need your birth date, address and phone number.'

She giggled and said, 'OK, then. I don't see why not,' and sat down. Then, to my horror, she grabbed my notebook and started writing. The moment of imminent heaven was turning to imminent hell as she noticed what was written in my book: 'I love Michelle Seymour' was written in a jagged deranged scrawl about fifty times on each page, interspersed with 'Michelle, ma belle, these are words that go together well'.

I waited for the book and pen to be thrown back at me but instead she raised her face to mine and arched a wicked eyebrow. 'What a very avant-garde style you have,' she said, as she coolly handed over her birth date, address and phone number.

This girl was special.

Take it nice and easy, Ror. Don't rush it. A four-to-five-week plan. A casual suggestion that you go for a drink. Not an invitation to go out; just a suggestion you meet for a drink. A quiet drink – but not too quiet so as to sound menacing. A swift drink or two, but not too swift that you undermine the importance of the evening out. Sit opposite her at first, and then move round to sit next to her. Casual touching of thighs or arms. Not so much as to make it noteworthy, but simply the mere contact of two people occupying the same space. Perhaps resting hand on knee. Then the familiar sequence:

1) Inadvertent resting hand on hand.
2) Non-inadvertent resting hand on hand.
3) A hand squeeze, then remove hand immediately.
4) A hand squeeze, then leave hand resting on hers.
5) Hold hands.
6) Walk her back to bus stop/front door/taxi rank.
7) A 'Cheers for a fun evening' and a peck on both cheeks or briefly on lips. Then off.
8) Phone the following day to repeat thanks.
9) No contact with her for at least 24 to 48 hours.
10) Then call to say, 'Hey, we must do that again,' but with an inbuilt, cool-not-over-keen proviso, like '… but I'm busy (or away for a few days), so we can hook up when I get back. I'll call you Friday.'
11) Meet her again. A bit more formal perhaps. A bit more intense.
12) And so on and so on and then in about three to four weeks there will be an overnight, et cetera, et cetera, et cetera (with that last 'et cetera' a long, hot steamy 'et cetera').

The day came for step one. I knew that night was her evening off, so I phoned her.

'Hiya, it's Rory. Are you working tonight?'

'No, it's my evening off.'

'Oh, no.' I tried to sound disappointed. 'Shame. I was hoping to see you. Get some more inspiration for my book.'

'Sorry.'

'Hey, do you fancy meeting up anyway? A quiet drink some-where? Just a swifty. Or three.'

'Yes, that'd be lovely.'

The arrangement was made. In the Mitre 7 p.m. I couldn't believe it had been so smooth. My nervousness had managed to occupy itself elsewhere when I was on the phone to her. My low self-esteem had not sabotaged the project. Despite my assumption that someone as awesomely gorgeous as her would never go out with someone as repulsive as me, no catastrophe had befallen our first date – and it wouldn't have time to. No ex-boyfriend, no fiancé, no dying relative, no prior arrangement with her flatmate that she couldn't get out of, no car crash, no invasion by a foreign power and no giant meteor striking the planet had shown up or could show up to ruin the potential love affair of the century at source.

I now had a few hours to shower, get ready and practise 'Casual touching of thighs or arms'.

Six o'clock and there was the sound of a motorbike pulling up outside and spluttering to a stop. Door bell. One hour early and Michelle's at my bed-sit. This did not bode well.

I leant out of my first-floor bed-sit window. There she was. Michelle, magnificent in skin-tight leather.

This could only be bad news.

'Hello. Nice surprise,' I shouted down. I waited for the bad news.

'Sorry. Bad news, I'm afraid.'

'Hang on, I'll let you in.'

A moment later she was sitting on the edge of my bed filling the room with the smell of scent and leather. I sat in the armchair opposite aware of nothing else in the world but this perfect vision of a girl … and the corner of a *Razzle Readers Wives' Christmas Special* poking out from underneath the bed.

'The pub called to say that Mandy was ill and could I do her shift tonight,' she explained, twisting her mouth and endearingly biting her bottom lip.

'Oh, well, never mind. I was hoping we could get to know each other a bit better over a few drinks and maybe have a meal and … er.' I realised that it would probably be a bit presumptuous to outline my plans in too much detail.

She smiled and finished my sentence '… and end up back here in bed together?'

'Er, well, I hadn't really …'

She stood up and unzipped the front of her leather suit. 'Well, come on then, I've got an hour.'

It seemed she was wearing nothing else under her biker's suit. Sweet Holy Jesus, as we (lapsed) Catholics say. I decided there and then to do an instant and radical revision of my four-to-five-week plan.

I'm pretty sure it was the best hour available to mankind ever. Events had been so sudden and unexpected, I didn't have time to be as nervous, feeble and self-conscious as usual.

The Michelle Seymour phase of my life had begun.

* * *

Sleeping together (sooner than expected); holding hands (later than expected); going out like adults (sooner than expected, i.e. before my adulthood had begun), which included swimming, walking, hiking, pubs, restaurants and the cinema. We even went to the theatre once or twice. Actually I have never been a huge fan of the theatre and I occasionally managed to palm these evenings off on a mutual friend called Paul, who worked in the theatre and could get West End tickets cheaply. And they seemed to get on so it was an arrangement that worked well.

We did staying in (reading, chilling out, watching television, playing the guitar, singing and even tidying the flat). We did going on holiday together, meeting each other's friends, making new friends as a couple, meeting brothers, sisters and parents.

It was idyllic. People must have looked at us and thought, 'What a lovely couple! What a lucky couple! They have everything! A fabulous couple. Perfect for each other. So different but so complementary. So unlike each other but fitting together so perfectly!' Marriage, children and happy-ever-afterness seemed inevitable.

But there are no certainties, are there? Proverbially death, taxes and student nurses are the only certainties.

Our perfection had an inbuilt flaw that at first wasn't obvious. It should have been obvious. Obvious to me, at least. As the fatal flaw was me.

If I had seen us, what would I have thought? Would I have joined in consensual adulation? Would I have thought: 'He's a lucky bloke,' or 'He's punching above his weight,' or 'She's married beneath herself,' or 'What's a gorgeous girl like that doing with an utter wanker like him?'

The last one is probably what I'd have said if I'd seen Michelle and me staring lovingly into each other's eyes, sharing a joke over a bottle of wine or having a confident smooch on a country walk. And was that the tiny fatigue crack that would one day bring down the jumbo jet? That thought of why is someone so wonderful going out with me? I'm amazed she doesn't up and leave me for someone as wonderful as her. She could have anyone. And yet she's staying with me …

'I can't believe my luck to be with you!' I would say. Probably too often. 'You could have any bloke in the world and yet you stay with me.'

'Oh, shut up. Don't be silly.'

'You're simply the best.'

'But didn't you say that to JJ, sweetie?'

I was stumped.

'Have I told you about JJ, then?' I didn't remember mentioning her.

'Only about a million times.'

This was a shock.

'No, you're exaggerating. She's history. She'll be happily married with loads of kids now. She probably never gives me a thought, if she remembers me at all,' I said laughingly, desperately wondering what JJ was up to, whether she was married with loads of kids, whether she thought about me, whether or not she even remembered me.

Was that another flaw? Was I really waiting for JJ to come back? A vain desire that was stopping me from living in the present?

No, that was nonsense; Michelle was all I wanted.

That night we were meeting in the pub after she had been away for a few days in the Lakes with her family.

'This is the first pub we ever went to when we started going out.' I beamed.

'Yes, I know. Well, this is our sort of anniversary.'

'Yes, three years. Give or take. Now, c'mere, you, I haven't seen you for ages!' It was the longest we'd been apart in all our time together. I'd been busy and Michelle had said that it might do us good to be apart for a while.

She looked wonderful. But different. She looked like a different person in the same body.

'You look wonderful.'

'Thank you,' she said awkwardly.

Things had been drifting and we'd reached the treading-water stage where the relationship was not going in any direction with any energy. But our relationship was still a long way from breaking point, the going-our-separate-ways point, the split. Or so I thought.

'I think we should split up,' Michelle announced flatly as I returned with another drink.

'What?' I said.

'Break up. Split. Go our separate ways.'

'Er …' I had nothing to say. If I asked why, she would probably say, 'Because you're right, I'm too good for you. I'm amazing and you're a tosser, as you keep telling me on a daily basis.'

I mustn't ask why.

'Why?' I asked.

'No particular reason.'

'Apart from the fact I'm not good enough for you.'

'That's not true! And it's actually a very vain thing to say. I know you think it's self-deprecating but in reality, it's vain.'

'So, is that why you're leaving me, then, because I'm vain?'

'Oh, shut up!'

The next obvious question was another I wanted to avoid asking. It was certainly a predictable question but potentially a dangerous one, because of the potential answers. I must not ask, 'Is there someone else?'

'So, is there someone else?' I asked neutrally.

'It's so predictable you'd ask that question. No, there isn't anybody else. It is just possible that I can decide our relationship's not what I want without there being someone else. I might actually want to be on my own. I might not want a relationship of any kind.'

I was devastated. But if there was a microscopic crumb of comfort, I suppose it was the absence of a new lover. I weighed up the misery, public and private, of knowing that she was out and about with someone. Most likely someone I knew. On the other hand, that lack of new boyfriend meant she'd decided to end our relationship entirely because of me. Not by comparing me unfavourably to some new, muscular, handsome, sexy, rich, upper-class blond bloke, but by comparing me to no one. In a competition with a non-existent bloke, I'd come second. I was less than a nobody.

* * *

Still reeling the next evening, I was sitting in our pub in Camden Town. Our pub. Our friends' pub. Michelle was staying away.

Theatre Paul was first with his commiserations: 'I've only just heard about you and Michelle. I'm staggered. Let me get you a drink. Was it expected?'

'Well, *I* didn't expect it. But I suppose I could have read the signs.'

Paul handed me a pint and a welcome, but unrequested, large whisky. His concern was sweet and he looked genuinely distraught.

'I thought she was away on some family trip,' he continued.

'She came back last night. She told me straight away.'

'So, what's she doing?'

'Disappearing, apparently. To be on her own.'

'Oh, dear.' There was a pause. 'And that's actually quite annoying. I'm supposed to be going to the theatre with her on Thursday. It's a long-standing arrangement. An opening night. Pricey tickets. I don't suppose you want to come instead?'

I laughed. 'No, I'm sure she'll still go. Call her.'

'What am I supposed to say to her, though? About you two?'

'Well, there's no point in pretending you don't know.'

'You were just perfect for each other.'

I patted him on the arm and thanked him. 'Perhaps you could remind her of that when you see her. Tell her I still love her. Tell her I'll even take her to the theatre myself next time. If you can get me cheap tickets for a first night.'

He smiled and said, 'Well, I'm not much of a marriage-guidance counsellor, but if I can say or do anything to get you back together, I will.'

'That's a sweet offer, but I get the impression she's made up her mind.'

After another round, he left to meet someone in town and I felt sad to see him go. Or rather sad to be left alone. If I couldn't be with Michelle, I could at least talk about her to anyone and everyone who'd listen.

Before I could get too beery and maudlin, another friend came in and came straight over to me with a flustered frown. Jonathan was gay, and an actor. He had been a flatmate of Theatre Paul's and had known me and Michelle for most of our time together.

'Oh, dear,' he declaimed, 'anyone here need urgent cheering up?' He placed his hand on my shoulder. 'You look like you need to talk to a self-obsessed poof.'

'D'you know, I think I do,' I smiled.

'I just saw Paul.'

'Yeah, we've just had a heart to heart.'

'I supposed he talked about Michelle.'

'What else? In the circumstances, I suppose, it's the only conversation available to me at the moment.'

'Was it OK?'

'Yeah, he was great. He told me he was going to see her.'

'Oh, good. It's been so hard to keep quiet. Especially this trip they've just had in the Lakes.'

'Sorry, I don't understand.'

'It's only been a fortnight or so, I think, since they started—'

'You mean …'

'You're taking it better than I thought you would. I thought you'd be murderous. Rory, are you OK? You've gone very pale.'

If you've never tried it before, and I hadn't, you should know that murdering someone is problematic. The big problems are patently obvious and I won't bother going through them here, but a lot of the minor difficulties are virtually unseen at first. I didn't know where Paul lived; that was going to make killing him awkward to say the least. I knew roughly which area but not the house. Or the street. It was in south London, but it was late at night. I'd have to get a taxi. More problems; I had no money and taxis cost money and, in those days anyway, would never go south of the river (I couldn't blame them).

* * *

I flagged down a cab in Dean Street.

'I need to get to Clapham but I've got no money.'

The driver thought briefly then shook his head: 'I need to get home but I've got no money. That's why I'm driving a cab at this diabolical hour of the night.' He revved his engine and prepared to drive off.

I couldn't imagine Paul would ever not have enough money for a cab.

'It's quite important,' I pleaded. 'I've got this bottle of Laphroaig. It was a gift for someone [it was actually my intended murder weapon], but you can have that.' The cabbie took his foot off the accelerator and put the car in neutral. 'It's a single malt. From Islay,' I went on. 'It's a bit peaty for me. Tastes like TCP but it's—'

'Yeah, I know all about single malts, thank you; I *am* from Ilford,' he interrupted.

'I was going to smash it over the head of my girlfriend's new lover, but I'd rather you had it.'

I gave him a brief outline of the previous few hours and he was hooked.

'Right, get in. This one's on me. What a fucking bitch. And what a wanker he is. I mean, that is well out of order. That is *well* sneaky. What a fucking coward. The same thing happened to me. Only about six months ago. My little Dawnie. But they won't make that mistake again, the fucking bastards!' he went on venomously.

I began to worry that I may have made a blood pact with a friend of the devil's.

'Are they still together, Dawnie and her new bloke?' I asked, hoping that neither of them had gone missing in the Epping Forest area.

'Do me a fuckin' favour! *Neither* of them is together. If you know what I mean!' A chilling laugh followed and I hoped I didn't know what he meant.

'Once we've found his gaff,' the cabbie went on, 'I'll park out the way and hang round just in case you need back-up. I got a baseball bat in the back.'

Holy Jesus, maybe I've chosen the wrong cab. This could escalate nastily. I didn't really want to murder Paul but I did want to frighten him. The last thing he'd expect was for me to turn up, angry and armed. The anxiety caused by my lethal chauffeur was dwarfing mine. My only concern now was to extricate myself from this journey.

No doubt catching sight of my face in his rear-view mirror, he waded in: 'You can't go back now, mate. I won't let yer. You said what you said and he laughed in your face. Talk about addin' insult to fuckin' injury. The cunt's laughin' his cock off.'

This wasn't the London cab driver who'd once won BBC's *Mastermind*, I mused. But he reminded me that my anger was still there: a huge, blazing, solid lump in the middle of my torso.

After my chat with Jonathan in the pub, I had gone on to a birthday drinks do in Soho. My rage had made it difficult for me to walk or talk or think. I knew, above all, I should not sit and brood. It was difficult.

At the party, I could hardly function for anger.

'Are you on something, mate? You look out of it!' someone said. I felt I was in a foreign country where foreign people, jolly and friendly, talked at me in a foreign tongue.

I picked up a full bottle of wine from the table.

'Hang on, mate,' said Tommy, a close friend of old, 'that one's not open.'

'I'm taking it anyway,' I tried to say calmly, though it came out in a muffled wheeze, as if somebody else was saying it.

'You OK, pal?' Tommy asked.

'Yes, I'm taking it round to Paul's to smash over his head.'

Tommy looked worried. 'Oh, so you know, then?'

I couldn't take in what he was saying.

'I was going to tell you,' he continued, 'but …'

He knew. George and Colin looked over at me. They knew, too. All my friends knew. Everybody knew.

I smashed the bottle down hard on the floor. The noise was immense and droplets of wine and glass glittered across the tiles. There was a girly shriek and then silence.

I left and went into the nearest phone box (the days before we had mobile phones were so frustrating – just when I felt like sending off a highly abusive text, I had to stand in a draughty box that reeked of piss and carry out a grown-up conversation).

Fumbling in my pocket for change, and hardly able to hold the receiver for trembling, I managed to dial Paul's number. My inebriated body throbbed with my heartbeat and breath. I noticed I was bleeding from a small cut on my hand.

Breath and heart stopped as I heard the click of Paul's phone being answered. I hadn't prepared what I was going to say to him; I had no idea if I would even be able to speak, but I knew that when I heard his voice I would remember his slippery deceitful words from earlier in the evening and my words would flow like lava.

'Hello?' said Michelle's voice. 'Paul's phone.'

I was dumb.

'Hello? Hello? Can you hear me? Anybody there?' She sounded cool and lethally beautiful.

From my end of the line, I heard a croaky voice stutter, 'Hello, Michelle, what are you doing there?'

'Oh God!—' The phone was, I presume, grabbed from her and Paul came on the line.

'What the hell do you want?' he said with an unmerited cockiness.

'I wanted to ask you if there was anything you'd forgotten to tell me in our cosy chat earlier this evening?'

'Listen, I invited Michelle round here because I felt sorry for her. We're enjoying a nice glass of whisky and we don't want to be interrupted by the rantings of a drunk.'

He seemed feistily confident. Well, it was gone midnight and a tough eight miles of Central London and a world-famous river stood between us. And I didn't know where he lived. So he probably felt safe.

'You're a cunt, Paul.'

'If you're going to speak to me like that I'm going to put the phone down.'

'You're a cunt, Paul.'

'Right, I'm putting the phone down.'

'If you put the phone down, I'll come down there and kill you.'

'Fine. Bye.'

The line went dead.

Shit, shit, shit, shit, *shit*! Me and my mouth. Now I'll have to go down there and kill him. But there was one more phone call to make.

'Oh, sorry, Sue, did I wake you?'

'It's nearly one o'clock!' said the breathy voice of Barking-Mad-Sue, as she was affectionately known. Sue had been Paul's long-standing girlfriend a few years earlier.

'I know. I'm sorry but I feel a right twat. I'm wandering round Clapham Common like an idiot. I'm on my way to Paul's party but I can't remember his exact address.'

'It's a bit late to be going to a party.'

'He said any time. It's bound to be an all-nighter.'

'I don't get invited to his parties any more,' she sighed. After several more redundant and nostalgic exchanges, I got the required information and set off.

And now the die was cast and I was in a cab and on the way. The taxi driver had calmed down and seemed preoccupied as we sat at red lights, watching no traffic cross the road ahead of us. Buying Paul's present, the whisky, had used up all my money and now I'd have to give it to the driver. The journey seemed endless; long enough, certainly, for my anger to subside.

'And she answered the fuckin' phone, did she?' said the cabbie. 'She was probably lying in his bed when she spoke to you. You probably interrupted their shag. What a pair of cunts.'

My anger returned.

The driver parked at a discreet distance from the house and refused to accept the agreed fee of one bottle of twelve-year-old single malt whisky. 'This one's on me, son,' he said, with tears in his eyes. 'I can't believe my Dawnie done this to us.'

I was relieved to see him go (the considerable problem of getting back to north London in the dead of night was not on my immediate agenda at this point).

The elegant mews house seemed quiet. A nice house; one I'd never be able to afford. Ditto his gleaming new motorbike outside. No wonder she left me. The kitchen was downstairs at the back of the house and faced onto the narrow street. The window was open. That could be useful. There was light coming from upstairs. I knocked loud and cheerily. I heard an upstairs window open and Michelle's voice: 'Oh, fuck!'

'Hi. I'm here for the party. I've brought a bottle.' After hurried footsteps, doors slamming and much scuffling, I heard Paul's voice on the other side of the door.

'I'm not opening this door to you, so you may as well piss off.'

'You will open this door to me, you cunt. Otherwise your motorbike's coming through your kitchen window!'

'Just go away!'

Damn. Shooting my mouth off again. I went over to the bike and tried to lift it. It was massive and wouldn't budge. After a lot of twisting and bending I managed to get a wing-mirror off.

'Open the door, or your bike's coming through the window—'

'Leave us alone!'

'Bit by bit,' I added, and threw the mirror into the kitchen, where it clattered to the floor with an impressive din. Immediately I heard bolts being slid back and locks being turned and the door opened a few inches, restrained by a chain.

Paul's face appeared in the gap. 'Look, this is going nowhere, Rory. Just do us all a favour and go home.'

'I told you not to put the phone down on me.'

'This is absurd!' he said and closed the door fully once more. He was right, of course, but I didn't realise that until years later. At that moment the magma of rage was still churning in me. I was shaking and struggling to talk calmly. I'd made up my mind. I had to get inside the house. I didn't want to attract the neighbours' attention.

'Just let me in. I'll come in and we can have a chat.'

'You're not coming in!'

'Well, just open up the door a bit. I can't talk to you like this.'

'I'm leaving the chain on,' he said.

I could hear the lock turning again. I had to time this well. The door was about two inches ajar, the chain not fully extended, when I leant back and stamped my foot against the door as high and hard as I could.

The chain was wrenched from its screws as the door banged inwards, catching Paul just above the eye. He jerked backwards and fell over. I stepped over him and went into the kitchen, putting the bottle of Scotch on the table. Paul followed me, pale but for the bruise on his left eyebrow, which was oozing blood. Some agonised and futile pleadings from Michelle echoed down the stairs.

'Stay up there, darling. I'll be up in a sec.'

'"Stay up there, darling. I'll be up in a sec!"' I mocked. 'How fucking cosy! I've brought you a bottle!' I held up the whisky and smashed it down on the floor. The stout bottle bounced off the carpet tiles and spun meekly away under the table.

Paul sniggered. That was enough.

Fights of this type are usually just one clear punch and a lot of heaving, grunting, bear-hugging and posturing. The first punch was mine and it was a good one. Paul went down like a house of cards. He came up again, covering his head with his hands. I pummelled him with blows as he grabbed at my shirt. There was a lot of tearing and scratching but the fight began to dwindle after about an hour and a half, or it could have been five seconds. Then somebody else came into the kitchen. A slightly built, well-spoken man, who apparently was Paul's housemate, Gerry, whom I'd never heard of before.

He tried to drag me off Paul, saying limply, 'Come on, Rory, stop this! I live here, too, you know!' He got a good, clean, but accidental, punch for his efforts, and it was over. The three of us stood in silence, each with varying numbers and sizes of bruises and bleeding scratches, our shirts more or less evenly shredded.

'I need to go home,' I said, and burst into tears.

'Gerry, get your car and drive him home!'

'Sure.'

In retrospect, this was a rather noble gesture on their part. They could really have shafted me by just abandoning me. Or calling the police. To this day, I still can't work out why they didn't call the police.

Gerry spoke for the entire journey about the fickleness of women, love, sexual jealousy, forgiveness, the geographical prejudices of cabbies, the wonder of traffic-free London streets at 3 a.m., the disinfectant taste of Islay malts, uninterrupted but for the occasional sob of 'I'm sorry. I'm so sorry' from the passenger seat.

He kindly dropped me off near my house but I couldn't go home. I couldn't sleep. Guilt and shame, like anger, were jangling through me and I had to walk. I couldn't stand still. I didn't want the feelings and events of the night to catch me up.

I walked up Camden Road to Finsbury Park, passing several important landmarks of my London life: Camden High School for Girls, Arsenal Stadium, Ladbrokes on Hornsey Road and the Ocean Wave fish'n'chip bar.

With Wordsworthian splendour, the sun rose over the City of London and I had the best view in the world, standing on the bridge that takes Hornsey Lane across Archway Road. This *was* the Archway. Suicide Bridge, it was known as locally.

Suicide. At that point I felt lower than I ever had done and yet suicide seemed a remote and completely alien concept. I leant over the parapet and gazed down at the A1, already busy with traffic. A sudden pang of vertigo made me recoil instinctively and step backwards into the road behind. A horn blared and brakes screeched.

'Watch where you're going, you pisshead!' yelled the driver.

I could hear my mother's voice: 'Your guardian angel must have been looking after you.' I clung to the railings of the bridge. Lungs panting, heart pounding. I'd packed a lot into the last twenty-four hours. Near-murder, near-suicide, near-death.

I started walking towards Highgate, thinking of angels and suicide. Of course, it's a sin. A mortal sin. It was the same as murder. The fact that it was you being murdered was irrelevant; it was you doing the murdering.

Angels and sin.

Would my late religion never leave me alone?

And then, as if on cue, there it was, squatting massively in front of me: St Joseph's Roman Catholic Church, Highgate. Sturdily forbidding, not quite at the top of Highgate Hill but nevertheless dwarfing the surrounding land, an upright finger of authority and menace. But inside there was only coolness, serenity and placid harmony. I sat in the front pew as the early morning sun illuminated the stained-glass windows with almost unbearable beauty.

'*Agnus Dei, qui tollis peccata mundi, miserere nobis,*' someone whispered. It could have been me. 'Lamb of God, who takest away the sins of the world, have mercy on us.'

I cried and thought of Michelle, and of JJ. I looked round at the interior of the building, resplendent in the morning light of early

May, and something made me shudder. Not fear. Not pain. Not cold. Just something unearthly.

Did I have a sense, perhaps, that within less than six years, I would be getting married in this very church to a girl I hadn't yet met? And later, my two children, a wonderful boy and a heavenly girl, would be baptised in the very font that stood, solid and majestic, a few feet away from me?

Me, have children?

Surely that would never happen.

Chapter 19

Grown-up Boy Becomes a Daddy

After all the waiting, I was unprepared for the scene of chaos.

It was terrifying.

I had no idea what mayhem would be caused.

I had arrived at four o'clock the previous afternoon; it was now twelve hours later. The dullness in the hospital at that time of night was clinical. Visits to the vending machine or the lavatory had ceased to relieve the boredom.

Then chaos. Sudden and frightening.

From nothing, from nowhere, there was screaming, shouting, people hurrying and struggling to be heard under the noise, bellowing warnings and instructions. There were tears, clenched fists, faces contorted with pain.

And then there was the filth.

The dark slime and stench of faeces, urine and, of course, blood.

The fight seemed to go on for ever. I tried to hold her down and she gripped my arms so tightly I could feel the numbness begin.

Blood began to seep from the scratches.

I looked around for help from the bystanders but they held back, indifferent to the struggle.

Above the sounds of the battle, I heard the wailing of ambulances close by.

Then suddenly silence.

I looked up and noticed for the first time it was dawn.

A gloomy dawn.

No sun. Just how I like my mornings.

A lovely, gorgeous, miserable gloomy day.

A dim grey trickle of light seeped from the drizzly London morning into the glare of the room.

No sun.

But a son.

Everybody sighed and a new sound, a high-pitched wheezy cough, was made.

'Joe is a boy,' said the midwife, handing me a tiny, spluttering parcel of life.

'Joe is a boy,' I said to Mary and placed him on her chest. She held him and smiled with the satisfaction of a difficult job well done, though she was too exhausted to take in the immensity of the moment.

'I was so shattered, it could have been a fish they dumped onto my chest,' she told me later.

So this was it, I thought as I examined the moist wrinkles on his squashed purple head, I was a father.

I had a child.

I was no longer the end product. I was one of the producers.

I was no longer centre stage in my own life. I stepped back and let the spotlight shine on my stunning, wriggling, puckered, crying, purple, blotchy bundle.

Before the tears had pricked their way to my eyes, a nurse grabbed the child and whisked him away.

'Got to check for jaundice and give him a vitamin K jab!' she said matter-of-factly in her act of kidnap.

'Never again,' Mary said.

'I thought you wanted a big family,' I reminded her.

'He'll be big one day,' she said closing her eyes.

A far-too-jolly slap on the back made me jump.

'Well, boy or girl?' It was Father Hubert.

'Hello, Father. Hope you didn't come up here specially?'

'Sure, no,' he said, 'I was doing the rounds anyway; I thought I'd pop in to see if there were any familiar faces. It's nice to be up here in the labour ward. I spend most of me time down there with people who are on their way out.' He chuckled.

'Of course, I see,' I nodded.

'Will I be seeing all three of you back there at HQ for the baptism in the not-too-distant future?'

This event seemed a million years away but the priest was eager for an answer.

'Definitely, Father. We'll be back. If we're not too shattered to make it up the hill.'

'Ach, sure, we can always come to you,' he said, adding with what I think was a laugh, 'There's no escape. We know where you live! Ha ha ha.'

At ground level I bumped into a close friend who was eager to catch up with news of mother and child. I explained that both were sleeping and we should do our celebrating away from the bedside. The Roebuck Inn is literally 30 seconds' walk across the road from the hospital. We got there at two minutes to three, just as the landlord was closing up. The panel above the door informed us that he was called Raymond Byrne.

'You're not about to shut, are you?' I asked, hoping I sounded desperate but not alcoholic.

'Sorry, lads,' said the Irishman. 'Three o'clock it is.'

'But I've just had a baby.'

The publican chuckled. 'Of course, you have!'

'It's true. A little boy.'

He stopped in the middle of bolting one of the doors and asked, 'What's he called?'

'Raymond,' I said without hesitation. He roared with laughter.

'OK, fellas, that cheek has got to be worth a drink! Come on in.'

There was something very unsettling about sitting in a closed pub drinking, while not fifty yards away my wife was lying asleep and my newborn baby was in a glass cot being prodded and poked by doctors. I ached to be with them, but it was the practice in that hospital that they didn't want grinning new dads hanging around the ward, simpering and drooling soppily like weirdos. We were kicked out as soon as possible.

'I'm sure there'll be times when you're with your wife and kids when you'll be gagging to get to a pub,' said our host.

'You're probably right, Raymond, you're probably right!' I agreed and ordered three more drinks.

'Coming right up,' said Raymond, looking up from the pumps to say, 'Oh, by the way, I'd better tell you: my name's not Raymond. Raymond's the governor. The landlord. I'm just a skivvy. But it was a nice try.'

It was as agreeable a baby-head-wetting as I could have wished for. We stayed until opening time and the skivvy unlocked the doors and let us out saying, 'Before you go, just one question.'

'Go on,' I said.

'Have you really just had a baby?'

I assured him I had and he laughed incredulously.

'It's just that they all try that one. They all rush over from the hospital at closing time saying they've just had a baby, trying to blag a late drink. I usually give in and say what the hell, then they always buy me a drink. So, boy or girl?'

'A boy,' I said proudly.

'Name?'

'Joe,' I told him.

'Ach, would you get out of here! That's my name!'

Chapter 20

Good Catholic Boy Goes to the Doctor's

Of course, I knew what doctors were from the age of four at the latest. And I knew lots of them by sight and by name. I had seen them lots, I just hadn't ever been to see one. The reason for this was that all the doctors we came in contact with went to the same church as us. They were Catholics and, for the most part, Irish.

Doctors were, in the hearts and minds of mothers, nuns and church workers, second only to the clergy. Dr O'Carroll, Dr Claghane, Dr Golding, Dr Fahey, Dr Herlihy and Dr Heffernan all practised within a twenty-mile radius of our small Cornish town and they were, needless to say, the best doctors around.

There was an Indian doctor with outstanding qualifications who would occasionally be tolerated by the elderly and infirm of the parish with some reservations.

'Ooh, he does talk with such a funny accent. It's like having Peter Sellers in the room. Nice hands though. Very soft.'

And a tall but nervous young Kenyan doctor who 'seemed very thorough', the parish ladies would aver, adding surreptitiously, 'Black as the ace of spades, though! Lovely teeth, mind.'

My earliest memories of 'the doctor' were all about pink medicine and diarrhoea. I don't recall which was the worse to have.

Acne in those days was so rife and so common that the doctor thought it bizarre that anyone should think it worth a medical consultation. But when you're ugly, as I was, and you're *self-conscious* about being ugly, as I was, what you didn't need was a lot of spots, which I had, which made you end up on top of everything else feeling self-conscious about having a lot of spots as well as being ugly, which I did.

'I'd make more money out of finding a cure for acne than a cure for cancer, you know,' snapped the matter-of-fact Dr Leahy as he handed out a generous volume of some sulphur-based skin-drying lotion.

(I look back and wonder what he'd think about the possible financial benefits of inventing a blue instant-hard-on pill before a cure for either cancer or acne.)

But as an adolescent, especially a Catholic adolescent, there was one thing I suffered from acutely and chronically: guilt. Guilt was brought on by masturbation. This could also bring on the occasional meaningless tiny pimple on the penis; or, in medical jargon, a tiny pimple on the penis. But magnified by guilt and the recent perusal of an article in a Sunday colour supplement about the increase of venereal disease, a tiny willy-pimple becomes the rampant onset of syphilis. For months of sleepless nights and self-loathing I wrestled with the anguish of this private stigma. I read copiously on the subject and became an expert, counting down the seconds to when the tertiary phase exploded into my blood and I went blind, mad and dead.

It stopped me concentrating on work; it ruined my playtime and affected my sleep. I had to do the unthinkable and tell my parents. There would be huge implications for school and church and even family. Would I be sent away? Would I be arrested? Sent to jail? Would I be thrown out of the Catholic Church; excommunicated? That would probably be the easy way out; at some stage I'd have to face my brothers and sisters, my schoolmates and teachers, the nuns and the priest and, inevitably, that nice Dr Fahey. My parents were delightfully sympathetic and took my anxieties seriously. Looking back, I'm surprised they didn't burst out in gales of spluttering laughter and derision or summarily dismiss me with a 'don't be ridiculous, get back to bed'.

They, also, didn't bite my head off with angry shame on hearing that their son had … I can hardly write its name … syphilis.

'You haven't got syphilis,' said Dr Fahey matter-of-factly, adding with an amused grunt, 'Sorry to disappoint you.'

I smiled weakly and my father patted me on the knee.

'Have you had sex in a public lavatory with an archbishop?' asked the nice Irish Catholic doctor.

It was a question I wasn't expecting to be asked at any stage in my life. Even if years later I did end up having sex in a public lavatory with an archbishop, I still don't think I'd be expecting the question.

'It's a medical fact that that's the only way you can catch syphilis,' he went on bluntly, aiming a wink and a smirk in my father's direction.

'I've, er, never had any sex …' I stammered till the nice doctor thankfully interrupted me.

'Apart from masturbation, of course?' he said, a bit too loudly for my liking. I could feel my face bursting with red humiliation.

'Er, I suppose.'

'Well, don't worry about that. Everyone does it and if they say they don't, they're lying.' He beamed at my father who also seemed redder in the face than usual.

'You haven't got syphilis,' Fahey went on, 'or gonorrhoea, NSU, crabs or genital warts. You obviously have too much guilt and you should stop reading medical encyclopaedias.'

My faith in and admiration for doctors and my father went up significantly that day and I went back to school deliriously happy in the knowledge that I was suffering from nothing more than guilt.

Which, the doctor had added, was totally incurable.

Many years later I was back with the wise doctor when I was troubled with an itchy arse. When I say I was troubled with an itchy arse, I do mean *my* arse. Other people's itchy arses have never really bothered me that much.

'OK, let's see this itchy arse of yours,' he said. His blunt manner had not forsaken him over the years. 'Drop your trousers and pants, get up on the couch and lie on your side, facing the wall, with your knees up to your chest, thank you.'

I did as I was instructed and he began to put on some rubber gloves.

'Right, here goes. Breathe shallowly for me,' he said as he inserted his fingers and, as far as I know, his whole hand, into my ring. It felt strange having something inserted there – my first and only time, I'll have you know – but not uncomfortable. Then the most horrendous and embarrassing thing happened. I shat myself. I felt myself excreting the longest turd I have ever produced. It came out long and slow and smooth, and I felt ill with the expectation of what I would see when I got up and what that nice Irish Catholic doctor would say when he saw how enormously I had defiled his couch, his floor, his room, his life!

He spoke immediately though the wait seemed interminable. 'Right, pop your things back on.'

I got up delicately and looked around. Where were my faeces? Where was that champion of turds? I'd just de-logged massively and there was no trace! Dr Fahey had taken his gloves off and was standing by the sink rinsing his hands. Had he cleared it all up? In that time? The room looked spotless. The man was a genius. A great doctor who would surely make a good living on the side as a cleaning lady.

'Er, sorry, doctor,' I offered feebly.

'Don't apologise; it's no big deal,' he comforted.

I was about to say, 'No big deal? It was a stool of basking-shark proportions, what are you saying?' but he carried on talking. 'Strange feeling, though, isn't it, when someone pulls their hand out of your bum? You think you've done a poo. Same sensation: the feeling of

your sphincter muscles closing on something smooth and long slid-
ing out of the anus.'

'If you say so, doctor,' was my limp but relieved response.

'You've got pruritis ani. I'll give you some cream. Right, off you go!'

So that was it; I had pruritis ani. That is Latin for itchy arse. I go
in there, tell him what I've got and after ten minutes and him shov-
ing his hand up my Gary Glitter, he translates it into Latin. Pruritis
ani, my arse.

Well, at least I hadn't redecorated his surgery with shite.

Chapter 21

The Ship of the Fens

'Doctors know fuck all,' announced Jonesy, Wales's foremost painter and decorator and bit-part actor, as we left the cathedral by a side door leading onto a pretty, narrow, cobblestoned street.

'What makes you say that?' Danny inquired, fingering his arm to check the patch was still in place.

'The fact that he's a twat,' I answered.

'That's not nice,' said the Welshman, lighting a cigarette and puffing his first drag offensively in my direction. 'I told you, though,' he went on. 'I said that when I was next in church it'd be for a funeral.'

'Your own funeral, you said,' Danny corrected him.

'Well, I didn't think it'd be Nobby's. That's what I mean about doctors, you see. They know fuck all.'

'How come?' asked Danny.

'Well,' Jonesy informed us, 'three months ago, coming up to his fiftieth, Nobby decided to go to his quack for an MOT. You know, a complete medical check-up. Well, he passes with flying colours. Blood pressure good, weight good, cholesterol good, ticker good. Everything. An example to all fifty-year-olds, says the medicine man. Now, look where are we today. At Nobby's bleeding funeral. Doctors, eh? They know nothing!'

'Nobby was killed in a car crash, though,' I reminded him.

'Exception that proves the rule,' Jonesy went on meaninglessly.

'It's a very sad day, there's no doubt about that, but let's be positive,' I urged. 'Nobby was a positive person, he'd be looking for something good at this moment.'

'Some good boozers in Ely,' Jonesy said, a bit more animated now.

'And this, don't forget,' I said, pointing up at the magnificence of Ely cathedral. 'It's amazing! Just imagine building that in the eleventh century.'

'Building what?' Jonesy asked, scanning the end of the lane for boozers. 'Oh, the church.'

I carried on enthusing. 'But it's stone! That's what's remarkable. Stone!'

'Well, what do you expect?' said Jonesy, who had dabbled in the construction trade. 'They didn't have plasterboard back then.'

'No, but when you think about it,' I persevered, 'they didn't really have stone back then. People lived in mud huts or wooden shacks.'

'Nothing much has changed in the Fens then,' sniggered Danny.

'The blocks of limestone used to build this cathedral were dragged here from about fifty miles away,' I pointed out.

'Really?' Danny asked. 'How do you know this stuff?'

'I'm reading it off this information board here. And that would have been by horse and cart, or possibly by hand. It's incredible.'

Danny was prompted to think about this and eventually asked, 'Why didn't they build better houses for themselves, then?'

'This is the point. The church was the most important building in a community then.'

Jonesy looked interested. 'Not the pub, then?'

'No, definitely not,' I answered. 'That would have been wattle and daub.'

'Good name for a pub,' said Jonesy.

I continued my homily. 'God's house had to be the best house. The biggest house, the most beautiful and often the most terrifying. They would have thought nothing of dragging boulders around for God's house. To people then, the Church was everything. The Church was unquestionable. For them, God was responsible for all good things and all bad things, as it happens.'

'Only because the priests and bishops and monks kept them in the dark,' Danny butted in, 'and fed them with superstition and threats of hell and damnation.'

'Yeah, I know,' I conceded, 'but whatever the reason, you didn't question it.'

'Well, I've never questioned God. I just ignore him,' said Danny categorically.

'Well, that's easy for you, isn't it? You had a secular upbringing. You had no faith to abandon. When you're brought up a Catholic, it's very hard to give it up. One of the hardest things I ever did in fact.'

'Harder than whitewater liloing in *Rory and Paddy*?' asked Danny, sensing a challenge.

'Even harder than that.'

'Harder than explaining away that text you sent to Claire Webber when her husband found it?'

I ignored this and said, 'Listen, you don't wake up one morning and think: "Right, that's it. I'm not Catholic any more. Bye bye, Church." It took me years to do it. Literally, for about three years every Sunday morning I'd lie in bed trying to summon up the courage or the will to do it. And it took me years to get over it.'

'But you question everything,' Danny argued. 'It doesn't seem to bother you. Global warming and man-made climate change? You question that.'

I nodded. 'Yeah, well, that *is* bollocks. Only the feeble-minded believe that crap. Hen-pecked men who read the *Guardian*, mainly. It's just a convenient lie to enable governments to rip you off and groom you into unthinking civil obedience. Like recycling, which makes not one jot of difference to the environment. It just creates more pollution, in fact. And a few pointless jobs and lots of money, of course.'

Danny started laughing. 'Ha, bravo! You see, straight in with the questioning of a popular belief. Shakespeare?'

'Overrated. Generally very boring. All his plays are too long and wordy. There are bits that are beautiful to read, there are bits of amazing insight and wisdom, but they should never be performed. Especially not in a modern setting or in contemporary costumes to make them seem more "relevant". Especially not *Hamlet* uncut. That's a fucking nightmare.'

'Caviar?'

'Fish-flavoured rat shit.'

'*X Factor*?'

'The death of culture.'

'No, the death of culture is no smoking in pubs,' Jonesy contradicted.

'*Big Brother*?' Danny went on.

'The end of civilisation.'

He shook his head. 'Blimey, you're going to tell me next you don't believe in the omnipotence and infallibility of Stephen Fry.'

'No,' I agreed, 'that would be going too far. That's like saying there *is* no Arsène Wenger!'

'In the words of the dear departed Nobby,' Jonesy interrupted, 'drink, anyone?'

'Good idea,' said Danny. 'Yeah, let's try the Wattle and Daub.'

We trudged off in search of booze but I couldn't help stopping to look round at the building behind us. I wondered if it made any difference to your faith to have a place like this to worship in. I thought back to the modest rectangle of inter-war functionalism that was my home church in the nondescript town of Redruth.

Chapter 22

Good Catholic Boy Is Superior

Wally Freeth, the boy from next door, was a show-off, that much was well known. And he liked nothing better than to spin a tall yarn. But on this occasion he was telling the truth, the whole truth and the nothing but the truth. He was adamant. And his revelation was truly stunning, prompting equal parts excitement and terror in my six-and-three-quarter-year-old brain. One Sunday afternoon Wally Freeth announced that he'd found out where Redruth legend Kitchie George lived.

In 1720, Daniel Defoe toured Britain and declared that Redruth in Cornwall – my birthplace – was 'not worthy of note'. To us Redruthians, the very fact that he noted it was not worthy of note was noteworthy enough. And it's a shame DD didn't hang round for another ten years as from 1730 onwards, for a hundred years or more, Redruth was going to be world-famous.

Its name is derived from the Cornish for 'red ford' or 'red river'. Various streams in the area are a reddish-brown colour, testifying to the presence of minerals containing copper or tin. And with the advent of steam engines, which helped move men up and down the pits and pump out water, Cornwall's ancient copper and tin mining industries flourished. (In fact, as any Cornish schoolboy will tell you, the first working steam locomotive was designed and built by local lad Richard Trevithick. Sadly, though, he was from the deadly rival town of Camborne, two and a half miles away, so we Redruth men don't like to harp on about this too much.)

By the mid-nineteenth century, Redruth was a boom town. It was the world capital for tin and copper. Its population in 1861 was over 11,000; huge for the time. It had more prostitutes than any other town outside London, Birmingham, Liverpool and Manchester (my, how things had changed by the years of my youth). But when the global price of copper and tin plummeted around 1886 – due to other tin and copper mines opening worldwide – Redruth had to wave good-bye to its wealth, prestige and all those night-time lovelies, and was plunged, once more, back into relative obscurity.

And had Mr Defoe returned 250 years after his first visit, he might well have thought 'not worthy of note' a lavish compliment. Redruth in the sixties and seventies was a one-horse town. But with no horse.

The terminal drabness of the Close Hill estate, the council estate on which I was born and where I was brought up for the first seven years of my life, meant Redruth existed unremarkably until 2008, when it was reported internationally that police had to enforce a curfew in the summer holidays to stop rowdy yobbos terrorising the streets. (Fucking noteworthy now, Mr Defoe, or what!?)

But growing up is an exciting thing to do wherever and when-ever you do it. Children can always make their own adventures. A lovely sandy beach was walking distance from our house; the fire station was at the bottom of the hill from us, and at least once a week the fire engine would fly by, sirens blaring, and we'd run to the end of the road to catch a glimpse of it; a fish and chip van came round once a week, and occasionally someone would fall to their death down an unfenced, disused mineshaft. Oh, and 1963, it snowed. And then one night in 1965, there was an earth tremor which set off our neighbours' burglar alarm and the police came round. This was barely after we'd got over the excitement of *having* neighbours with a burglar alarm. (Theirs was the only house that ever got burgled round our way; my dad sagely informed us that it was the alarm itself that alerted the burglars to the presence in the house of something worth stealing.) Then there was the time Ed Hocking shat in a piece of newspaper and brought it into school to show us. (I think he comes up for parole any time now.) The list is endless.

And, of course, there was the living legend that was Kitchie George; Redruth's premier tramp. Perhaps more of a hobo. A man of the fields and ways. A dosser. A wino. A vagabond. Though there were rumours that he was merely an adherent of an alternative lifestyle: an ascetic who lived apart from humanity, neither needing nor accepting charity.

Another, rather more generous, story had him as a commando in the Second World War who had seen selfless active service and who had subsequently lost his mind due to the horrors he'd witnessed. But we didn't like these stories; we wanted to keep him as a bogeyman.

The only item of clothing of his you could see was a huge ankle-length overcoat, permanently held tightly closed across his middle with a piece of parcel string. On his feet he wore boots. Or maybe they *were* his feet; perhaps the boundary between foot and boot had become blurred. Wild, black hair covered most of his face, featureless but for two vein-reddened billiard-ball eyes. This and the fact that his clothes, with age or dirt, were either black or dark brown and made him seem not like an elderly male human dressed in clothes, but an alien being; a charcoal-coloured yeti; the Abominable Coalman.

Harmless as you passed him in the car on a sunny day, slumped by the gate of a field or in a hedgerow, but an evil presence at night: 'Kitchie George'll get you!' was an oft-heard reprimand or curse.

'What does he look like?' my little sister would ask, and my two brothers and I would give her a graphic description, with all manner of horrific embellishments. The conversation would inevitably descend into general bickering when Stephen, the eldest of us, thought Michael's and my rococo details were detracting from the realism of the man.

'No, he hasn't got three eyes, Rory, or a tail; you're just being silly.'

This in turn would lead to an argument about who had seen him most recently. Or who had seen him the greatest number of times. Or, best of all, who had seen him from closest up. We'd then be hard pushed to remember a recent sighting of him at all. Or, in fact, any actual sighting. By us or by anyone. The truth was that very little was actually known about Kitchie George. No one knew where he came from and no one knew where he went at night. If he did, in fact, sleep, where did he sleep? If he did, in fact, live, where did he live?

Well, now we knew. Wally Freeth had found out.

President Kennedy's assassination a few months earlier hadn't really impinged on us. We knew he was special and holy and great because he was Irish and a Catholic and had been shot, but apart from that I don't remember much about the events of Dealey Plaza, 22 November, 1963. But I'll never forget what I was doing when Wally Freeth told me he'd found Kitchie George's hiding place and was going to show me.

'You're not going,' were my mother's emphatic words.

'Why not? Wally's going. And so is Charlie Owens and four of the Tregonings,' I pleaded.

'In that case, you're definitely not going. I don't want you mixing with them. Especially not rooting round in a tramp's hovel!'

'Ah, please, Mummy! S'not fair!'

'And anyway, you can't go tonight. We're going to Benediction.'

'But we've already been to church today!'

'That was Mass, this is Benediction.' She was adamant. Benediction it was.

I never really understood what was happening at Benediction. It was gloomy and downbeat. There was lots of incense and bells and more Latin hymns and prayers than usual. The sacred host was exposed – this was supposed to be a big thing – and blessed with the sign of the cross. This was the blessing. The benediction, in fact, from the Latin *benedictio*, meaning 'a blessing'. The service was quite short, I recall, which was the main blessing.

'If Wally and that lot aren't going to Benediction, why should I go, then?' I asked, defiantly.

'They're not Catholics!' Mum replied, as if it were self-evident. I couldn't think of any speedy or useful reply to this. Eventually I came up with, 'Why can they do some things that I can't do?'

'Well, you do lots of things they can't, too. Like go to Mass and Benediction; which are a damn sight better than poking around in hedges.'

The benefits of this didn't seem all that obvious to me.

'If they're not Catholics, what are they?' I persevered.

'Well, if anything at all …' she laughed nervously, 'they're Prods. Protestants.'

'Are Catholics better than Protestants, then?'

She smiled. 'What a question! Of course. Now go and get ready.'

But I wasn't to be put off. 'Why am I a Catholic then?'

'You were born Catholic. You were baptised a Catholic. Now let's stop this palaver and get ready for church!' Her exasperation was beginning to show.

'What if I'd been born Proddy?'

'Just thank God you weren't and that's an end to it!'

She left me alone in the room, pondering my superiority over most of the people I knew. I was baptised a Catholic. That's important. Not 'christened'. Although Catholics are Christians, they see themselves to be a superior form of Christian. The Russian word for 'peasant' is *krestyanin*, which is derived from 'Christian', and the French for 'Christian' gives us 'cretin'. Say no more.

Jews, Hindus and Muslims didn't come into the equation. You must understand that when you're a young Catholic boy growing up in England in the fifties and sixties, the only other religion was Protestantism. If we ever met anyone at church, school or socially, who was from India, Asia or Israel, they would be Catholic Israelis or non-Catholic Israelis, Catholic Muslims or non-Catholic Muslims. And we all knew that 'C of E' wasn't the same as Protestantism, it was just code for 'No religion at all, but just too lazy to wrestle with the concepts of atheism and agnosticism'.

Was I better than Wally and Charlie? They were good fun but definitely a bit common. They swore, which I never did. And probably never would do. Or, if I did, it was mainly the word 'bloody', which hinted of danger, physical threat and, possibly, fatal injury. I intuited its intensity.

But: 'That's a horrible word. I hope I never hear you using it,' we were told. 'And it's blasphemous, anyway.'

Now this was new. My mother went on, 'It's a corruption of "By Our Lady", so it's even worse than it sounds!'

That is fascinating, I remember thinking. And deeply disappointing.

Charlie swore more than Wally, so I assumed he was even less Catholic than Wally. Or more Protestant. According to Wally, Charlie had once used the f-word.

This was shocking but also exciting and hilarious. (I didn't know at the time what the f-word was but it was obviously, deliciously, non-Catholic.)

Wally once dropped his trousers and showed me his bottom, which again was daringly funny. But common. And inferior.

'Are we Christians, then?' I asked my mother.

'Of course we are. Roman Catholicism is a branch of Christianity,' she answered tentatively, as if worried that the next question would be: 'Was Jesus Christ a Catholic then?'

'Was Jesus Christ a Catholic then?' I asked.

A nervous laugh from my mother. 'Well, he was Jewish really.'

'Oh,' I said, not really knowing what that meant. 'I'd have thought if anybody was going to be a Christian, it would be Christ.'

'He founded the Church that we now know as the Catholic Church. Well, he told St Peter to,' she said, picking her way through the jungle of religion and theology.

'Are Jews Catholics then?' seemed to be the obvious follow-up question.

She laughed. 'No. Jews don't even believe in the New Testament! They don't believe in Jesus Christ.'

'So, Christ was a Jew but he didn't believe in himself! So are Jews Christians?'

'No. Not at all,' she paused and turned something over in her mind. 'Though they're very special people, the Jews.'

Mmm. There seemed to be a hierarchy appearing, in which Catholics were at the top, Protestants were clearly at the bottom and Jews, I sensed, were somewhere up high. Second maybe?

'What are Muslims?' I went on.

'Listen, love,' my mother finally gave in. 'I'm not the person you should be asking these questions. I'm not really qualified to answer. It's good that you're asking, though. It shows you've got an inquiring mind. You should question things. It's good to question things.'

'Why is it good to question things?' I asked innocently.

'Just shut up and finish your homework before Benediction,' came the reply.

Instead of doing my homework I decided to look up 'Religion' in the encyclopaedia. This was a shock. A 'By Our Lady!' shock. Religions: there were hundreds of them. Well over half the population of the world had had the misfortune to be born non-Catholic (I was assuming, of course, that things like Hinduism, Zoroastrianism, Shintoism, Buddhism and Quakerism weren't all different forms of Roman Catholicism).

And there was something called Mormonism, which sounded like a scary, congenital defect, like thalidomide.

'Who do Muslims worship then?' I asked my father, thinking he might fill in the multiple gaps that were appearing retrospectively in my mother's answers.

'They have a God called Allah.' he said, barely looking up from the rugby league on the telly.

'Is our God better than Allah?'

'Well, I suppose he's the same really,' said my father, more agitated by St Helens *v.* Wigan than Allah *v.* God.

'Exactly the same, or better? Or worse?' I persisted.

'Listen, love, why don't you go and ask your mum. She's better at all this.'

But I wasn't finished. 'Is it better to be a Catholic than a Muslim or a Methodist?'

'Oh, yes,' he said distractedly, adding, to someone on the screen (I assume), 'Ooh, you daft clot!'

'*O, Salutaris Hostia,*' boomed the a cappella voice of Father McEvedy, hitting the right notes but unfortunately at the wrong times. '*Quae caeli pandis ostium, bella premunt hostilia, da robur, fer auxilium.*' Even with the priest's minuscule choral abilities, there was something quite magical about the words. They were full of hope and meaning, until you translated them to English – 'Oh, salutary victim who expandest the door of the sky, hostile wars press; give strength, bear aid' – when they became hopeless and meaningless.

I loved the smell of incense. I still do. To be fair, Benediction wouldn't have been so bad if it didn't happen on the same day as Mass. Mass in the morning, Benediction in the evening, and the whole day in between informed by goodness. There were no gaps in the day for feeling careless joy or unbridled mischief. No looking in Wally's elder sister's handbag and examining all manner of saucy but inexplicable curios. No playing football in the private field and running away from Lenny the Louse, the bad-tempered groundsman, or distracting the driver of the 'pop van' while Charlie tried to sneak a dandelion-and-burdock from the back of the lorry. Nothing sinful. Nothing inferior. Nothing non-Catholic. Nothing fun.

'*Panem de caelo praestitisti eis*,' Father Mack continued. I bet Wally and Charlie didn't know what that meant. 'You have given them bread from heaven.' But then I'm superior to them, aren't I?

Everybody, it is said, remembers exactly what they were doing when Wally Freeth announced that he'd found the lair of Kitchie George. As I was getting ready for Benediction (a perk of my superiority), I didn't see it.

Funnily enough, years later I found out something that did nothing to diminish my disappointment, albeit retrospectively, about that night.

Kitchie George *did* exist. He *was* a famous Redruth character. Tramp, hobo, vagabond, bogeyman, call him what you will.

But he had died in 1938, about twenty years before we were born.

Chapter 23

Sinner Boy Commits Another Deadly Sin: Gluttony

What's happened to mirrors? Are they being manufactured differently these days? Why are they such poor quality now? Are mirror-makers using cheaper materials, cutting corners or not lavishing the skill, patience and craftsmanship that produced those fine mirrors that I grew up with?

Whenever I looked in the mirror back then, they clearly showed a slim, optimistic man, beaming with confidence and glowing with an inner strength.

This particular hotel bathroom contained the worst mirror I'd ever encountered. Perhaps I should mention it to the management; have someone from Maintenance come up and look at it.

The reflection clearly showed a sagging wreck of what was a thirty-year-old human being: bowed, spindly legs could hardly support the bloated torso, which was the colour of candlewax and the texture of mashed potato. The head didn't look as if it belonged on the body. It had clearly been the result of a botched head transplant that work-experience surgeons had half-heartedly stuck back on without bothering to join up bones, nerves and sinews. The face was a shade known as perilously-close-to-heart-attack purple. The eyes were two scarlet slits; stab-wounds that the surrounding skin strained, wrinkled and puckered to keep shut lest the creature bleed to death.

Was that really me? How did I become this? What did I do last night? I leant closer to the mirror and looked again. Ah, not as bad as I originally thought. There was a gentleness, a softness, a smoothness to the face. No, it was just my breath steaming up the glass. Once it cleared the beast reappeared, more brutish than before. The mirror cut me off just below the navel, which was probably a good thing. I was naked, and what I'd seen so far rather scared me; perusal of my nethers in that state would probably have sent me over the edge. And, wait …

Oh my God!

I looked closely. There was a brown, lumpy streak from my temple down my cheek to my chin.

I must have shat myself.

Through the side of my head?

And what was this? Just underneath my nipple. A spot? A pimple? A blister. It was pink and hard. Almost scaly. There was another one on my side. And another. I was covered in them. But, wait, one was blue. There was a green one, too. And orange. Oh my dear Christ!

'Darling, what exactly did I do last night?' I croaked in the direction of the bedroom. No reply. 'Darling?'

The reply was not quite what I expected. A girl's voice but not understandable as English. A sort of slurred mumble.

Whatever I was doing last night, she had clearly been doing as well.

'I feel like death and I've got a weird rash all over me, and shit on my face.'

Another strange and alien mumble from the girl.

'What about you, how are you?' I asked as I opened the door and stepped back into the bedroom.

'Me good,' the Polish chambermaid said, then turned round and saw me. 'I come back later!' She fled.

I picked at the orange scab on my arm and looked closely at it. It looked like a sweet. I tentatively put it in my mouth. Thankfully it was a Smartie. Yum. I'd clearly fallen asleep having opened a packet of them.

I walked back towards the bed. The carpet crunched with pizza crusts, Smarties, pistachio shells and three sharp-pointed Toblerone tubes. The bed was a mess. A girl-shaped duvet lay the wrong way round on the bed, with the feet end at the headboard and the head end dangling painfully off the bottom of the bed. I shook it.

'Wakey, wakey! Let's get a coffee. I feel dreadful.' No answer. A terrifying realisation came over me. I pulled the duvet back.

Oh my God.

There on the bed was …

Nothing.

The girl-shaped duvet was a girl-shaped duvet.

The phone rang. I jumped.

'Hello?'

A cheery female voice asked, 'Hi, how are you today?'

'Er … fine.' I laboured to recognise the not unpleasant voice on the other end. 'Er, who's that?'

'It's me. Glynis!'

'Oh, Glynis. Sorry, lovely. You didn't sound like you.'

Who the fuck is Glynis? I thought.

'I thought you'd forgotten me!' she giggled. 'You can't ever forget Amsterdam, though, can you?'

What's she talking about? I've never been to Amsterdam.

'Hey … er, Glynis. I've never been to Amsterdam!'

She laughed. 'You are silly. You're *in* Amsterdam now. I left you in your hotel room ordering the whole room service menu.'

' Glynis, can you call me back a bit later? I'm feeling a bit peculiar.'

'Sure thing. Speak soon, ciao!'

Glynis. She sounded cute but she could sod off with her 'ciao'. I hate that. I decided a long, frothy aromatic soak would do me the world of good.

Back in the bathroom, I turned on both taps fully and looked for the little bottle of foaming bath oil. There was none. What sort of hotel is this? While I waited for the bath to fill, I went to the mini-bar to see what goodies remained. Nothing. I was starving. Perhaps I should ring down to room service. I looked again at the mini-bar. What about a drink? That's a good idea. A stiff one first thing to sharpen the senses, that's what I needed. No, still nothing. Even the Bailey's Irish Cream had gone. I must have been spectacularly out of it last night to have downed that as well.

I searched round the desk and coffee tables, the bedside tables and under the bed. Under the bed. Aha! There it was. A miniature bottle had made it through the night. I reverently unscrewed the top and took a swig.

'Yeuch!!'

At least I'd found the foaming bath oil.

One cold, overflowing bath and several very frothy gargles later, I was feeling a bit more human. Not quite human, yet. Certainly hominoid, but not exactly Homo sapiens. Perhaps a few brain cells on from Australopithecus.

Using the misshapen remains of my memory, I was vaguely able to piece together what life must have been like for a being such as me in the misty depths of yesterday. The gaps were filled in by Glynis on the plane home the following day.

* * *

Evidently, I'd gone to Amsterdam to work on a TV pilot. It was a daytime game-cum-quiz show entitled approximately, 'Answer correctly or show us your arse'. (It's possible that some of the pithiness of the original Dutch title gets lost in translation.) A production assistant from the English production company, the very comely Glynis, had accompanied me to the Netherlands and was 'looking after' me. The pilot, I recall, had gone well, with the Dutch crew speaking better English than most of the British crews I'd worked with.

In the evening Glynis and I had gone out for dinner, but prior to that I had visited a 'brown' café called Mary-Jayne's and had scoffed down four cakes called 'Fairy Headbangers'. (They were exceedingly good cakes and had they been his, Mr Kipling would have found a whole new generation of customers. But probably lost his licence.) It seemed a million years since I'd sat nervously in Timothy Blaine's college room the night Claudia, his girlfriend from London, had shown us innocent excited students a small lump of cannabis resin. In those days I think I was too frightened even to touch it.

Anyway, the effects of the cakes had kicked in at the worst possible moment: the moment we ordered our meal. It was an above average Thai restaurant and Glynis suggested the mixed starter for two.

'Yes, fine,' I agreed and turned to the waitress. 'Er, the mixed starter for two for my friend and I'll have the mixed starter for six, thanks.'

* * *

'You were laughing a lot,' Glynis recalled, 'and leering at the girl on the next table.'

'Oh, dear,' I said, still with no memory of the event, 'at least I wasn't dribbling.'

'Oh, you were,' Glynis corrected, 'salivating like a rabid hippo. In fact, at one point her boyfriend asked you to stop staring at her. I thought he was going to hit you.'

'Oh, no. What did I say?'

'You said, "Don't worry, pal, I'm a poof!"'

I shook my head. 'What happened then?'

'The two gays on the table behind us called you a "Sad English pig!"'

Oh, dear …

Then, apparently, to my extreme consternation, a gentleman on a nearby table had left without finishing his meal. In fact, it was barely touched, and I had expressed my disgust that people should waste good food like that, especially with millions of starving people in the world; one of whom was me, come to think about it. So I had got up and sat down at the abandoned table and started eating.

'What the hell do you think you're doing?' a man had yelled approaching the table, red-faced with anger. 'This is my table. I've just been to the toilet!'

Glynis had clearly smoothed things over and back at our table our main course had been served. It consisted of the set banquet for five and copious bottles of Singha beer. I had ardently spooned food into my mouth, in between giggling fits and leching at the girl on the next table. Waitresses and other diners had steered clear of our table lest a stray body part be hoovered up into my busy jaws.

Once the feast had been laid waste to, the waitress had tentatively approached and given us the menus for dessert. By this time, I had already forgotten that we'd had dinner.

'Ah, menus. Excellent,' I had beamed at the waitress. I had then turned to Glynis and suggested, 'We could have a mixed banquet for six, if you like; there's never enough food in these combos.'

'We've already eaten, Rory,' had replied an exasperated Glynis. 'This is the menu for desserts.'

'No dessert for me; I'll just have some Thai fishcakes and spring rolls.'

'We have vegetarian spring rolls, pork or chicken,' explained the waitress.

'Yes, they'll be fine.'

Glynis had escorted me back to the hotel and up to my room where I'd predictably tried to snog her and asked her to stay the night. She told me she had smiled demurely and politely declined, saying something like, 'Fuck off, you must be joking!'

And then to cap it all, she claimed I had announced suddenly, as if having a flash of divine inspiration: 'Aren't we stupid! We were supposed to go out for dinner tonight but we forgot to eat!'

Glynis had left as I was ringing down to order two pizzas.

'I left you and escaped back to my room. God knows what you did. You sounded completely dazed when I phoned you.'

* * *

After my bath, I realised I really was hungry (unbelievably), and decided I should perhaps go down for breakfast. Dressed, clean, tidy and presentable – despite evidence to the contrary in the mirror – I opened the door and was about to head for the lifts when I noticed a trolley outside my room. On it was a continental breakfast. Fab, I thought. I was obviously sentient enough to order my breakfast the night before.

I wheeled the trolley into the room and saw that there was something on the lower shelf. A full English breakfast, with additional rollmop herrings and four bottles of Amstel Gold. Magic! I tucked in with zeal but was disappointed to find that the eggs and bacon were completely cold and the sausages anchored to the plate with congealed fat. This was absolutely unacceptable. I phoned room service and complained vehemently.

The man at the other end was apologetic. 'But, sir, I'm sure the breakfast was perfectly hot when we delivered it to your room at 7.30 a.m. as requested.'

'Oh,' I said. 'What time is it now?'

'Six o'clock in the evening, sir.'

* * *

My doctor was not amused when I told him this story a week later.

'But I do love my food, doctor.'

'And other people's, by the sound of it. Now, listen, ingesting illegal substances is bad enough but when they're appetite enhancers, too, you really should think twice. It's a miracle you're only four stone overweight. Right, put your clothes back on.'

'Thanks, doctor,' I replied glumly. As I dressed, I looked across the room and noticed that the doctor had one of those faulty mirrors as well.

I was in a bad place, I thought. If only I could be born again.

Chapter 24

Grown-up Boy at Baptism Again

So, here I was again in the wholly superior surroundings of Holy Joe's church, Highgate, awaiting those special words …

'… And I baptise thee, Joseph Rory, in the name of the Father and of the Son and of the Holy Ghost.'

And everybody says 'Amen'.

(Except for my little boy of course.)

He's just a cute, pink bundle of chuckles; not the unsightly, screaming, wriggling splodge that I was when I was his age. Or do your own children always look completely different?

Everyone is given a candle.

(Except the boy; he's too young to play with fire.)

The priest says, 'Shine as a light in the world against sin and the devil.'

Everyone says, 'Amen'.

It's the Hebrew for 'so be it'. I'll teach him that one day. If he's interested. Possibly if he's not interested. Let's wait and see.

The ceremony is over and my boy is clean.

Pure. Spotless. Unblemished. Immaculate. The sin of Adam has been washed away. He is stainless. He is stain-free. He is without stain.

'Oh dear, look at that stain. I think he needs his nappy changed.' I chuckle as a pained grimace contorts the little face.

But his soul is white, blindingly bright white and full of grace.

Though in my opinion, it always was. My child was born without the sin of Adam. So his soul does not have to be cleansed of that blemish. There is no soul more spotless than a non-existent soul. I didn't want my son to grow up in a world where a God doesn't allow him into the world because he's dirty from someone else's sin. In fact, this whole baptism thing is a sham. I only decided to go ahead with it for my parents. Mary's family was largely indifferent. It was hinted to us with sly obliqueness by one of the priests at Holy Joe's that only children baptised in the faith could attend the Catholic primary school, the best in the area, but I wasn't falling for that. I'm sure there were others just as good in the area. And if there weren't, it wouldn't hurt to go through a bit of a silly ceremony in church. It was only up the road and it was an excuse for another family booze-up. What would I say to my children if they started asking my awkward questions like, 'What is grace?'

Would I deliberately misunderstand the question and say dismissively, it's a prayer you say before and after meals?

'What is a soul, Daddy?' Would I say, it's a fish? Or it's that thing on the bottom of your shoe?

'What is sin, Daddy?' Would I say, you'd better go and ask your mother?

'Have you sinned, Daddy?' No, but your mother has.

One thing at a time. Today was about my first-born. The boy Joe. My job was not to think about my hypocrisy in putting him through it, my job was to hold the camcorder steady and record the event for our future joy and, no doubt, his future embarrassment.

And oblivious to the fact that for the first, and only, time in his whole life he is free from sin, the recently baptised Joseph Rory is carried up the dark aisle of the church. The door creaks open; a shaft of light glances across the baby's face. The light, which is to illuminate the path of goodness and ward off evil, makes the baby wince and as he leaves the church into daylight he starts crying. And I find that I'm crying. The boy is oblivious to the fact that this day the world revolves around him. Lots of worlds revolve around him now. Mine definitely does. Some are crushed by the weight of parental responsibility and the child suffers. But that day I felt that one weight was being lifted from my shoulders. I was no longer the centre of my universe. The lights were no longer trained on me. I could withdraw slightly into the shadows and hope nobody noticed me.

'And who are you?' said the registrar, peering over the top of her glasses.

'I'm the baby's father.'

Her tongue clicked with irritation and continued sarcastically, 'I assumed you were but you are a person in your own right, aren't you? You do have a name of your own, don't you?'

'No,' I was tempted to say. 'I'm not and I haven't. I'm the baby's father; that's enough, isn't it?'

The little congregation walked the short distance downhill from the church to my house. Our house. Our children's house, in fact. The place we'd moved to so we could have children. The family home, yes, that's what it is.

Chapter 25

Good Catholic Boy Moves Upwards

A proper family home, it was. And brand new. It was 1964 and I was eight when we moved house. We moved away from boys like Wally and Charlie, away from tramps' hovels, away from f-words, away from Protestants with Cornish accents who'd say things like 'Right on' and 'Eeeeoooo' and 'I'll see 'ee myrrh'.

It didn't occur to me at the time that the majority of people I knew in Cornwall, at church and at school, didn't speak with a Cornish accent. They were mainly from up country (i.e. England) or Irish, and the few who *did* have Cornish accents were second-generation Italians or Poles.

The new house made us feel as if our lives had started again. Because of my father's work, as an MoD research chemist, my parents had had to move down from St Helens in Merseyside, in the early fifties, to this remote outpost in west Cornwall. A dream move, you might think, from the grim, industrial hinterland of the north, to a small Cornish town a mere mile from the coast. But for a young married couple used to an extended family and a network of close friends and the open cordiality of northerners, it must have seemed bleak, cold and unwelcoming. And it certainly wasn't the plan for my siblings and me to be brought up on the Close Hill estate, so when the time and money were right, we moved.

We went upmarket (before the expression was invented, of course). We moved from an end-of-terrace council house in 'Curfew estate' to a brand-new, detached bungalow. Not only was it a bungalow, which was the height of posh, but it also had an upstairs. This made it technically not a bungalow, but because the bedrooms upstairs were built into the roof, it looked like a bungalow from the outside and felt like a house inside. This was 'cool', an expression, I think, that was still in its first incarnation in the mid-sixties.

So me and my two brothers, Stephen (two years older) and Michael (one year younger), had the upstairs room, while the rest of the upstairs, the roof-space, was a walk-in loft that my parents planned to convert to another bedroom one day (I can report that this conversion is yet to be done forty-five years on). My parents had the large bedroom downstairs and my sister, Catherine (four years younger), the small one next to it.

There were seven houses in our road. Well, six along one side of the lane and one round the corner, on a tiny side road. We were the last of the six on the angle of the corner, with the house round the corner next to us. It was a very desirable place to live, apparently, as these few shiny new houses were surrounded by nothing but fields. It was like being in the country (which is what most people think Cornwall is anyway).

Ours was the biggest house of the group because of its whacky upstairs bit, and our bedroom overlooked a football pitch. This was the home ground of Illogan Royal British Legion FC and, but for an annoyingly placed hawthorn tree, we had, every other Saturday, an unimpeded view of some atrocious football.

The first house in our street, where it joined the main road, belonged to the Holroyds. They were from Yorkshire which, in our Lancashire 'red rose' household, was normally considered a bad thing, but was rather good in this case. They were friendly and outgoing in that 'northern way', and they united with us against the alien Cornish in whose land we found ourselves.

Next to them were the mysterious Brownlows, who kept themselves to themselves. This was considered a very 'good' thing, apparently. Just as good, we intuited, as being open and friendly and always in each other's houses, like northerners. The Brownlows were treated with a distant respect, polite nods and the occasional, not too smiley 'Morning!' They had been professionals (whatever that was) in the Home Counties (whatever they were), so they were obviously 'a cut above' (whatever that was). Next to them were the Tresidders. Now this couple was Cornish, but he, Basil, wore a suit. He was a solicitor. This was apparently a good thing. Not just the fact he wore a suit, or that he was a solicitor, but that we should have one living just three doors down the road. Solicitors, like accountants, councillors and insurance men, were talked about in our house in hushed, semi-reverential tones. Not with the same unquestioning awe that accompanied mentions of priests and doctors, of course, but still with substantial deference. (When you've had dealings with solicitors, accountants, councillors and insurance men in your adult life, it's hard, looking back, to understand why they should ever have been viewed with anything but suspicion and contempt. But we were young then, and so was the world.)

Next to the Tresidders were the Palmers, a nice family. Nice parents and nice children. Nice neighbours. Probably the most similar to us. But, sadly, not Catholic, or they would have been our lifelong soulmates.

Then came our immediate next-door neighbours, the Nicholases. Cyril and Greta and their two girls, Helen and Penny. They were from Devon, which, as we all knew, just like St Helens, was in England, not Cornwall. This made them virtually posh and particularly good people to have next door. He was a lecturer at 'the college' and occasionally wore a hat with a feather in it: the height of raciness.

Next came us on the corner and round the corner in the last house of the neighbourhood lived the Kendricks. Now they actually *were* posh. They spoke with the accent you only used to hear on the BBC news. Mr Kendrick was 'high up' in an 'office' (whatever that meant) and she was a freelancer (whatever that was).

So, all in all, the move was, in every respect, a huge improvement. We were nearer the beach, nearer our school, but further away from the influences of the Close Hill estate. We were further from church as well, but that was not a problem because, although the changes brought about by the house move were to have a considerable influence on our upbringing, the church was the one thing that stayed exactly the same. The routines it involved and the people it brought us into contact with were to be a constant for many years to come.

Constants, in fact, began to feature more in my life. Or possibly I just noticed them more. Like fish on Fridays. Unmistakably Catholic, that. If, in later years, someone said something like, 'We used to always have fish on Fridays,' I would immediately identify that person as Catholic. The phrase 'fish on Fridays' is like a Masonic handshake to Catholics.

Technically, 'fish on Fridays' really meant 'no *meat* on Fridays'. And 'no meat' meant eating fish. That is, only the meat of a fish. Whether there was a long-lasting health benefit to this or not, it was certainly true in those days that Catholics would eat more fish than your average non-believer, Prod, heathen or savage. And I've no way of knowing whether or not this informed my lifelong passion for fish and seafood (on balance, I think, probably not).

Hake, monkfish, sea bass, bream, John Dory, zander, red mullet, grey mullet, witch (or Torbay sole), halibut, Norway redfish, snapper, brill, turbot, coalfish, marlin and swordfish are just some of the fish that I'd never heard of, or got to eat, until I was at least thirty.

A rare treat was tinned salmon, which is a bright red, sloppy, salty substance that, coincidentally, shares some of its name with an actual fish. Thankfully, the Fridays of my childhood usually meant haddock or cod, which to all intents and purposes are the same fish.

And occasionally plaice, which is basically haddock or cod that's been flattened out with a rolling pin. Once or twice, the haddock or cod might be in batter, from the chip shop. This was a real treat, especially as the fish and chips in Cornwall were invariably fried in beef dripping.

But in general, for us and for most children of the time, fish was rectangular, covered in orange breadcrumbs and came, not from the ocean, but from the Co-op. What would the sixties have been without fish fingers?

Bizarrely, looking back I don't ever remember questioning fish on Fridays or complaining about its dullness. Predictability didn't seem to be a bad thing. Routines just *were*.

Dad would give us a lift to school in the mornings. He had to be at work by eight thirty, which meant we were dropped off at school by ten past eight at the latest. This meant we were first in school every morning, which I didn't mind, but it meant we'd have to be up every morning by seven thirty at the latest. And this is what happened five days a week during term-time. It was predictable, it was a routine. I didn't question it or rebel against it; it didn't comfort me or stifle me. It just was.

At the end of the day there were similar rituals. We wouldn't have our evening meal until our father got home. And then it was on the table within minutes of him coming up the drive; the car door slamming became a Pavlovian bell to us salivating children.

Eagerly awaiting tea one Monday (cold roast meat, chips and peas), I was looking out of the window and down the street to see if Dad was on his way, hoping to somehow hurry him along. The first thing I saw was Cyril Nicholas from next door, sweeping into his driveway in one racy curve, hardly slowing down. He honked in a chipper 'Hi, honey, I'm home' way as he came to a halt at the back of his house. About two minutes later, at the far end of the street, Mr Holroyd arrived home and drove up *his* driveway. Within seconds,

Mr Brownlow and Mr Tresidder drove into the street and disappeared up *their* driveways. Then my dad's car turned into the lane and my thoughts turned to food.

But the next day (bacon, egg, chips and peas), I observed the same thing. All the dads of the neighbourhood turning up with mechanical precision at the same time. And the next day and next. The parallel routines of the daily lives on our street made our world seem like a well-oiled machine that would purr on indefinitely.

I didn't notice the repetitious tedium at the time but, a few years later, I would look back at those days and think, 'That's not living, that's existing. That's being a faceless cog in an oppressive machine.' I would rail (predictably) against the predictability of it all; the stifling bourgeois conformity.

I remember there was a popular American protest song around at the time which allegedly satirised the endless, identical boredom of life in suburbia. It was called 'Little Boxes' and described, in a sort of sanctimonious whine, houses and lives 'all made of ticky-tacky, and all looking just the same'.

I was nearly taken in by the song but there was something I sensed at the time about those days, something that many more years later I would desperately miss and long for: the *warmth* of the routine, the *safety* of the predictable, and the comfort, the warm snuggly *comfort*, of the tedious.

Chapter 26

Grown-Up Boy Finds Life Can Be Serious

I liked the song 'Little Boxes'. Not because of the social comment in the song, but because I could play it. My hobby, if you like, from the age of sixteen was playing the guitar; well, learning to play the guitar. Any guitarist will tell you that you only stop learning when you die. As soon as I was able to play a few chords on the guitar, I wanted to be a rock star. My life took a slightly different path and now that I'm in my fifties, I've had to adjust my sights. I've just about taken on board the fact that I'm not going to be a rock star, but I *could* be an *ageing rock star*. Dylan's in his seventies and Jagger's in his sixties so there's still loads of time for me.

About twenty years ago I thought I'd make a start on my rock career and took a band on the road, and to the Edinburgh Festival twice. Because of the limitations of my guitar playing, it was a country and western band. And because of my background in comedy I thought I couldn't get away with straight songs, so I ended up doing a load of comic songs country-style. Privately I was aching to write serious songs, sad songs, songs that would move people to tears or rebellion but I always bottled out at the last minute and made them funny.

One song I wrote was, I suppose, my own version of 'Little Boxes', a twenty-first-century version, perhaps. It too was about the boredom and routine of people who lived on an estate where all the houses, cars and even people looked the same. The song is a tender love ballad with a pretty tune and it's called 'The Milton Keynes Tragedy'. And the first verse went:

And I wake up
And she's sleeping
And her little heart is beating
And she's breathing
Soft and gentle
And her breasts
They gently rise and gently fall
And I think about
The night before
When we made love
Upon the floor
It's been ten years
Since we were wed
But still it's paradise in bed
Because I love her
And I get up
And I wander
To the kitchen
Where I make her
Some coffee and I wake her
To tell her that I love her
And she looks at me and says ...
Who the fuck are you?

Another of my repertoire was 'Country Singer', a song that celebrates the aspirations and tragic upbringings of most country stars. It's a song for a woman singer and it kinda goes like this:

I always wanted to be a country singer
From the day that I first sat on Momma's knee
A star who stood in lights down at the Opry
That's all I ever wanted to be.
But I do not think that I will ever make it
As the greatest country act under the sun
It's a long hard road to be a country legend
When there's so many things I've never done …
I've never been killed in a car crash
I wouldn't know a rooster from a chick
I've never got pregnant by my brother
Or choked on my own sick … (etc)

'The Hunting Song' purports to be a serious song about animal rights and the iniquity of blood sports.

We don't believe in blood sports and we don't believe in zoos
And animal experiments don't seem right
But some critters are dangerous and that is why we choose
To do the thing we do each Friday night …
We hunt the beaver, we hunt the beaver
Beavers are by far the best to hunt
We hunt the beaver, we hunt the beaver
And when I say a beaver, I really mean a …
Beaver.

* * *

But one day, I did write a serious song, moved by a real-life tragedy that befell some close friends of ours.

One thing I learnt as a parent is that you don't start learning things till you're a parent. A lot of what you learn is exciting and magical, while some of it is very painful.

And then there are a few new things that are unexpected. And shocking.

Nick James was a parent. And so was his wife Lily. They were the first parents in our set of friends and acquaintances. They were the trail-blazers in many aspects of our young lives. They'd been, if you like, our guineapigs for every new experience.

Slightly older than his contemporaries, Nick had been the first to go to university, to take drugs, to graduate, to get a full-time job, to get engaged, to get married, to get a mortgage, to own a house and to have a child.

Whereas most of his friends went into TV, radio, theatre or advertising, Nick had done law at college and ended up via the bar in a job in the 'city'.

It seemed impossibly grown-up to us when Nick announced that Lily was pregnant. When I heard, I felt it was an almost outlandish event; something that was, and always would be, beyond my reach.

All the girls cooed and fussed and talked about names, and all the boys asked roughly the same question: 'Who's the father, then, Nick?'

Lily became a curiosity at social gatherings with her growing bump. Nick's laddish friends shook their heads wryly and brooded over the life-changes that Nick would have to make. No more Wednesdays of five-a-side footy and curry. No more lads' sessions in the Bull on the first Friday of the month. Nick took it all in his stride and rightly pointed out that our time was not far away.

He and Lily were very close to being the most annoying couple on the planet.

Very close, but they were so nice, you just resigned yourself to the fact that they were perfect. They were healthy, good-looking, energetic, positive, generous and forgiving. Compared to them, I felt I was an angry, gnarled, venomous, parasitic, destructive worm.

And now they had a baby as well. A boy. And guess what; he was a beautiful baby boy.

* * *

The office phone rang. I was nearest to it so I answered it.

'Rory, it's Sally Mills here,' said the usually loud and jolly Sally Mills, in a very serious and croaky voice.

'Sally Mills!' I said and people round the office looked over with smiles or tuts, knowing that a silly and probably semi-obscene conversation was about to take place.

'How are you, gorgeous?'

She continued in a whisper: 'Willow died last night.'

'Oh, dear,' I said, purely as a reflex; I didn't know who Willow was. 'Hang on, Sal, say that again.'

'Willow's dead.'

I was still at a loss to make meaning out of this. The bustling office was noisy and I had just happened to pick up the phone because I was standing next to it. Maybe it was meant for someone else. But no, she had said Rory. I heard sobbing from the other end of the line.

'Willow James died this morning. It's heartbreaking. It's unbelievable.'

The puzzlement on my face had attracted attention from around the desks and people started to quieten down. Who's Willow? I thought.

'Listen, Sally, are you OK?'

Nothing.

'Are you still there, Sal?' Nothing.

'Willow's died,' I said to the office, more as a question than a statement.

One of the girls stood up. Open-mouthed and white-faced, she slapped her palms to her cheeks and blurted, 'Nick and Lily's baby. William.'

The sickness in my stomach was instant. And extreme. I slid down into a chair.

Everybody in the office stopped what they were doing and looked at each other. The silence was eerily total. The silence that follows a plane crash.

Seven months old.

Horror.

*　*　*

Well, God? Anything to say? The child is everything we were taught. Everything is about the child. Unborn and born. The Catholic Church is against contraception because it would mean the death of a baby. Now what, God? We'd bought Willow some baby clothes. Quite chic ones. They were so cute. Proper clothes, but little. That's all I could think about. Baby clothes.

What should we do with them, God?

Burn them?

Sell them?

Chuck them away?

Give them to someone who's just had a baby? How would that feel?

Have these; we don't need them any more.

Why not, has your baby grown out of them?

No. He'll never grow into them.

*　*　*

Few of us had ever heard of cot death before. It was a new one on us. Sudden Infant Death Syndrome. How many more nasty surprises had adulthood got up its sleeve?

Our boy was born within a year of this sad shock and I often wondered how we'd cope with anything similar. Suppose it had been our child? Supposing one night for no apparent reason your healthy baby decided to stop breathing? Pondering these things, I doodled a song. A sad one. A serious one. 'The Cot Song':

You slept there so peacefully, safe in your cot
Your breath was so soft and so warm
The night was so gentle, we simply could not
Predict the approach of that storm.

We silently leant in to give you a kiss
We tiptoed across the floor
A sudden strange silence said something's amiss
Our baby was breathing no more.

Chorus:
Where did you go, baby, who did you see?
Did you go looking for Mummy and me?
Did you see a sweet beauty, who cast a strange spell
And beckoned you down a dark stairway to hell?

The world disappeared then, our screams and our tears
Were all that seemed to remain,
A minute that seemed like a million years
Of suffering, sadness and pain.

Chorus:
Where did you go, baby, what did you do?
Was someone mysterious waiting for you?
A thin, bony stranger in a scary, black cape
Who grabbed your hand tightly and blocked your escape?

Mummy breathed in, put her sweet lips on yours
And filled your small body with breath
And snatched you away from the gaping red jaws
Of a frightful, sad, mystery death.

Chorus:
Where did you go, baby, who did you see?
Did you go looking for Mummy and me?
Did you see a sweet beauty, who cast a strange spell
And beckoned you down a dark stairway to hell?

You suddenly woke up with a sigh and a cough
And you started crying as well,
Our baby was back, the search was called off
We'd had a sneak-preview of hell.
But some aren't so lucky and we have a whole
Lifetime of thank-yous to give
And next time you leave us, remember to breathe
Remember to breathe and to live.
Remember to breathe and to live.
Remember to breathe and to live.

Chapter 27

Little Box

It was a dismal, icily grey day.

It would have been whatever the weather.

The pretty country church was disguised by drizzle draping its mournful granite.

'God, if ever I needed a fag it's now,' said Danny, struggling for breath and patting his patch. He was clearly still on a promise of love etc from the gorgeous, so far unattainable Rachel.

'That was bad,' said Strobo joining us. 'That was cold. That was just wrong. God, if ever I was going to take up smoking, it would be now.'

'Do you want a patch?' offered Danny.

'I want something. I want the last hour wiped from my memory.' He shook his head and breathed in exaggerated puffs of the frigid air to try to relax. 'Say something funny, then,' he said to me almost defiantly.

'There isn't anything funny left in the world today,' I replied.

'I think everybody cried,' Danny pointed out.

'Everybody,' Strobo confirmed, his customary blinking emphasising his own tears. 'The vicar as well. I've never seen a vicar in tears at a funeral before.'

'The vicar was a woman,' said Danny.

'Well spotted, Sherlock!' I said.

'Steady. I just thought maybe it gets to a woman more. She may have a child of her own.'

'It's the coffin,' blinked Strobo. 'The coffin. That's what did it.'

'Oh shit. Yeah. That got me.' Danny agreed.

A coffin so small that one person can carry it. I recalled our friends Nick and Lily James who lost their baby about twenty years ago. An unspeakable shock. They lived in Australia now. Four children all healthy and happy. Do a lot of work for cot-death charities. I wondered if they ever really got over it.

'Fuck me, that was horrible. Fags and booze now!' It was the unmistakable wheezy baritone of Jonesy, Wales's foremost painter and decorator and occasional dramatic amateur.

'It should have been me. Children shouldn't die. It should have been me,' he droned on.

'But you are a child, Jonesy,' Danny said.

'No need for that,' said the Welshman, lighting up and blowing a challenging cloud in Danny's direction.

'Nice to see you in a suit, Jonesy,' I said trying to lighten up the conversation. 'Black, was it, once?'

Jonesy ignored this and shook his head. 'Fuck me. Did you see that coffin? That was the saddest thing in the world. Sadder than the 1993 Grand National.'

'Ah, I knew you bring us down to earth, Jonesy,' I smiled.

Jonesy went on: 'I wonder if the coffin-makers charge more or less for a child's coffin. Coz, if you think about it, there's less wood so it should be cheaper. But on the other hand, they probably don't have to make them so often so there's no, er … what's it called?'

'Economy of scale,' Strobo answered.

I shook my head in despair. 'I'm almost impressed, Jonesy, that on such a sad occasion you can still think about the financial welfare of coffin-makers.'

Jonesy looked genuinely upset and said quietly, 'Well, what *else* do you think about?'

This question hung unanswered on the frosty air.

'Surviving your children, that can't be right, can it?' I thought to myself, or possibly said out loud.

'I couldn't imagine it,' said Strobo and Jonesy added, 'I couldn't help thinking about my own son. Asking myself questions.'

'Like who is he? Where is he? What's his mother's name?' Danny chuckled in a valiant attempt to cheer us up.

'That's not nice.'

'It's got to be wrong. It's got to be against all God's laws,' I said to Strobo.

'A lot of people would say it's an act of God,' he replied.

'Which God acts like that?'

'Maybe it's a sign,' Danny suggested. 'A sign of God.'

There was no sign of God today.

Chapter 28

Sinner Boy Breaks a Commandment: Thou Shalt Not Commit Adultery

'Hi, it's me. I've parked in Montague Close,' she said, clearly flustered.

'You alright? You sound flustered,' I said, trying not to sound flustered.

'You're the one who sounds flustered. Are you having second thoughts?'

I thought. My thought was: it's only adultery if both parties are married, surely.

I thought I heard a voice say: *You know that's not true.*

And then I heard mine saying, 'No, course not. Look, we can have this conversation when you're here.'

'I'm about five minutes' walk away.'

'OK. I'll see you in a minute. Can't wait.'

She's the married one so she's the one being sinful, surely.

You mean she's taking a huge risk and you're not. You don't know her husband or her children, do you? To you it's just a game in which you score points over an innocent stranger.

'Shall I come in the back or front door?'

'Sorry?'

'Front or back?' she sounded a bit scared.

'Come to the front. Should be OK. I'll open the door and leave it on the latch. Walk straight in and come downstairs.'

She rang off and I went to take the wine out of the freezer. I opened it, poured a glass and sipped it. I thought of her husband. I didn't know him but she said he was at best a bit of a bore and at worst a bit of a bastard.

Oh, so it's alright then …

I looked round the room. Everything was fine. I'd even hoovered the carpet. We might end up there, I thought.

How thoughtful of you. And crude.

A loud banging at the door. I jumped. Shit, I'd forgotten to open the door. I raced down the hall and opened it. An anxious girl swept past me.

'I thought you said you were going to leave the door open? I've been knocking for hours!'

'Sorry,' I said, attempting a kiss.

'I need a drink. Your neighbour saw me. What if she recognised me?'

Ah, you see! Some things you can't prepare for.

'Are you sure?'

'Well, she said hello. And I said hello back to her!'

'Let's have some champagne,' I said firmly.

Yeah, that's right. Alcohol, that's what you need. Help you get through these tense moments. Help you feel better about the fact you're proposing to cheat on someone.

Though, I'm not actually the one cheating, I thought, as I poured her glass of wine and tried to sound indifferent.

'There's no need to worry about her. There's no reason to think she'd recognise you or know that you're married.'

It's alright for you, you're not the married one. You're the bit on the side.

'It's alright for you,' she said with unexpected vehemence. 'You're not the married one. You're the bit on the side!'

'Well, not yet,' I said, attempting a joke. Which failed.

'I'm not doing this lightly, you know. I'm taking a big risk which I wouldn't be doing if I thought you thought I was just a one-off quickie. If I end up single after this, I'd expect you to be there for me.'

I didn't particularly want to hear this.

You didn't particularly want to hear that, did you?

I couldn't think of what to say so I thought actions might speak louder. I tried to cuddle her but she pulled away and went over to the mirror, looked at herself and ruffled her hair.

'God, I'm looking old.'

Yes, she is, isn't she? And so are you.

She is, I thought, and went and stood behind her. I was looking old too.

'You look lovely,' I said. 'Good enough to fuck.'

'You charmer,' she said, turning round with a smile. We kissed passionately and our nervousness began to ebb away.

'Where's er … *he* today?'

'He's at some conference. Or meeting or something. Birmingham. Or Milton Keynes. I don't know.'

We sat down on the sofa and Claire put her glass of wine on the coffee table. The lipstick smudge stood out in incriminating scarlet.

'You'd better not forget to wipe that off before your next bit of stuff comes round.'

I wasn't in a relationship at the time but it had occurred to me that that's the sort of thing that could trip you up.

Ah, you see. Thinking like a two-timer already.

The physics of intimacy, the holding, kissing, touching, stroking, fondling, squeezing and rubbing grew in speed and intensity. Items of clothing were removed. Pre-sex undressing takes longer the faster you try to do it. Buttons are forgotten and delay the shedding of shirts; zips are not fully undone and jam halfway leaving you trapped in your jeans; and shoelaces snarl up into a solid knot. All the while the volatile passion fades and the inhibitions starting trickling into your brain.

'Why don't we go upstairs to the bedroom? It's ridiculous doing it on the sofa.' Claire grunted as she struggled to free her foot from her inside-out trouser leg.

'I think it's sexy and illicit doing it here,' I lied.

'It's illicit enough, anyway. We might as well just go to the bedroom.'

We started kissing again which meant the awkward and graceless struggle on the sofa continued. In the time it took for a contorted and strained position for copulation to be finally achieved, my desire and ability had waned. I kissed her forcefully and hoped my physiology would catch up.

'You've lost it,' she said vaguely, but precisely.

'Let's just have a break and a chat and a drink and get back in the mood,' I placated.

'I thought we were in the mood. I am. Well, I was.'

I seized on this admission. 'Do you want to stop, then?'

'You clearly do.'

My manhood, which was quickly reverting to childhood.

Why was I the nervous one?

Maybe you're frightened that this will turn out to be a bigger commitment than you'd planned. Just a one-night stand? Forget it. Make love to her now and there could be no return.

'Maybe I'm just too nervous,' I offered.

'Why should *you* be nervous? I should be the nervous one!'

'Let's have a breather just for a minute or so.'

It was too late. She was getting up off the sofa, clearly miffed that she had risked so much for nothing, not even physical satisfaction. The lack of sex seemed to make her feel more exposed and more rejected. She stumbled as she got up from the sofa and nearly fell as she tripped over her tangled tights. She now seemed downright humiliated. And angry …

'Please don't go straight away,' I pleaded, probably unconvincingly. She said nothing but continued to collect her things. I could feel the anger radiating silently from her.

I had committed adultery without committing adultery.

Nice one!

'Let's cuddle,' I murmured.

'Or do you want to get rid of me and fumigate the whole room before your next appointment?' she snapped.

'Don't be daft, this is the best part. Holding each other afterwards,' I said, squeezing her to me.

'Afterwards? After *what*? We haven't done anything!'

Just enough, I'd say.

'We should go to a hotel next time. You could relax more,' I suggested encouragingly.

She snapped.

'Hotels? Credit cards with names on? Items listed on bills? Other people? Chance meetings with friends? My husband's friends whom you don't know by sight. Whom I don't know by sight? Bar bills that fall out of pockets. Receipts? Receptionists who may remember my face later? The phone call to my house informing Mrs McGrath that she may have left a wedding ring on the bedside table of Room 441!?'

'I'm sorry, I didn't think it through.' I felt unclean.

'Oh dear, you've got my lipstick on your tummy!' she said, lightening a little.

'It's not yours.' This attempted joke was a mistake. Her lightening had turned to thunder.

Ah, getting a bit cocky now. You've under-achieved and she's about to go and you decide to come over all macho and arrogant. That could be dangerous, old bean!

'Oh thank you very much. Right, I'm going. I've wasted enough of my time!'

We said a cooler 'goodbye' than I'd expected or hoped. I closed the front door behind her and leant my back against it after she'd gone.

Adultery without the sex, eh? Bummer.

She had a lot more to lose than I had, I thought. The imbalance is too great. That's where the tensions start. Perhaps I should stick to single girls. Or wait till I'm married, then it'd be a real affair. Real adultery. I crossed the room and looked in the mirror.

You look like a piece of shit.

I looked like a piece of shit. One that was fast disappearing down a drain.

Chapter 29

Good Catholic Boy
Goes North on
Humanitarian Mission

A piece of shit floated quickly into sight and disappeared down the watery drain.

'Look, there it is,' I exclaimed excitedly, 'my poo. That's my poo!' We looked through the grid into the pipes below and there it was. I realised years later, when watching some repeats of a programme I did for ITV 1, that this was probably the only time in my life that I got any sort of pleasure from watching shit I had produced.

My brothers and I were gathered round the hole just outside the lavatory at the bottom of a narrow, grassless, cinder-spattered yard by the wooden gate that opened with enticing mystery into the 'back alley'.

The outdoor lavatory was exciting enough, and the fact you could see your business go down the drain seconds later by looking down the grid outside, but the toilet also had a wooden seat. A continuously smooth bench with a perfect circle cut into it. A seat that, unlike the plastic and ceramic of lavatories in Cornwall, always felt warm and comfy.

Granny had been taken into hospital suddenly. My mother's mother was seriously ill. We had to go and visit her. She was in St Helens in Lancashire (or possibly Merseyside, it doesn't matter now). We were in Redruth in Cornwall. There were 338.2 miles between us. This was long before the new A30 and the M5, and the M6 was still having teething difficulties. We had a dilapidated car that struggled to make the three miles to school every day. It was going to take us about ten hours. It was seven in the evening. We were going to have to drive through the night.

It was the first day of the summer holidays when a lot of northerners would be leaving their dirty, smoggy old northern towns to come to the sea and sunshine of Cornwall; we were going the other way. What an adventure!

I don't remember if I felt any concern about how mum was feeling about her mum, or about how Granny was, or about the considerable ordeal it must have been for my dad driving at that time of the day, that number of miles in that car. It just seemed dangerously but thrillingly impromptu.

It was the first time I could recall going anywhere in the car at night and I fell asleep hypnotised by the flakes of light that streamed past the car, as moths caught the beam of our headlamps. It was a fitful sleep and we'd wake periodically to learn that we were passing through dreaming towns with exotic names like Okehampton, Bridgwater, Tewkesbury, Kidderminster and Crewe.

Day broke with a bang and steam pouring from the engine and brown water splattering the windscreen. The hosepipe had burst, we were informed by the AA patrolman.

'I didn't know there was a hosepipe in a motorcar engine,' one of us said.

'Neither did I,' Dad replied.

The episode meant a two-hour delay to our journey, which must have been painfully unwelcome to my mother, who was worrying about Granny in hospital, and my dad, who was no motor enthusiast to say the least. He had the additional worry that the tax disc had expired the day before and this unexpected journey meant he couldn't renew it till we'd arrived in Lancashire. Again this meant nothing to us and the delay was highly welcome because it meant we could stop and have a sandwich in a roadside café. And a drink of pop. I chose limeade. My first ever. I remember it being the best drink in the world.

About an hour after the restart, the journey dwindled into boredom and the engine failed to explode again. Games like I spy and seeing who was the first to shout 'Heil Hitler' whenever we passed an AA patrol box soon wore thin and we took it in turns to do the 'are we there yet?' whine. It was probably a little less boring for my dad who, conscious of his expired tax disc, was more than a little alarmed to see the roads on the outskirts of Bristol lined for about three miles with police officers. They were there for an expected royal drive-past, it transpired, and we got past the cordons unarrested.

* * *

Lancashire was different. The rows of sooty, red brick terraces of St Helens seemed alien to us, fresh from our spanking new bungalow in the middle of fields a mile from the sea. 'Hey, it's just like *Coronation Street*,' said Stephen excitedly. The big old house in Hardshaw Street was enthralling. A kitchen and a *back* kitchen. No bath, but when it was required, an iron tub was filled with hot water from the boiler. There was a large, beautiful room with a piano that no one ever seemed to use. And light bulbs with clear glass so you could see the glowing filament inside. It was wondrous to see the working of a light bulb. Why didn't we live in a house like this with only one toilet and an outside one at that?

And the mornings were a delight. First of all the smell. A wonderful combination of aromas unlike anything we'd experienced in Cornwall. We were told it was a mixture of smells from two legendary local institutions: the warm, rich bouquet of malted barley from the

Greenall Whitley brewery in Hall Street (established 1880) and the homely, mouth-watering fragrance of freshly baked pies and cakes from Livesey's bakery.

But making the morning even more special was orange squash; delivered to your doorstep by the milkman in third-of-a-pint bottles with shiny, green-foil tops. Heaven.

We were allowed to go to the newsagent's, the butcher's and the baker's *on our own*. The people in the shops were funny and friendly and made us laugh with the jokey conversation in broad Lancashire accents. Total strangers chatted amiably to us as they cleaned their doorsteps and polished the brass fittings on the doors. This was a fab place to be spending the summer holidays, away from the sun and the beaches and the tourists.

We visited Granny, of course, who had improved slightly and was delighted to see us. This was the only serious bit of our stay. The rest of the time we visited aunts, uncles, cousins and family friends, who took us to parks with small zoos, boating lakes, playgrounds and paddling pools. They were clearly amazed to meet Cornish children and bought us toys and sweets and ice-creams. Cousin John made us each a bow out of bamboo and string. They were fantastic even though they didn't work and we had no arrows. Uncle Tom showed us the more accessible bits of his factory, which he said was world-famous for its glass. St Helens, he informed us, was the glass capital of the world; whatever that meant. He worked at Pilkington's and his son, our cousin Thomas, worked at UGB (we never found out what that was but the 'g' probably stood for 'glass'), and some other cousins worked at Triplex, who made safety glass. 'Pilks invented the float glass process,' Uncle Tom told us eagerly, and eagerly we listened. 'It's a way of making high-quality flat glass by floating molten glass on a bed of molten tin. And the tin ... well, that's Cornish, is that!'

One evening Uncle Tom, Thomas and Uncle Jimmy, who was known to be a bit mischievous and fearless, having once been a cook in the army and driven double-decker buses in Liverpool, decided they'd drive us children to Southport to the fairground.

'I'll take you on the big dipper.' Uncle Jimmy winked at me rather disconcertingly. It seemed he had singled me out as the fearless, mischievous one.

'Now, just look after those boys' – our sister Catherine was considered too young for this venture – 'and make sure you don't stop off at every alehouse on the way!' one or several of the womenfolk admonished.

'Of course not,' smirked the three men.

'What's an alehouse, Uncle Jimmy?' I asked when we were well en route.

'It's only a pub,' he answered, taking his eyes off the road to wink at me again. A pub? I was none the wiser.

We'd been driving about twenty minutes when Jimmy said, 'Hey, look at us driving to Southport and we haven't even got the lads a bag of crisps and a bottle of pop!' This sounded very good to me and my two brothers; especially when we worked out that 'the lads' were us.

'Ooh, yes,' agreed Uncle Tom, who turned to us and asked, 'Who wants a bottle of pop and a bag of crisps?'

'Me, me, me' was, of course, the communal answer.

We stopped in a place called Rainford and the men went into a building called the Bridge. Thomas came out with three bottles of lemonade and three bags of crisps. Not just any old crisps but 'cheese and onion' flavoured, which were new and we hadn't had before. We were hyperactive with excitement and climbed all over the car, inside and outside.

The same routine happened at three more places en route in buildings called weird things like Prince Albert, and the Kicking Donkey. This was the best trip we'd been on and we hadn't reached the fairground yet. On our fourth stop Stephen suggested that the places we were stopping at were the prohibited 'alehouses' or 'pubs'.

This was an exhilarating thought. What did people do in these places? And why did Mummy and Aunty Jane and Aunty Anne and Aunty Reenie think they were so bad?

'Why don't we climb up on the window ledge and look in?' was Stephen's daring suggestion. This seemed such a naughty thing to do: climbing on a high, dangerous window ledge; spying on people who might be involved in something we might not like to see or want to see. Yes, let's do it! With courage plucked up, we managed eventually to get a brief glimpse into the murky goings-on in a public house.

Our cousin and two uncles were sitting round a table playing cards. They each had a drink with them. Was that it!? Was that the mystery of the 'alehouse'? We were bitterly disappointed that there had been nothing more world-shattering or racy going on. Pubs, we decided, were the most boring things in the world and when we were grown-up it was highly unlikely that we would ever be going into one.

The big dipper at Southport pleasure beach was gigantic. I couldn't wait to go on. Stephen and Michael declined but I was determined to have my first 'rollercoaster' ride.

'Come on, Uncle Jimmy,' I badgered, 'can we go on the big dipper first?'

Jimmy looked up at the huge and elegant waves of the super-structure and his usually reddish-purple face went decidedly pale green.

It was the first and best fairground ride of my life. I screamed myself hoarse next to a grimacing, white-knuckled Uncle Tom.

* * *

There would be no escaping the shadow of the church while up north, and in St Helens the churches had immense shadows. Lowe House was a massive structure; an imposing cathedral-like church so unlike the tiny modern buildings we were used to in Cornwall. Similarly Sacred Heart and Holy Cross. These were serious churches. You didn't mess with them. They left you in no doubt who was the boss. Similarly the amazing construction that is the Metropolitan Cathedral of Christ the King in Liverpool. This fascinating but odd-looking building (latterly known as Paddy's Wigwam or the Mersey funnel) was unfinished but for one of the side chapels. I remember still the stunning stained glass in there. These buildings demanded severity and solemnity and in each we dutifully said prayers for Granny and lit votive candles for her.

And it worked.

Granny got better and came to Cornwall to convalesce and eventually decided to move there permanently and live near us, which was nice but it meant we didn't go back to St Helens, that strange, exciting and friendly place way up in the north of a country called England.

Chapter 30

Grown-up Boy Splits

'Well, you'll never guess what. Maureen Culdrose is getting divorced,' Mrs Shaw is saying, and reaps the expected chorus of horrified and incredulous gasps. Mrs Fulton takes up the sanctimonious baton and waddles with it. 'And her with her holier-than-thou posturing and her perfect marriage to "my Gerald", blessed by the Bishop of Liverpool, no less!' The women form a malodorous and obstructive huddle on the steps of the church. Miss O'Driscoll pulls her outer chin inside the others and stretches the edges of her mouth downwards in a just-stepped-in-dogshit grimace and opines, 'Well, it's those poor children I feel sorry for. It's always the children that suffer with the selfishness of their parents.'

The conversation is now back with Mrs Shaw. '… And I've heard whispers that that pretty little creature that the Kenwrights' boy is about to marry is a divorcee!'

'Married twice before, I've heard,' adds Mrs Chadwick, 'once to an Arab!' Sharp intakes of breath all round.

'"Pretty little thing" nothing, she's a stuck-up madam!'

Mrs Fulton continues to vigorous nodding of heads: 'It's too easy for them nowadays. If you marry, you're married. That's it. It's a life commitment. If you don't like it, do something about it. Marriages aren't easy. They're not supposed to be easy. These youngsters just don't know what hard work is!'

There is no good divorce.

Ours was the worst in divorce history.

Or so I thought.

Well, it involved me and my wife and my children.

It was the only one in divorce history to involve me and my wife and my children so how could it *not* have been the worst in divorce history?

I spoke to friends, colleagues and acquaintances who had been through it and heard heartrending stories of desolate birthday teas in motorway service stations and of Christmas presents left on the window ledge. I was told horrendous tales of abuse, violence, robbery, brainwashing of children, stalking, revenge, kidnap and secret emigration.

Mine was certainly better than any other divorce I heard about.

Positively civilised.

Almost caring.

In comparison.

But still, for me, the worst divorce in divorce history.

I could not foresee the disruption, mental, physical, practical and logistical, that divorce would cause.

And that was before any financial considerations.

And we had to deal with lawyers.

This doesn't help. They want everything to be concrete. They like facts and realities, not mushy feelings and squashy desires. Their aim is to talk only of property and values and times and dates. This is meant to make it seem clinical and neutral but it only makes it seem venal and uncaring. However well it is handled by both parties, however firmly the interests of the children are put first, solicitors are the only people who benefit from divorce, despite their pious perorations to the contrary. Their job is to make money out of other people's misfortunes, however they dress it up.

The law has come up with useful but seemingly arbitrary grounds for divorce into which you have to fit your circumstances.

No category seemed to fit for us.

1) Adultery: No, despite endless opportunity and near misses, I never did. I'm not counting extramarital flirtation and I'm not putting the sin of thought on a par with the sin of action; in that universe no one is innocent. Some would say that if one's marriage is fairly robust it could quite easily survive the odd indiscretion. But others would say if the marriage is so robust the odd indiscretion would not be necessary. A fragile marriage may not even survive a bit of extramarital flirting.

2) Unreasonable behaviour: Impossible to define. Whose behaviour is reasonable?

3) Desertion: This is fairly concrete, I suppose, but not applicable in our case.

4) Two years' separation with consent: OK, but it takes two years. And a lot of painful uncertainty.

5) Five years' separation without consent: Time-consuming and not applicable in our case.

* * *

Of course, there is no Catholic divorce. Whomever God has joined, let no man put asunder. Matrimony is a sacrament and cannot be dissolved and therefore it has to be endured till one of the spouses dies. It's obviously taken seriously by God. In the Bible, Moses is given not one, but two, commandments to cover this. Number seven, 'Thou shalt not commit adultery', and number ten, 'Thou shalt not covet thy neighbour's wife'. No chances being taken here. Murder, I notice, only gets one commandment.

But the Church's firm stance on marriage is not about the happiness, emotional and physical, of the spouses, it's about the children. And mothers. Matrimony, lest we forget, come from the word 'mater', mother. The point of marriage is to have children in a structured, supposedly loving, environment. You got married, had children and you looked after them. Staying together was the best way to ensure their security. If you and your spouse had stopped getting on with each other, if you'd begun to hate each other, so what? Just concentrate on the children. Just get on with it.

Despite all the time and effort we put in, despite putting the children first, it didn't work and there was a lot of pain for the four of us. And someone somewhere would be passing a judgement.

'I heard that McGrath boy's getting divorced.'

'Terrible; they've hardly cut the wedding cake.'

'He always was a bit flaky though, wasn't he?'

'And those poor children. Still so young.'

'It's very selfish.'

'And the tragedy is, his wife was a Catholic girl.'

'Terrible.'

Chapter 31

Another One Bites the Dust

'His wife was a Catholic girl. I never knew that. Devout, as well, apparently,' I was saying to no one in particular but Jonesy chose to hear me.

'What's that got to do with anything?' he moaned. 'She never liked me. I used to help Peter the Heater when he first started putting boilers and radiators in. She said I was shifty and idle.'

'So a Catholic and a good judge of character then, Jones?' Strobo smiled.

It was a bright May morning; the best time of the year. The promise of summer was in the breeze. It was no day for a funeral. Peter Cockburn had been a well-known character all over town. A cheery soul who bred laughter wherever he went and there was consequently a huge turn-out.

'I doubt if this many will turn up to my funeral,' continued Wales's foremost painter and decorator and occasional bit-part actor.

'Oh they will, Jonesy,' smiled Danny. 'The entire city will turn up just to check you have actually gone.'

'That's not nice,' said Jonesy petulantly as he puffed a mouthful of cigarette smoke in Danny's face.

'Careful, I haven't got a patch on today,' Danny said stepping back.

'Does that mean you're now officially a non-smoker?' I asked, and Strobo continued, 'And is Rachel is going to give you an "access-all-areas" pass?'

'We're getting closer,' Danny admitted with surprising coyness.

'I hate death.' Jonesy was whining on in between drags.

'How do you know, you've never tried it?' Danny pointed out.

'Yes, I have. Quite a few times,' Jonesy said. 'Died on stage in Oldham in 1983.' He looked pained at the memory. 'Horrible it was. The crowd turned on me. The entire audience chased me out of the theatre.'

'Poor Jonesy. Did they catch you?'

'No, he outran both of them,' I said.

'I'll ignore that.' Jonesy went on pompously: 'This is a solemn day and we should be remembering Peter the Heater. Poor old bugger. He's the last person I thought I'd be seeing off. Just like that, as well. No illness, no warning, no nothing. How old was he?'

'Ninety-eight,' answered Strobo.

Jonesy shook his head theatrically. 'That's no age to die. I can't believe it. He didn't have my health problems.'

Danny clapped him heartily on the back. 'I'm sure you've got a good few years left, mate.'

Jonesy suddenly looked very grave, 'They've given me three months.'

'That's to pay your council tax, Jonesy. That's not medical,' I said.

He ignored this and went on plaintively, 'I'm the enigma of the medical world, I am.'

'You're the enigma of the vegetable world, Jonesy.' Strobo laughed but Jonesy persisted in his narcissistic hypochondria.

'Listen, you lot, I'm on heart medication, I'm diabetic, I'm numb down one leg, I've got asthma, I'm nearly blind with macular degeneration, I've got dangerously high cholesterol, my teeth are dropping out with gum disease, I'm overweight and I drink and smoke too much and I have occasional continence problems.'

'I hope that's not your speed-dating speech,' I said.

Danny stepped in quickly to change the subject from the walking dead to the really dead. 'Old Peter had a packed life, though. I'll say that.'

'Yes,' I agreed. 'Saw active service. Killed a German or two.'

Jonesy seemed genuinely interested in this.

'Really? Second World War?'

'No,' I replied. 'Car crash in Munich, 2001. He shouldn't have been driving, really. Something distracted him on the autobahn – his guide dog jumped on his lap.' Danny laughed and Jonesy concluded that we were taking the piss.

'Sorry, Jonesy,' I said. 'It's my way of handling grief.'

Jonesy put on his ominous preacher-man voice: 'In the midst of life we are in death.'

'Well, you are. You live on Thorpe estate,' Danny pointed out, and I tried to raise the tone of the debate. 'Without death, is life meaningless?'

Jonesy replied instantly. 'Without ale, life is meaningless.'

'And women,' Danny added.

'I don't think so,' disagreed Jonesy. 'I don't mind living without women in my life.'

'You've got no bleedin' choice, Jonesy,' Danny reminded him.

Jonesy shook his head and muttered, 'Christ al-fucking-mighty, you're disrespectful to me!'

'Please don't take the Lord thy God's name in vain,' I said straight away. 'That's one commandment broken.'

Jonesy didn't look impressed. 'Does that mean I'm going to hell?'

'Not dressed like that,' Strobo cut in.

'That can't be a commandment, can it?' asked the Welshman. 'That's hardly a sin, is it? Saying "Christ"?'

Danny agreed. 'Yeah, I thought the commandments were about big things. Deadly serious, you know, like capital offences.'

'OK, then,' I said, being teacher. 'Let's see if we can remember the Ten Commandments. Number one?'

'Thou shalt not bet on any horse ridden by Lanfranco fucking Dettori,' was Jonesy's suggestion.

'Er, which version of the Bible are you using as your reference, Jonesy?'

'Thou shalt not kill,' was Danny's effort.

'Thou shalt not kill, very good. That's number five. Number one is: thou shalt have no other gods but me.'

'Well, that's easy. I don't actually believe in God but if I did then I'd be happy to believe in that one,' Danny explained. 'You know, that old friendly bloke with a beard and long, white robes.'

'But hang on,' Jonesy interjected. 'We don't know that God was like that, do we? How about if God was a woman?'

'No, that's just not possible. God can't be a woman.' Danny was vehement.

'How do you know?'

I gave Jonesy my answer. 'If God was a woman she wouldn't have created Adam and Eve. She would have created only Eve.'

'Yeah, and a dildo,' added Danny, 'and what about periods? If God was a woman, she wouldn't have created periods.'

I thought I'd move the conversation along a bit faster. 'Number two: thou shalt not take the name of the Lord thy God in vain. Number three: keep the Sabbath holy. Number four: honour thy father and thy mother. Number five: thou shalt not kill. Number six: thou shalt not commit adultery.'

'No probs. I'm not married,' smiled Danny.

'But you have shagged a married woman, so technically you have committed adultery,' I corrected him, recalling one or two awkward episodes in my life.

'Who?' Danny challenged.

'Carla Barnes.'

'She's not married.'

'You were best man at her wedding!' Strobo pointed out.

'Ah, but our little er … "thing" was before she was married.'

'Only an hour before.'

'Bollocks,' Danny said emphatically. 'You're doing that exaggeration-for-comic-effect thing.'

'Oh, alright then. Now, number seven: thou shalt not steal.'

'Never stolen,' claimed Jonesy, his eyes shut piously till Danny jogged his memory.

'Come off it. What about the time you worked in the Millers'? You were always pouring pints for yourself.'

'That's stealing from the brewery, those bastards at Greene King. That doesn't count!'

'Yeah, actually now you come to mention it,' I said to Jonesy, 'I do recall that bit in Exodus when God says to Moses, "Number seven: thou shalt not steal except from those bastards at Greene King."'

'Isn't there one about covering your neighbour's ass?' Danny asked.

'Covet,' I corrected him. 'Thou shalt not covet thy neighbour's wife and thou shalt not covet thy neighbour's belongings.'

With some justification Jonesy pointed out, 'They're bloody dull when you think about, aren't they? I mean apart from "Do not steal" and "Do not kill" you can more or less ignore the rest.'

'Yeah, you could have a point there, Mr J. But I think it's important to have a code to live by.'

'Don't go religious on us, please,' implored Jonesy. 'Just because you can remember all the commandments and all that Catholic shit …'

'Not just knowing the commandments but all that Catholic shit probably does make me more conscious of what is right or wrong. It makes you think twice before you do something bad.'

'And then you do it anyway and then go and confess it,' Danny cut in quickly.

'I think that's unfair, Daniel,' I said dishonestly.

'Why didn't you become a priest then?' Jonesy asked me search-ingly. 'You know all the stuff and everything. You're always preaching on about some things …'

'Well, I did once go to a retreat to reflect for a weekend on this and many other universal questions, but for now, let me just say, why don't we go and drink to the memory of Peter Cockburn?'

'I've got a question,' Jonesy said. 'Considering what he did for a living and all, it's surprising Peter the Heater didn't get cremated!'

We pondered this and other weighty questions as we made our way to the nearest licensed premises. 'Mulligan's bar,' Strobo said.

'Not an Irish pub,' whined Jonesy.

'Irish is good,' I said definitively.

Chapter 32

Good Catholic Boy Is Irish

A man goes into a grocer's shop in Tralee and asks if he's got any pickled onions.

The grocer checks the shelf and says, 'I've none out here but come back to the stockroom with me and we'll see if there's any there.'

The grocer and the customer go to the back of the shop to a huge stockroom, every shelf of which is packed with bags of salt.

'Now, let's see,' says the grocer, 'pickled onions.' And he proceeds methodically to check the shelves. 'Right, salt … salt … salt … now, what's this here? Oh, salt … More salt. What about this aisle … salt … salt … salt …' After an intense half-hour the grocer concludes that he is indeed out of pickled onions.

'No, I'm sorry. I'm out of pickled onions.'

'Never mind, I'll try elsewhere,' says the customer cheerily and goes to leave the shop. As he gets to the door he turns to the grocer and says, 'Hope you don't mind me asking, but do you sell a lot of salt?'

The grocer thinks. 'No. To be honest with you, I sell very little salt. Hardly any at all.'

'Oh,' says the customer.

'But, funny you should ask, though,' continues the grocer, ''cause the man who sells me salt, now, he sells a lot of salt!'

* * *

This is an Irish joke.

I like Irish jokes.

My friend Dara doesn't.

(Dara, skip the first bit of this chapter.)

Being a learned Dubliner he is, rightly, worried that the word 'Irish' becomes a semantic shortcut for 'thick and uncultured'. Not being Irish myself, I see Irish jokes more as a celebration of the flexibility of language and a messing around with internal logic. In the 'salt' joke, you have an absurd situation but at no point can you say that either participant is stupid. And Dara, being Irish, has never had the experience of Irishness that I have.

I've already told about the priests, the nuns and the doctors, and I'd concluded, or been led to conclude, that Irish is good. Irish is special. Irish is the best.

Despite more than a century of jokes depicting the Irish as stupid, if you grew up as a Catholic in Cornwall in the sixties, the Erse, the Gaels, the Hibernians, the people of Eire, of Erin, of the Emerald Isle were loving, friendly, devout and, moreover, wise, brainy, knowledgeable, intelligent, clever and holy.

But certainly not thick.

Anyway, if you examine Irish jokes with a fine-toothed analysis, you'll discover that more often than not the Irishman is the winner. It's all about the logical side-step.

So you ask a man in deepest, rural Ireland, 'How would you get to Killarney from here?' and he replies, the joke goes: 'Well, if I was going to Killarney, I wouldn't start from here.' Now that surely, if looked at under the microscope of reason, is not a stupid thing to say at all. It means that the route to Killarney is a difficult or complex route from your chosen starting point. Presumably the Irishman will give you the directions, one point of which will certainly and implicitly be a better, easier, starting point for the journey.

I feel I'm on strong ground here as, when recently working in Ireland, one of our crew asked how to get to a place called Mileek. The knowing reply was, 'If I was going there, I wouldn't start from here.'

My father, who naturally would be a few genes more Irish than me, was well aware of the inherent pseudo-racism of these innocent gags and he would regale us of the time he'd been out with his native Redruth friends and had told a bunch of Irish jokes but substituted the word 'Cornish' for 'Irish'. The jokes had gone down badly. One of the locals had failed to understand them as jokes at all.

* * *

Around 1972, our home town of Redruth was going to get a bypass. Actually, it already had a bypass, but the town was such a shit-hole they were taking no chances. The construction of the new Redruth bypass, as the new road was going to be called to distinguish it from the old Redruth bypass, which was simply called the Redruth bypass, necessitated the influx of considerable casual labour. This meant, in effect, that hundreds of Irishmen descended on the area. A tiny yet comparatively devout handful of these would attend Mass on a Sunday from time to time. These were real, rough, dyed-green-in-the-wool 'Paddies'. They were apparently better known as 'navvies' due to some obscure connection with canal-building in the last century. These were not the twee, anglicised Irish that we'd grown up with: priests, nuns and the busy devout church-cleaners and flower arrangers of the parish. These were rough, hairy-knuckled hunks of men who turned up on a few Sundays and filled their own pew. What struck me most was the blotchy redness of their faces and their prodigious eye-brows. They were uniformly stuffed into Sunday-best suits which they'd clearly bought several stones ago. Clean but unironed shirts and ties strained to contain stomachs, necks and chins. But what most exciting, to us altar boys, was their cavalier disregard to the celebrant and the liturgy. 'Speak up, fella!' boomed an Irish voice from the back as Father McEvedy began one of his pious ramblings. This was excellent stuff. 'Give us a good song now, ladies' was bellowed as the organ groaned to life and the alleged choir stood up.

Until I got sacked for truancy and fraud, I worked for five days on the construction of said new bypass. I was a casual labourer and my immediate boss, Hughie Devine, took the word 'casual' to its Irish extreme and was a joy to be with and reinforced my feeling of pseudo-Irishness on a daily basis.

'Ah, here he is! Look at him with his head of curls and Irish mush. You're a navvy, now, make no mistake, Rory, lad.'

Which brings me finally to me!

Me?

Yes, of course, I'm Irish.

A good friend of mine, whom we shall call 'G' (because he's quite well known and might get annoyed if I reveal his real name, Griff Rhys Jones), will argue, and has done at length on several occasions, that, in general, I come from the same place as the person I happen to be talking to, especially if that person is a girl.

'Rory's Cornish, you know,' G declaims to a third party, usually within my earshot. 'Well, he was born in Cornwall but if necessary that includes Devon, Somerset and most of the West Country. Of course, his parents are from St Helens in Lancashire, so let's not rule out his being from "oop north". Even a Scouser, if the situation demands it. And he's an avid Arsenal fan, so that covers most of the Home Counties and the south-east and he might even throw in a few Cockney credentials. He now lives in Cambridge which, of course, means he actually comes from East Anglia, don't you know! Norwich, Peterborough, Ipswich and all those other well-known East Anglian places like Birmingham. Oh, and he once filmed some obscure history documentary for some equally obscure TV channel and spent a lot of time in Scotland and Wales so that covers most of the British Isles. Oh, and his first name's Patrick and he likes a Guinness, so he's Irish as well; but only should the need arise, you understand.'

My first name *is* Patrick but there's a good reason for that. Not only was it the name of my paternal grandfather, but I was born on 17 March.

St Patrick's Day.

Yes, Paddy's Day when all over the world, from Rio de Janeiro to Kathmandu, the streets flow with black stout and green lager; in bars like Dirty Nelly's in Brisbane, Mulligan's in Nairobi or Filthy Flynn's in Leningrad, the shamrock hats are donned and the bars echo to twinkly-eyed laughter, the clinking of Jameson's glasses and the strains of the Pogues, U2, the Chieftains and Val Doonican, and a day when not a lot of work gets done in Kilburn High Road.

In fact, not only was my paternal grandfather Irish but so was my maternal great grandmother. Now, by my calculations, that makes me three-eighths Irish, which must be equivalent to, though I'm not great at metric calculations, 98 per cent.

Certainly that's what I thought, or wanted to think, when I was a schoolboy because every Catholic schoolboy in Cornwall wanted, surely, to be Irish. I was certainly more Irish than some of the people I once met in O'Neill's bar in central London on Paddy's night: an Australian called Lars McDougall; Mitchell C. Biegelman the Third, an American who claimed to be half Irish, quarter Slovak and quarter Navajo Indian; or Ryan Rosario, who was a third Irish, a third Jamaican, half Sri Lankan and quarter innumerate.

The truth is, everywhere in the world, people want to be Irish.

Apart from the birthday presents, St Patrick's Day meant the added excitement of wearing shamrock to school. Those of us in the know, or with friends or distant relatives in God's own country, would be sent authentic Irish shamrock. From Mayo.

'Where's Mayo, Mummy?'

'In Ireland, of course. Where else would shamrock come from?'

Anywhere in the world, in fact. Well, anywhere with a wettish climate. We didn't know that then, of course, but this dull, straggly weed is extremely common and can be any one of about a dozen species. It is said to take its name from the Gaelic 'seamrog', meaning 'little clover'. Like a lot of clovers, it is trifoliate, which is gardening nerd-speak for three-leaved. St Patrick, who it is believed came from Wales, used to use it as an image of the Holy Trinity when he went preaching and converting around Ireland in the fifth century. Though before then, the druids of Ireland considered it sacred or mystical because they considered three to be a magic number. They loved a triad, did the Druids. (I think, to this day, we all find a threesome a little bit special.)

Anyway, off to school we'd go with this scraggy green plant pinned to our lapels and dribbling down our shirts, explaining its significance to the boorish, inferior, Protestant children on the bus, with amused disdain.

Before school there'd be a special Mass and we'd get to sing 'Hail, Glorious St Patrick'.

'Hail, glorious St Patrick, dear saint of our isle / On us thy poor children bestow a sweet smile' it began. 'Our Isle' no doubt meant Ireland but for our purposes this was extended to include Great Britain, Europe, the World, the Galaxy, the Universe etc. 'Bestow' was one of those 'hymny' words we never understood and were never explained to us. We just learnt them and sang them and they were sacred, mystical and, largely, meaningless. 'Hail, Glorious St Patrick' contains quite a few of those words: infidel, wiles, throng, kindled, exiles and undiminished. And 'wert', as in 'where the shamrock still blooms as when thou wert on Earth'.

The chorus went: 'On Erin's green valleys / On Erin's green valleys / On Erin's green valleys look down in thy love.'

In the Republic of Ireland, being Irish is not uncommon. The same can be said for being Catholic. Everyone's a Catholic, everybody goes to Mass, learns the same hymns and knows the same prayers. Catholicism is just something you do, and then at some point in your life you stop doing it. Well, some do. But in Wesleyan Cornwall being Catholic is rare. You're in a huge minority and this gives you the feeling of exclusivity and superiority. And, of course, paranoia. Your religion and your 'Irishness', however bogus, feel more precious and much more part of you. The faith is hard to walk away from, and so is your faint feeling of Irishness.

Being called Patrick Rory McGrath and being born on 17 March counted for something. Not least being captain of the Irish team for the traditional St Patrick's Day Irish *v.* English football match. The tradition was that the Irish team wore green sashes and the English wore red ones.

Sister Michael picked the teams.

This was another tradition; as was the fact the Irish team had the eleven best players and always won.

Except one year.

One year. I think it was 1965; the St Patrick's Day match was officiated by a lay teacher. A young woman, though half Irish and a good Catholic, of course, she wasn't au fait with the traditions of the event. She picked the teams based on the nationality of the individual. This meant we had the absurd situation where the English team was full of English boys and the Irish team was full of Irish boys. The English were by far the better team and beat us 12–3. (Now I know this *sounds* like a drubbing, but I'm convinced one of their goals was a good yard offside.)

This was unacceptable, and Sister Michael and Sister Stephen were called in and it was decided there may have been some confusion about team selection. An understandable and quite innocent mistake; no need to contact Sepp Blatter. The nuns decided a rematch was the only fair remedy with more attention being paid to the two line-ups.

Kieran Fitzgerald, the school bully but the best footballer, was as fiercely English as a Cornishman could be. He had scored five for England in the first game, but what was someone called Kieran Fitzgerald doing playing for the reds? He had to be given a green sash. Another two footballing prodigies from the English side were Michael Myskiewicz and Salvatore Babbagallo. They surely had to be on the Irish team, if only on the grounds that they couldn't possibly be English. We'd had David Pugh on our team in the first match. He was Welsh but spoke what was known then as 'dead posh' so had to be relocated in the English team.

It occurred to me years later that by this reasoning, if St Patrick had been around then, *he* would have ended up on the English side, encouraging his team-mates no doubt in his thick Welsh accent against the hated opposition of Irish, Cornish, Poles, Italians and Nigerians.

After Sister Michael had approved the reshuffle, the list of names for the two sides was drawn up. The Irish team now had fifteen players and the English had seven. New players, who hadn't taken part in the original match, were bought in and adjustments were made till everyone was happy with the teams. What a game it turned out to be; an excitingly close match which the Irish won 8–1, despite the courageous heroics of the English goalkeeper, nine-year-old Barbara Smith.

The shadow of Irishness has stayed with me long after my Catholicism had died out. I still find myself wanting Ireland to beat England in football and rugby. Not that it has happened that much. I like Guinness. I like the 'fiddling and jigging' music. And I have had a wank while thinking of one of the Nolan sisters. (I think it was Maureen.)

Dara, when he can be bothered, is good at making me snap out of it.

'Now, Rory, I'll break it to you gently, but I think there's something you're going to have to know. Being born on St Patrick's Day does not make you Irish. You are English. Totally English and typically English!'

'How can you tell?'

'Because I fucking hate you.'

I laugh and order two pints of Guinness.

And a Magners for Dara.

'I'll tell you something, though,' he whispers. 'It would have been Linda Nolan for me. She was the naughtiest of them all!'

Chapter 33

Sinner Boy Breaks Another Commandment: Thou Shalt Not Take the Lord's Name in Vain

Bobby Harker was the Head of Light Entertainment Radio (HLER) at the BBC. He was my boss in my first proper job and I was going for a script meeting with him. This would be a landmark in my comedy-writing career.

Reading Spike Milligan books, listening to *The Goon Show* on the radio (under the bedclothes so my parents wouldn't know), then *Round the Horne* and later *I'm Sorry I'll Read That Again*, had whetted my appetite for comedy, particularly radio comedy, which would often be verbal and totally surreal. I'd written sketches for school revues and the main impetus for my desire to go to Cambridge was to get in the Footlights and have a career in comedy.

It was a brave plan and totally naive. Footlights was moribund when I arrived in Cambridge, and the drinking and the largely unsuccessful pursuit of girls siphoned off a lot of the zeal that might have gone into comedy writing and performing. But I met some people there who went on to work for the BBC and proved useful contacts and after a year of post-graduation bumming around, unskilled labouring and sending jokes and sketches into BBC Radio,

I was eventually offered an in-house writing contract for the Light Entertainment department. From writing scripts for other people, starting with the likes of Frankie Howerd, Windsor Davies, Don Maclean and Roy Hudd, I ended up with a group of friends writing and performing in our own sketch show called *Injury Time*. It was concerning a sketch for this show that our producer, Graham, and I were visiting the 'boss' in his office suite.

Bobby took the script off Graham, the producer, and asked us to sit down.

'Right, let's have a little look at this scallywag,' he said with a chuckle and, repositioning his bifocals, he began reading enthusiastically.

This is what he read.

PAYING THE LAST BILL
THE SCENE IS THE UPPER ROOM OF A TAVERN. IT IS DARK OUTSIDE. THE TWELVE APOSTLES ARE SEATED ROUND A LARGE TABLE. IT IS CLEAR FROM THE PLATES, GOBLETS AND FOOD REMAINS ON THE TABLE THAT THEY ARE AT THE END OF A LARGE MEAL. JESUS IS STANDING AT THE HEAD OF THE TABLE. HE HOLDS UP A PIECE OF BREAD.

JESUS: This is my body. (HE THEN HOLDS UP A GOBLET OF WINE) And this is my blood.
A WAITRESS APPROACHES THE TABLE AND BANGS DOWN A SAUCER WITH A PIECE OF PAPER ON IT.
WAITRESS: And this is your bill.

All traces of a smile had disappeared from Bobby's face.

PETER LOOKS AT THE BILL.

PETER: That's steep! (HE PICKS UP BILL AND HANDS IT TO THOMAS) One hundred and forty-five? Is that right, Thomas?

THOMAS: I doubt it. (THOMAS HAS A YORKSHIRE ACCENT)

JESUS: We'll have to pay this somehow!

JUDAS: I love you, Jesus. You're, like, awesome.

JESUS: Yes, alright, Judas, not now.

JUDAS: You're my hero.

A waxy paleness began to replace the normally rosy complexion of HLER's face. He looked over the top of the manuscript at me and Graham to check he wasn't imagining the whole thing. He looked back at the text of the sketch.

PETER: As your rock, and all that, Jesus, might I suggest two ways of doing this? Either we itemise what everybody had and charge them accordingly, or we just divide the total equally between the thirteen of us.

JUDAS: Twelve of us! I don't think Jesus should pay ... Especially as in a few days' time, he ... er ...

PETER: What?

JUDAS: Nothing.

JESUS: D'you know what? I had a funny feeling that something odd might happen tonight. I had a dream that one of you would betray me for a bag of money.

(THEY ALL SEEM AGHAST AT THIS SUGGESTION)

JUDAS: (UNDER HIS BREATH TO JESUS) I bet it's that Simon the Zealot. Shifty character. You know what they say, 'Scratch a zealot and you'll find a Nazi underneath.'

PETER: (TO JESUS) What the hell are you talking about?

THOMAS: One of us betray you? No. Very doubtful, is that!

PETER: Here, what's that item on the bill? Mary Mag?

JESUS: Oh, she was that servant girl; the one who came in to wash my feet.

PETER: Oh, that's what she was doing under the table! (HE SNIGGERS CRUDELY)

HLER sucked in a lung-bursting volume of air and expelled it with a whistle.

JESUS: Right, come on, everybody, it's roughly twelve each.

PHILIP: But I didn't have a starter!

MATTHEW: And I didn't have any wine.

JUDAS: We should have ordered water, then you could have done that trick of yours, Jesus.

JESUS: What? Walking on it? (LAUGHTER ALL ROUND)

JUDAS: Walking on it! Ha ha ha. That's priceless, Jesus.

BARTHOLOMEW: I should only pay half, 'cause I had the vegetarian option.

PETER: You poof! You should pay more then. You're putting us fishermen out of business. (MURMURS OF AGREEMENT)

JESUS: OK, we'll separate the wine from the bill and split that among the drinkers.

JUDAS: We should have gone BYO then you could have brought in five loaves and two fishes and you could have done a miracle. Tuna sandwiches for five thousand coming up!

JESUS: Shut up, Judas.

JAMES: Listen, Jesus, I ought to shoot. Babysitter and all that. I'll stick this in (HE WAVES A NOTE) and if it's more I'll see you right next week.

JUDAS: (SOTTO VOCE) Next week?

MATTHEW: Same here, Jeez. Great night, there's a tenner. Oh,
    and if you ever need any cheap tax advice, let me know.
PETER: (TO WAITRESS) Do you take cards?
WAITRESS: What have you got?
PETER: This one says 'Happy Easter' and this one …

Harker shook from head to toe as if his grave had been trampled
over by 3,000 elephants. The sheets of paper in his hand started to
tremble and looked as if they could at any moment quite easily burst
into flames.

WAITRESS: Cash or I'll call the guards.
PETER: Well, I'll put this in. It's more than I owe but sod it,
    I need a piss.
JUDAS: I'll put this in but I'm strapped. I'm down to my last
    thirty pieces of silver.
JESUS: Thomas, have you put in enough?
THOMAS: I doubt it. (THE APOSTLES START LEAVING
    ONE BY ONE, EACH CASUALLY AND RELUC-
    TANTLY CHIPPING IN A FEW COINS TO JESUS)
ANDREW: That's me. There'd better be some change.
BARTHOLOMEW: Three from me. Didn't have wine.
JAMES: And me. I'm off for a fag.
(EVENTUALLY THE APOSTLES HAVE FILTERED OUT,
    LEAVING JESUS ALONE WITH THE WAITRESS)
WAITRESS: Come on, I can't wait all night.
JESUS: (COUNTING THE MONEY) There we are, that's a
    total of eighty-five.
WAITRESS: Bad luck. I need one hundred and forty-five.
JESUS: Jesus Christ … This is the last bloody supper I come to.

* * *

Harker banged the manuscript down hard on his desk, shot upright in his chair and began to rant in a commendable impression of a Home Counties Hitler.

'Disgusting!' he said thumping his fist on the table.

'Unbroadcastable!' Thump.

'Disgraceful!' Thump.

'Obscene!' Thump.

'This will never go out!' Thump.

'Full stop!' We waited for one more thump but he just slumped exhausted back into his chair. Graham, the producer, gave a placatory nod.

'I know what you mean. That's why we came in to run it by you. It definitely needs toning down.'

'Toning down?' Harker fumed. 'It needs bloody incinerating and the ashes buried at the bottom of the ocean in a lead strongbox!' He stared at us both with aggressive disbelief. 'Listen, Graham, old chap, this is *not* going out on BBC radio – or anywhere else, I shouldn't wonder.' It was as if he and his family had been personally attacked.

'You're the son of a vicar, Bobby,' I ventured. 'Do you think that's coloured your judgement?'

'For Christ's sake, pardon my French,' he snapped. 'Rory, my boy, this sketch will offend every Christian worldwide.'

'Mmm, I didn't know the listening figures were that good!' I said, attempting a smile.

'I knew I could count on you to be facetious till the end, Rory.' Harker glowered at me for a moment. 'Now listen, the Last Supper is sacred. Its symbolism, its iconography, is at the very core of Christian belief and ritual.'

He was not going to be appeased but Graham interrupted bravely: 'The satire here is not about Jesus or the Last Supper or Christianity; it's about that universal situation, a very modern, urban situation, when a bunch of mates end up having a late-night meal – usually a curry. We've all been there and there's always an argument about the bill. Who ate what, who should pay what, who drank what, et cetera, et cetera, and however you divide it up, there's never enough. That's what this sketch is about. Setting it at the Last Supper, for me, just points up the satire a jot; makes it punchier.'

'Bollocks,' was Harker's succinct appraisal of Graham's defence. 'I've never heard such arrant bullshit in my life. It's balls and you know it! This sketch is just an excuse to do puerile jokes and have a dig at the Gospels. Rory, my dear chap, were you seriously thinking you could get a sketch broadcast on BBC Radio Four in which Jesus Christ, the Son of God, the day before his crucifixion, says, "This is the last bloody supper I come to"?'

Graham attempted some feeble mitigation. 'It was originally "This is the last *fucking* supper, I come to", so we've already begun to tone it down.'

'You're better than this, Rory,' said my boss, trying a new tack. 'You don't need to do this, you can write better than this.'

I didn't necessarily agree with him.

Harker tried again. 'Maybe this is about you, Rory, this sketch. You are a lapsed Catholic; perhaps you're getting your own back on your upbringing. Maybe this is a two-fingered salute, and not a very subtle one, aimed at your parents, your teachers, your priest?'

'Mmm,' I conceded. 'I'd never considered that.'

'I mean, would you have written the same sketch about Jews?' he asked pointedly, thinking he was now winning the debate.

'It is about Jews. They were Jews.'

'Don't split fucking hairs with me, young man! OK, Muslims, then?'

It was a good question but one that, back in the early eighties, would never have been asked. It would have been meaningless.

I didn't know enough about Muslims to write a sketch about them, and the listeners wouldn't have known enough about Muslims to have understood it, let alone to have found it either funny or offensive.

Now, of course, it would be unthinkable for anyone to write a piece of comedy deliberately lampooning Islam. But with the strangely distorted morality of the end of the twentieth century, the Last Supper sketch would probably have been OK. It was 'only upsetting' Christians, after all, and they're a docile bunch who won't kick up a fuss. We're not offending Muslims or homosexuals or disabled people, so we'll be fine, goes the thinking.

'But, surely, Bobby,' I lumbered on, 'taking offence is a choice. I can write a sketch like this and it may or may not be offensive depending on the person who sees or hears it. They can choose to be offended by it if they want, but they can also choose not to be offended by it. It's patronising of us to decide who will be offended by what. Why don't we let them decide?'

Harker began shaking his head vigorously. 'I've heard you trot out this "You-can-only-*take*-offence" argument over and over again, Rory, and it may be absolutely right but it's a sophisticated argument that I don't think the wider public is ready to accept. Ninety-nine point nine per cent of the population of this country are as thick as pig-shit, don't forget. They must be, otherwise television wouldn't exist. And it's not the main listening public I have to convince, anyway. It's the listeners' panel and the board of governors and they're an uptight bunch of … er, so to speak. Let's put it this way, Rory, what would your parents think if they heard it? Would they be offended?'

I was stumped by this question. Yes, they would be offended. And they probably wouldn't accept the 'you-can-only-take-offence' argument. They were good, kind people who would not understand what would make a loving son of theirs create something so unpleasant to their ears. Perhaps their background and upbringing would prevent them from making the choice about whether they were offended or not. Was there a lesson here for the sinner boy?

The 'Last Supper' sketch, as the 'Paying the Bill' sketch became known, never did go out, so nobody had the choice to be offended or not offended by it. Not even my parents, thank God.

Chapter 34

Good Catholic Boy Loves Mary

Danny folded his arms tightly and patted and rubbed himself vigorously on the upper arms as if he was very cold and trying to get warm.

'Nicotine patches?' I asked.

'No. Haven't got one on today, actually. If you must know, I'm bloody cold and I'm trying to keep warm.'

'Ah, I'll tell you what. May is the best month of the year in England. If you disagree, I'm happy to discuss it with you, but to save time let me just tell you now, you're wrong.' I was feeling expansive about the onset of spring as we walked along the riverbank from town to Danny's place. 'May *is* the best month in England. The trees. The blossom. Breathe in those scents. The birds. The vibrant shades of pale green.'

'What the hell are you on about?' asked my shivering companion.

'May. It reminds me of the innocence of my childhood. It reminds of Mary. May, the month of Mary. Not my first wife. But the Blessed Virgin Mary. It's warm but cool. It's still, apart from a light breeze.'

'But it's March. Today is the twenty-fifth of fucking March!'

'So what,' I continued. 'I still think May is the best month of the year in England.'

'So, what's this about the Virgin Mary, then?'

'It's Lady Day today. You ignoramus. The Feast of Annunciation. When the angel announced to Mary that she was with child and that child shall be the Son of God.'

Danny shook his head. 'Where do you get this stuff from?'

'I was born to it. Infected at birth,' I answered, but Danny was clearly troubled by the whole notion.

'How can anyone believe in virgin birth?'

It was an unanswerable question but I was in a good mood and thought I'd play the angel's advocate.

'Faith, my child. Do you believe that two plus two equals four?'

'Yes, because it does,' answered the slightly puzzled Danny. 'Unless you do it by logarithms, then it's three point nine nine nine nine nine nine recurring.'

'Ah, I see,' I went on with mock sagacity. 'So you believe in a certainty. Do you believe that two plus two equals five?'

'No, because it doesn't.'

'So you don't believe in uncertainty,' I went on. 'That's where faith comes in. Anyone can believe that two plus two equals four but it takes a strong faith to believe that two plus two equals five. So we don't question the virgin birth, we just believe in it.'

'Tell me this, then; how could she conceive?'

'Well,' I chuckled, 'as always the Bible has the answer. It says she was "overshadowed by the Holy Ghost".'

Danny laughed as well. 'I've never heard it called that before. "Fancy coming back to mine while I overshadow you?"'

'It's like "knowledge" in Genesis,' I explained. 'In Genesis, shagging is "knowing". Adam "knew" Eve.'

'Well, of course he did. They were the only two people in the world. It wasn't going to be long before one of them broke the ice. "Hello, I'm Adam." "Hi, I'm Eve. Nice to know you." And he says, "Yes, it probably would be, let's find out!"'

'But at least,' I said, 'Adam would have been confident she was a virgin.'

Danny thought about this. 'Yeah, that would have been a right downer. Imagine, you're with the only girl in the world, she's naked and up for an overshadow, then you find some bastard's already been there.'

'I see what you mean,' I said. 'Who could have got there first? The gardener of Eden, maybe? There must have been one. Dirty Derek, the gardener of Eden, sniffing around with his dibber and a sack of mulch in his hand.'

We laughed and suddenly became conscious of the strange looks we were getting from passers-by.

'No, but it was different with Mary,' I went on. 'It was the Holy Ghost what did it. Her husband Joseph had gone blind.'

'Oh, he'd gone blind, had he?' Danny went on, obviously enjoying the discussion. 'And we all know why men go blind! Well, you find out your missus is being knobbed the Holy Ghost, you've got to make your own arrangements.'

We'd reached Danny's doorstep and I was keen to change the subject; strangely enough, I was beginning to feel a little uncomfortable. 'Come on, make me a cup of coffee, then!'

But Danny had warmed to the theme and wouldn't let it go.

'Wait, hang on, I just thought of something. If God the Father is the father of Jesus and the Virgin Mary is the mother of Jesus and God and Jesus are technically the same person, doesn't that mean that Mary is the mother of her child's father?'

'Mary was immaculate and that's the end of it. Now, are you going to open the door or not?'

He wasn't.

'Immaculate. As in Immac, the stuff for getting rid of unwanted pubic hair?'

'I'd never thought of it,' I said, and as bad luck would have it, just as a frail-looking vicar was walking past, Danny said a bit too loudly, 'I wonder if Our Lady had a minge.'

We were at last in the house.

'Right, can we stop talking about Our Lady's pubes now?' I asked.

No, we couldn't, it seemed. 'Well, it was before the Brazilian and the Hollywood,' Danny went on, 'and she was Middle-eastern so I expect we're talking hairy. A good old coconut.'

'I think "immaculate" refers to the conception. Nothing else,' I informed him.

'I see,' he said. 'The Holy Ghost gave her a good old over-shadowing!'

'Yes, and it was immaculate.'

'I've never quite managed that.' Danny sniggered. 'I've had a few pretty good ones, a few nine-out-of-tens but never an immaculate one.'

* * *

Despite the scurrilousness of our conversation, the positive memories of Lady Day, of Mary and the enchanting month of May, only thirty-six days away, remained vivid in my mind.

I thought of my favourite prayer: 'Hail, Holy Queen, Mother of Mercy, hail, our life, our sweetness and our hope.'

Isn't it beautiful?

I loved getting a 'Hail, Holy Queen' (or 'Salve Regina') for my penance. Not just to relieve the monotony of the 'Hail Marys', the 'Our Fathers' and the 'Glory Bes', but because I loved the words. I'd always try to sit in the pew facing the statue of Mary while I recited it. The soothing, beatific Mary, in spotless white and celestial blue robes; holding the baby Jesus or a lily, or both; glowing with purity, lambent with compassion, radiant with love.

'To thee do we cry, poor banished children of Eve. To thee do we send up our sighs, mourning and weeping in this vale of tears. Turn, then, most gracious advocate, thine eyes of mercy towards us. And after this our exile, show unto us the blessed fruit of thy womb, Jesus. O clement, O loving, O sweet Virgin Mary.'

Absolutely beautiful.

I may not cry now or get a lump in the throat, as I recite that prayer, but I still struggle not to get a warm tingle.

Wonderful.

And completely meaningless.

Well, meaningless, that is, to the five-year-old who learnt it. 'To thee do we cry, poor banished children of Eve' (who are the poor banished children of Eve that we're crying to?). 'To thee do we send up our sighs, mourning and weeping' (of course, as an infant, you assume 'sighs' is 'size' and 'mourning' is 'morning', making that bit particularly batty). 'Show unto us the blessed fruit of thy womb, Jesus' (what blessed fruit will be shown to us? Apples? Kumquats? And why is thy womb called Jesus?). O clement, O loving, O sweet Virgin Mary (who is Clement and how did he sneak into the 'Hail, Holy Queen'?).

But it didn't matter that it was meaningless. That was its strength. The allure of mystery, like the Latin Mass. It was the participation in all that cabbalistic mumbo-jumbo that set you apart from your common or garden Protestant. (And most Protestants *were* common, of course.) It was its strength also for those teaching us and indoctrinating us. Teach them something by rote while they're too young to understand it. It worked for a while but as you get older and discover what it is that you've learnt and been saying all these years, it makes you angry and resentful. It makes you begin to question everything. But the beauty of the words remain.

O clement, O loving, O sweet Virgin Mary.

Mary, of all the names ...

In my class at primary school there were ten boys and fourteen girls. Being outnumbered by females was seen as a bad thing at that age.

Of the fourteen girls, five were called Mary: Mary Maloney, Mary McCarthy, Mary Clemmo, Mary Simmons and Mary Brown. We could massage this figure up to seven, that is fifty per cent, by including the Marias: Rawicki and Tardelli.

My happiest memories of church must be the various festivals dedicated to Mary.

Every year towards the end of May, which as we know is the best month of the year in England, one Sunday was set aside for the May Procession: priest and altar boys first; then the children in ascending order of age; then the grown-ups. The procession would wend its way from the primary school to the church for Mass then from the church to the convent next door for sandwiches and drinks. This was a special celebration for the Virgin Mary, the Holy Mother of God, Our Lady Queen of the Angels, Star of the Sea, Blessed Alma Mater and so on.

A chosen infant, usually a girl, often called Mary, would carry, on a little white silk cushion, a charmingly crafted coronet of freshly picked flowers with which she would crown the statue of Our Lady in the church. All the younger children would carry quaint little posies of wild flowers: bluebells, primroses, daisies and dandelions, which they would scatter like organic confetti along the processional route. In my memory these days were unquestionably happy occasions, of bright colours, dappled sunlight, petals and leaves, sunny hymns to the Virgin, and laughter and games at the big, communal 'do' afterwards. It engendered a real feeling of togetherness with the other parishioners, a feeling of community, exclusivity and distinction.

This select veneration of Our Lady is something peculiar to Roman Catholics. Other Christians don't have this special relationship with the Mother of God and this makes us feel more in touch with the human side of religion, the soft, warm, sympathetic, squidgy, fluffy, mumsy, mimsy, gooey side of Christianity. Everything was safe and perfect on May Procession days.

'Except that it always pissed down,' my brother once reminded me. But in my mind it *was* sunny and *we* were sunny and we sang sunny songs:

'Immaculate Mary, our hearts are on fire, / That title so wondrous fills all our desire / Ave, ave, ave, Maria. Ave, ave, ave, Maria.'

According to the Bible, Mary was singled out by God to be the mother of Jesus. And we know that by some clandestine skulduggery, some Almighty series of nepotistic shenanigans, Mary was somehow born without original sin. She was therefore not capable of committing a sin and could not even be tempted to commit a sin. (A tough act to follow and a hell of a pressure on all the millions of Marys who came after her. I must know at least a hundred Marys in person and some of them could have been, and definitely were, tempted to commit a sin or two, with some quite capable of committing a sin without any temptation at all.)

One in particular stands out: 'Do you, Rory, take Mary to be your lawful wedded wife?' intoned Father Hubert.

I paused expecting, from my betrothed, a comment like, 'You'll never get a straight answer out of him!'

It didn't come.

So I said, 'I do'.

And I did.

Chapter 35

Sinner Boy Breaks Another Commandment: Thou Shalt Not Kill

I used to think May was the best time of year. Not today. I somehow didn't expect it to be sunny. Sunny, like in my dreams. Always bad. And today was going to be a bad dream. Sunny; it didn't seem right. This was shocking.

'It's a lovely day,' I said, nearly adding, *at least.*

'Yes, it's wonderful,' she agreed as both of us struggled to think what impact or relevance the weather would have on our business today.

Did I hear a voice say: *There's no good day for murder?*

A glorious day in May. The May of petals and innocence.

There is no innocence any more. Not for you. Not now.

The recently cut lawns of the manor were impossibly bright green and sparkling with dew. The rhododendrons were heavy with coolness and purple. This wasn't the right day, surely, or the right place.

No right day. No right place.

We were silent as we walked up the gravel drive. The crunching of the stones seemed abnormally loud. Our presence there could not be kept secret. We felt ashamed.

That's all there is for you now: shame. Get used to it.

We held each other's hand tight with solidarity; we were in this together, tight with fear; we knew this was a huge event, tight with guilt. Neither of us was convinced that this wasn't a crime.

Like murder?

The woman who showed is into the waiting room was smart and business-like. She smiled too much.

Yes, no day for smiling, is it, today. You'll probably never smile again after today.

And she spoke in a whisper. Did she have to do that? Did she have to emphasise that we were all party to a guilty secret?

You mean you were expecting to be told off. To be punished. That's what you're used to. That's what you expect. And today you should expect it.

Everything in the consulting room was smart and clean and sickeningly ordinary. The doctor's words were bland and practical with no hint of disapproval, recrimination or accusation.

Apart from the hints in your mind.

'The tests confirm what you already know. I think we're talking thirteen weeks, which is absolutely fine,' she said nodding her approval.

Absolutely not fine. Absolutely disgraceful.

'Now, you've clearly gone into this thoughtfully and seriously and have come to a mature decision, a decision based on sound information and sensitivity to each other …'

A decision based on blind fear and craven selfishness.

We nodded and squeezed each other's hands and looked at each other without making eye contact. An outline of the technicalities followed but her jaunty voice couldn't lessen the grimness of the details.

This is the hard part. This is the bit about destruction.

I tried not to listen but occasional words leapt out and assaulted me. Words whose vagueness and obscurity just magnified the sinisterness: 'aspiration', 'dilation', 'curettage', 'suction' and 'evacuation of retained products'.

Blood. Flesh. Mutilation.

'Of course, we do give you time to reconsider. We do recommend you go over everything again. I'm sure you have done this already. Over and over again but give yourself just one more time.'

We nodded our 'Thank you, doctor' like star pupils trying to please teacher. But we wouldn't change our decision now. We couldn't.

So murder it is, then?

Endless hours we'd talked about it, without ever mentioning it. We'd examined the details, without really examining the details. We made meaningless, anodyne promises about how this would make us feel more for each other, cement our relationship, bring us closer.

Like having a baby?

But deep down we both knew that this was the beginning of the end. We would try to avoid each other now. We would keep apart. Not talk about it. Forget about it.

Pretend it never happened?

Pretend it never happened. If we could. If we could. Would we ever be able to escape the memory? The scar? The nightmare?

No, absolutely not.

The doctor twittered on about the legal and administrative formalities and I gazed out of the consulting-room window at May sunshine on pink blossom and cloud-shadows gliding across the grass. Two chaffinches landed on the lawn. The beautiful pink and blue male was a fluttering blur of song and dance as he courted his coy female, driven totally by the desire for immortality, to keep his species going, to have young. I hated that bird so much.

And you a twitcher? Go on. Give us the Latin name for a chaffinch, then.

I thought about children. Would I ever have children? Would I be present at their birth? Could I? Could I stand to see a bundle of life that I had helped create slither into the world full of hope, full of potential and full of the joy of living? Would I be able to look at them without shame? Would be able to gaze into their infinitely beautiful loving eyes and remember this dark day without weeping?

Well, let's see.

Then we had to sign some documents. I don't know what they were. I pretended to read them.

You didn't want to see it in black and white. Or was it in red?

My mind was full of questions that would not go away.

Worse still; answers that wouldn't go away.

We walked out through the packed waiting room trying not to look at anybody, trying not to make eye contact with all those people who were trying hard not to make contact with us. A surgery full of people who weren't really ill.

Just sick.

'Well then,' I said meaninglessly, knowing that anything with any meaning would be too hurtful to us both. 'Shall we have a coffee?'

'No, I'd better dash. I'm expected at the office. I'll call.'

'You must, of course. I mean, we'll obviously be seeing each other again, er …'

'Sure,' she said.

'Oh, one thing, Caroline, I must tell you …'

She interrupted. 'Carol. My name's Carol.'

Chapter 36

Holidays

The last supper took place on Holy Thursday, as we Catholics, lapsed or not, say. Maundy Thursday to the 'nons'.

This was what we called a 'Holiday of Obligation'.

Holidays. Holy Days. Notice the similarity? Holy day. Holi day. Holiday. Yes, they're the same thing.

Or they were a long time ago. At least for most people; but not so long ago for Catholics. The connection for Catholic children was more obvious but we still had to think about it. We had holidays that meant not going to school, and Holy Days that meant going to Mass. But then there were the Holy Days of Obligation that often fell in term-time, outside the holidays. On these days you had to go to Mass and refrain from servile works. Now none of us, except for those few who had been slaves under the Romans, knew exactly what servile works were. But apparently going to school was one of them. So on Holy Days of Obligation we had a day off school. The joy of getting home to tell Wally Freeth and Charlie Owens that we'd been told we Catholics would be having the next day off because it was (for example) the Annunciation, will stay with me forever. How smug we felt, how superior.

'I don' understand. Ow 'ee get a day off school?' a perplexed and envious Wally had asked.

'It's the Annunciation,' I replied.

'What's that?'

'Dunno, something to do with Our Lady,' I answered haughtily.

'Your mum?'

'No. God's mum,' I said making a mental note to find out what the Annunciation was.

'It's when the Angel Gabriel appeared to Mary and told her she was going to have a baby. And that baby would be Jesus Christ. Who is God,' my mother explained to me later. And I would explain to Danny later still.

The date is 25 March. It is still referred to even in the secular world as Lady Day, and until the calendar changed in 1752 it was the first day of the year. Twelve days were lost in the calendar change, so the first day of the year, if it hadn't been changed to 1 January, would have been 6 April, which, of course, to the Inland Revenue and my accountant, *is* the first day of the year.

There were several days in the year when the irritation and boredom of Mass would pay off in the form of time off school:

- The Immaculate Conception, 8 December. Back in those innocent, ignorant days we'd just enjoy the skive and not bother our little heads with the fact that the conception appeared to be over three months before the Annunciation and over a year before the actual birth.

- All Saints' Day, 1 November. Often called All Hallows' Day (from an old word for 'holy'), it's the day that follows All Hallows' Eve (Halloween). Forget the fun of witches, lanterns and apple-ducking, we had a lesson-free day to look forward to.

- Ascension Day, the fortieth day after Easter. This one could not be relied upon to fall in school-time because Easter tends to move around all over the place, but was often a welcome bonus between Easter holidays and half-term.

- Corpus Christi. The Sunday nearest to the sixtieth day after Easter is Trinity Sunday and the Thursday after *this* is Corpus Christi. (I know it's complicated but it was well worth it to know when your days off were.) Corpus Christi is when Catholics affirm their belief in the transubstantiation of the body of Christ (Corpus Christi) into bread, i.e. the communion wafers.

- The Feast of Saints Peter and Paul could be slipped in just before the summer holidays in some years.
- Christmas Day and Easter Sunday, all Sundays in fact, were Holy Days of Obligation, but it seems that everyone, even non-Catholics, had grabbed these for a day off work or school. Lazy heathens.

* * *

Catholic skiving went beyond Catholic school and individual days. In my non-Catholic secondary school, Catholics were, amazingly, exempt from RI lessons. (Religious Instruction. This was the same as RE – Religious Education, and RS – Religious Studies, but different from RU – Rugby Union.)

Our parents presumably thought we shouldn't be tainted with non-Catholic thinking, as learning about the history of the Bible, examining other religions and beliefs and comparing different faiths might lead us into temptation and sin or even worse, might lead to us running off to join the Methodists. So for at least an hour a week, my good (Catholic) friend Bob Sinfield and I would arse around the playground, wasting time, talking bollocks and feeling just that little bit superior.

One day, quite out of the blue, we got a special day off. We didn't know *why*, but two ten-year-olds would never dream of complaining that they'd been given an unexpected day off school. We were over the moon. We had to go to church and spend the day praying for some people in Wales. I think we went to the cinema after Mass. I certainly didn't stay at home praying.

I'll never forget it.

But not because we had a day off.

It still chills me to think back to that day, 21 October 1966. In a small valley town in Wales, called Aberfan, after heavy rain, a huge tip of coal waste collapsed and a slimy black avalanche engulfed the school next to it, killing 116 children. It was the last day of term. Seconds before they had been singing 'All Things Bright and Beautiful'.

Chapter 37

Good Catholic Boy Takes the Holy Sacrament of Eucharist

A holiday is not a holiday if you're at home, though, is it? To be in your own home, even on a day off, is to be surrounded by the perpetual nagging of the house. Every room screams at you to do one of those thousands of little jobs you've been meaning to do.

I eventually learnt that lesson and, before everything in Greece collapsed, we'd go to northern Crete for two weeks a year.

'It's so nice to be away from work and the house, isn't it?' says my wife.

'Yes,' I agree, 'nice to get away from those irritations, like Danny, Jonesy and Strobo.'

'That's not nice,' she says. 'I like Strobo.'

But distance doesn't remove you from your memories. No matter how far you go away, there's always something there to bring the past back. Or maybe it's a case of, 'Once a Catholic, always a Catholic'.

If you give up 'the faith', you are a lapsed Catholic. If you convert from Catholicism to Islam, you are not a Muslim, you are a lapsed Catholic. If you reject all forms of religion and belief in God and an afterlife, you are not an atheist; you are a lapsed Catholic. There is no let-up. There's no escape. There's always something there to remind you. Even in Crete.

Unlike most English tourists who go there, my wife and I try to learn a bit of Greek before we go. Like all English people, we say 'Please' and 'Thank you' more than is necessary and this brings a knowing smile from the waiter. He pours the wine and I say 'Thank you', which is *Efharisto*. Which just happens to be spelled 'Eucharistó'. (Can you see where this is going . . ?)

And every time I say it, I can't stop myself thinking of boiled eggs and short white trousers …

* * *

'What's for breakfast?' I ask.

'No breakfast for you today,' my mother tells me, 'you're on a fast. It's your First Holy Communion. And you'll get a big breakfast afterwards in the convent.'

Disappointment.

By the time you receive the communion bread into your body, it is no longer a slim wafer of tasteless bread, it is the body of Christ. During Mass the wafers have changed, transubstantiated. They have literally become, yes that's literally become the body of Christ. That's one of the main things that distinguish Catholics from Protestants. The Prods think the idea of a sliver of bread turning into God in your stomach is a bit too much of an imaginative leap. Anyway, the point is, you are taking God into your body and therefore your body must be as clean and empty as you can make it. God doesn't want to be sloshing round in your gut with a load of Coco Pops and toast.

'Now remember,' Sister Michael had told us, 'that it may feel like a small round piece of bread but it is the body of Christ. So no chewing or biting. You must swallow it down whole.'

Fear.

What if it sticks to the roof of your mouth? Could you use your tongue to dislodge it? Would it be a mortal sin to tongue Christ's body?

Jeanette Dalziel, who was sensible and decorous, asked the question for the class. 'What if it sticks to the roof of your mouth, Sister?'

'Good question, Catherine. If this happens then it is alright to dislodge it with your tongue.'

Relief. Followed by panic.

What if it goes down the wrong way and you choke to death? Or worse, you choke and end up coughing the body of Christ onto the floor?

'Did you have a question, Rory?' Sister's Michael's question made me jump.

'Er, no, Sister, thank you, Sister.'

Panic again.

* * *

First Holy Communion is taken young. It has to be. It has to be at an age when you can cope with the idea that a little wafer can, with a few mystical words from the priest, turn into the body of Christ. Many a faith has foundered and sunk on close scrutiny of this event. When you're a little bit older and are inclined to sling transubstantiation into the dustbin of irrationalism along with the tooth fairy, Father Christmas and the superhuman properties of Popeye's spinach, your elders and betters will try to persuade you that it's metaphorical, symbolic, merely a reminder of the Last Supper when Jesus sipped wine and broke bread with his disciples and said, 'This is my blood of the new testament, which is shed for many,' and 'Take, eat: this is my body.'

Even with only the rudiments of physics and human biology understood, Jesus' words at the Last Supper as metaphor is a far easier idea to grapple with than transubstantiation. But there again, to Catholics, the Last Supper is dripping with sacramental importance. This is not something to be messed around with. You don't make fun of the Last Supper. That would be a huge betrayal.

But when you're an eight-year-old boy, 'the host' is the body of Christ; it's real. Very real. Like the fear that you're going to choke and expectorate a little bit of Christ's body onto the priest's pristine robes.

'Do I *have* to wear short white trousers?' I ask my mother.

'Of course, you do!' she snaps.

I presumed this was to symbolise my state of utter cleanliness, spotlessness, freedom from sin; the only state in which to receive God inside you.

'Why?'

'Because everybody else will be wearing them,' she explains. 'You'll look absolutely lovely.'

So here I am in white shirt, red tie and white shorts, once more on the front pew of the church, queuing nervously for something I don't want to do. There is no expectation of exultation, no thrill at the unity I'm about to achieve with the Almighty, just a dry-mouthed anxiety about God sticking in my throat. I watch my fellow first-communicants go to the altar. One by one they kneel before the priest. The altar boy holds the brilliant gold plate under their chin to catch any bits of Christ's body that crumble off. The priest takes a host from the ciborium and says, 'Body of Christ.' 'Amen,' says the recipient; the host is placed on the tongue and it's over.

So far no one has choked. Angela McCann splutters alarmingly for a moment but after a theatrical gulp, the Lord is within her. And it's my turn. I kneel. The priest looms over me.

'Body of Christ.'

And the puny wafer is on my tongue and dissolving to nothing-ness before I've had time to finish articulating my 'Amen', let alone swallowing. It's over and I turn to go back to my pew, smiling radi-antly with relief that I didn't cough, choke, splutter, spit, retch, spew, die or bite Christ.

'Ah sure, did you see them all smiling when they got up from their First Holy Communion,' Sister Stephen was saying at the post-Communion breakfast feast. 'Sure, t'was a joy to see them looking so happy and holy.'

Then quite unexpectedly there were presents. One thing we hadn't been told about was a lovely reward. Do something good and holy and you will be rewarded. Of course. Most people were given rosary beads. Dinky, glittery silvery chains of beads, usually pearly white or blue, to help you keep count of your 'Hail Marys' when you were doing your penance. (Rather pointless in our parish with Father McEvedy, of course, as he only ever gave out three.)

But it was always nice to get a present, even if it wasn't as good as the solid silver St Christopher medal and chain that Jeanette Dalziel got.

Then the breakfast, which I recall was great fun. The ordeal of Eucharist was over and there was plenty of food. Everyone wore white so nobody stood out and no one told me off for spilling runny egg yolk down my shirt. The priest gave a short, dull sermon explaining what we had just been through. The gist being that the Eucharist was a thanksgiving, a favour or grace from God.

I'm not sure, after all these years, but I think he probably said that the word came from the Greek *eu*, meaning 'good' or 'well', and *charis*, meaning 'grace' or 'favour' and that *eucharisto* meant 'I thank' or 'thanksgiving'.

Eucharisto. Thank you.

Or, as they say in modern Greek, '*Efharisto*'.

'*Parakalo*,' replies the waiter.

'You look miles away,' my wife says, clinking her glass of retsina with mine.

'Sorry, I was. You don't fancy soft-boiled eggs, by any chance?'

'No, certainly not. I'm happy with just bread and wine.'

'Yes, bread and wine. Body and blood; what else could we possibly need?'

Chapter 38

Sinner Boy Commits Another Deadly Sin: Lust

She was stunning. There's something very suggestive about a beautiful girl in a shirt and tie, especially if the tie is not quite done up. Apart from their racy formality, the tie, white shirt and white coat emphasised her suntan; the sensuous skin of her face and neck was hazel and silk. And the darkness of her skin emphasised the bright green of her eyes and the sun-streaked gold of her hair. I looked at her badge. 'Marijke'. Mmm, possibly Dutch, I thought.

Did I have the balls to say it? Well, I had nothing to lose, I supposed, so why not? I approached the reception desk and cleared my throat. '*Hoe gaat het, Marijke? Ik hou van je.*' I once spent a lazy Bank Holiday Monday learning to say 'I love you' in most European languages. To date, it had got me one brief affair and two black eyes. I had a black eye on that occasion, though it was unconnected to European 'I love yous'. I didn't feel I was the best example of myself but Marijke seemed a sympathetic type.

With slow deliberation she looked up at me. How could such beautiful eyes contain so much contempt?

'What?' she spat in my direction.

'*Nederlands?*' I tried again.

'I'm Polish. Not that it's anything to with you,' she continued in near faultless English.

Polish? Polish, Polish, Polish: what was it?

Oh, yes: *'Kocham cie.'*

She huffed a scornful sigh, shook her head and without looking at me said, 'You love too much.'

It was a strange aside. The disdain in her voice stopped me taking it as a compliment, much as I wanted to, and I thought about loving too much. I thought about the previous weekend, which had been bizarre. One reading could have had it as the best weekend ever, but I wasn't so sure. It had been like an exhilarating fairground ride, but one that makes you throw up straight afterwards. The sort of weekend, I had thought, that only happened to other men. Now it had happened to me, though it felt like it belonged to someone else.

* * *

The weekend had started unpromisingly with Shady Sharon. I didn't like the name. A few boyfriends ago, she's acquired this soubriquet and she seemed to like it, though it went against her character. But it suited her physiology: she had dark hair, brooding eyes and a sombre smile. Shadowy, but not shady, I'd have said. Sharon was actually a shy girl (that's 'shady' without the 'ad', I suppose) and all the sweeter for it. I'd met her at the Edinburgh festival and we'd got on quite well, though she had a boyfriend, Nick, so our relationship had not progressed very far.

Down in sin-soaked London, however, on the run-up to the fateful weekend, we'd ended up getting much closer. She'd stayed at my flat for three nights. Tuesday night had been clothes-on-cuddling. Wednesday night had been getting down to underwear and heavy petting. She'd been getting progressively fed up with the boyfriend over the three days and Thursday, finally, we'd made love, which had been very lovely.

For me, with all the baggage I carried containing self-consciousness, nerves and self-loathing, a one-night stand took at least three nights.

I had some 'real men' friends who were better at this sort of thing than me. 'Peter A' was one. Under the terms of his one-night-stand rule, a one-night stand should, in order to be a good one-night stand, take at most three nights on purpose. This allowed for any first-night awkwardness or drunkenness. The second night you try to impress the girl with your stamina, prowess and technique, and the third night is all for you, to be just as greedy or as selfish as you like. Beyond three nights the 'relationship' is in danger – unless you so desire it – of becoming a fully fledged 'going-out-with' situation; i.e. the relation-ship is in danger of becoming a relationship.

I was not even nearing second-night accomplishment when I decided that Shady Sharon and I perhaps were not meant to be. (As cool as I tried to appear, the background presence of her boyfriend was definitely a factor.) I had had a failed 'encounter' with a married woman that had left me a bit tender if not neurotic about the other 'man'. I had concluded that it was time to move on and would tell her this, first thing on Friday morning.

* * *

'I think we need to have a serious chat about you and me. I think things are in danger of drifting and I foresee a certain awkwardness unless we have a proper heart-to-heart.'

Sharon's words stunned me. Her speech was almost word for word what I was about to say to her. She had clearly decided that we had better stop messing around and call it a day. She would go back to being a full-time girlfriend for Nick and we could remain 'buddies'.

'Amazing,' I said. 'I was about to say something similar. But I've also made a decision.'

'So have I,' she said.

'Based on the fabulous three nights we've had, I think something needs to be done,' I went on.

She smiled and hugged me with surprising passion, whispering, 'I think we're on the same wavelength.'

I hugged her in return and felt excited by her incandescence but was still determined to call it a day.

Sharon sat up in bed and announced her intentions: 'I'm splitting up with Nick. I'm fed up with him and now that I've got you, I realise that my relationship with him has been dead for a while. I much prefer you and think it's time to stop dragging it out with Nick. I'm going to phone him today and tell him we're finished, and that I'm going out with you. There.' She smiled sweetly and I felt awful.

'Well, that's not exactly what I was going to say,' I ventured.

'Go on, then. What?' she asked, her eyes aglow with an excitement that made me distinctly uncomfortable.

'I was going to say I think we should finish because of Nick. Just stop seeing each other. Just be friends. Because of Nick.'

Her concern quickly changed to delight.

'Perfect. Even better reason for Nick and I to finish. I'm going to speak to him today and when he gets back. Tomorrow I'm going to get him to move all his stuff out of my flat. We can have the whole weekend together!'

No, we couldn't. I was going to go to Cambridge to a party. It was the party of an ex-girlfriend of mine, Tina, who had just decided to get engaged. She had asked me to come up early so we could have 'one last drink', as she put it, before her fiancé showed up in the evening. Tina was an easy-going, no-nonsense girl and the fact that we'd been together for a while in the past seemed to make the presence of the 'other man' less unnerving.

'I've got to go to Cambridge today. For a party,' I said with some disappointment, as Sharon was grinning suggestively at me.

'Take me,' she said eagerly.

'Love to, but it's all boys. Old college do. Really boring. Stuffy old farts.'

She climbed out from under the bedclothes and moved sinuously over to me. 'Well, we've got till this evening before you have to go.'

'No, I have to be there by lunchtime. There's a sort of lunch thing. At lunch-time. It's a … er, a lunch, I suppose. Food and, er, lunchy-type things.'

She turned down her mouth with exaggerated disappointment. 'Ah well, we've got now. Let's get down to business then!'

We got down to business and afterwards I found it simply too difficult to finish with her there and then. She was a very attractive girl.

Why couldn't I just be honest with her? I should have said that she was lovely but that I didn't want to go out with her. Easy!

Instead, I decided it might be easier to call her from Cambridge later on that day, and break it to her gently on the phone, face to face, or voice to voice (or preferably voice to answerphone).

'I need to rush. I'll call you when I get to Cambridge later. Perhaps we can have a proper talk. You know, about the, er, our, er, future.'

'When are you back?'

'Tomorrow, I should think.'

'Where are you staying tonight, then?' Her question was a good one. I hadn't thought beyond a possible afternoon liaison with Tina, prior to her party. There'd be no chance of staying there with her new fiancé about.

'In college, I expect. Some crappy undergraduate room,' I lied nonchalantly.

'I don't want you chatting anyone up. You've got a girlfriend now!' she said with an unnerving squeak of joy.

'Yes, of course,' I said, thinking that sounded really strange.

And really distressing.

* * *

'Yes, I'm at the station now,' I shouted over a change-of-platform announcement.

'Come round any time after four,' Tina said. 'The sooner the better.'

'OK. I'll ring just before I set off to yours.'

Any time after four. Mmm, that gave me an unexpected two and a half hours. I could wander round sightseeing, go for a stroll down by the river, look up some old friends or go to my favourite pub, the Baron of Beef. The Baron it was.

I pushed open the pub door tentatively. As I'd approached the side door from the alley near the car park, I'd had an unpleasant body memory. Some time last year I had got drunk with a girl who worked in this pub and ended up in bed with her. I remembered nothing about the evening but I remembered the morning after. She'd brought me a cup of tea in bed and for some reason had ended up pouring it over my genitalia. I couldn't remember her name but I would recognise her again. I poked my head round the door and checked out the bar staff. The unknown girl was not there. With a lighter heart I went into the bar and looked forward to a couple of hours of cordial drinking.

'Well, hello! My prayers have been answered!' howled a voice in my ear.

'Maggie, what a—' I couldn't finish the sentence because Maggie's tongue had inserted itself into my mouth.

'It's a pint of lager, thank you,' she whooped, 'and why don't you get yourself one?'

The overpowering, hyperactive monster that was 'Montrose' Maggie McDowell was squeezed into a petite, flame-haired frame that buzzed with excitement and desire. This little Scottish girl had 'been out' with a prodigious number of men and I had been, and was continuing to be, prudent enough not to join the list. Especially not today, with Tina awaiting me for what could be our last 'cuddle' ever.

'You here for Tina's party then?'

'No, er … I've been visiting an old college friend,' I mumbled. Maggie was not one to share too much information with.

'Shame. You could've taken me.'

'You not invited, then?'

She cackled a particularly Scottish cackle. 'Ach, no. She hates me, that Tina,' she said, then added in a hushed voice, 'Me and James had a bit of a thing once,' as if it were something that the entire population of the city didn't already know.

'You're kidding!'

A mischievous smile appeared on her face.

'So you weren't thinking of paying Tina a quick visit this afternoon, then?' She winked.

'No, I think that would be a bit dangerous. I presume James is around.'

'No, I heard he's away till this evening.'

'No, definitely not. I have to go back to London. Quite soon.'

A shriek from Maggie. 'Aha, so I've got you till you go then! Come back to mine. For lunch. I'll drop you back to the station.'

'You don't drive.'

'We'll get a taxi to the station from mine. I'll come and kiss you goodbye at the barrier, it'll be dead romantic!'

'No, I'd better get a cab from here …' I sensed a Scottish net closing in. An awkward situation was developing where I'd have to go through the motions of calling a cab from the pub to the station, going in it to the station, paying it off and then walking back into town to go to Tina's.

After a few drinks and some jokey sex-talk, Maggie thankfully seemed less driven and I decided it was time to make my exit. As I was searching my pocket for loose change to phone for a taxi, the pub door swung open and a man said, 'Taxi for McDowell.'

Maggie grabbed me saying, 'Come on, that's your cab for the station, I ordered it while you were in the loo.' I was taken aback but pleased that I would be extricated from her clutches so effortlessly, even at the expense of a pointless cab journey. The journey passed in a flurry of urgent snogging.

After ten minutes the car stopped and the driver announced, 'Here we are: 31 Robertson Street.' Maggie's place. 'Three pound fifty, please.'

Before I could object, Maggie put her hand over my mouth. 'Half an hour. Come on. I just want you to see my flat.'

The tour of her flat started and finished with her bedroom. I did the best I could. The phrase, 'A bad workman blames his tools' popped briefly into my mind but the lively Scottish girl lying next to me seemed remarkably pleased.

'Someone's been scratching your back, mister!' she said admiring her own handiwork.

'It was one of the witches from *Macbeth*.'

She smiled a self-satisfied smile. 'Cab's here.'

At last, I was going to be free.

But not straight away.

Maggie got into the cab with me and came to the station.

She saw me on to the train.

The train to London. Where I wasn't going.

'That was a fantastic "lunch". Thank you so much,' I said kissing her through the train window.

'Och, my pleasure.'

'Look, you go off home now,' I said, 'and don't bother waiting for the train to leave. We'll say goodbye and I'll go find a seat.'

'No,' she insisted, 'it's away in two minutes. I'll wave you off.'

And, sure enough, in two minutes, the train pulled away and she waved me off.

* * *

'What the bloody hell do you think you're doing?' the railway official screamed. He was seriously angry. 'You fucking idiot! You're coming with me. Straight to the transport police!'

I got up from the bank of gravel and dusted myself down.

'It wasn't going very fast,' I said defiantly. 'It was hardly moving.'

'Jumping off a moving train onto the track is really dangerous! And not just to you, you damn fool.' This man would not be smooth-talked out of it. I was in serious trouble.

'I thought it was the Norwich train. When someone told me it was going to Liverpool Street I panicked and opened the door and jumped out. I thought it was still stationary; it was barely moving,' I tried again.

He shook his head. 'OK, the train *was* hardly moving. In fact, the bit of the train you were in was still at the platform. And yet you jumped out the other side. How bloody mad is that?'

'I didn't realise the platform was on the other side.'

We were walking across the sidings to the railway company's site office. He was holding onto my arm; not particularly firmly but enough to make me feel like a criminal.

'I'm going to have to report it. I'll make a call from here to the stationmaster's office.'

The station looked different from the other side; it's funny what you notice when you're in trouble. I felt like a VIP. The site office was a Portakabin by an open gate in a barbed-wire fence. A road ran alongside it.

'What road it that?' I asked.

'That's Stratford Street.'

'You're kidding,' I said. 'What, off Mill Road? I didn't know you could get into the station that way.'

'Well, YOU can't,' he said severely. 'That's staff entrance only. In fact,' he said looking round for a member of staff to shout at, 'that gate should be shut and locked.' But it wasn't. It was unlocked and

open. And it was the gate I ran hell-for-leather through before sprint-
ing up Stratford Street and disappearing round the corner.

'Oi, come here, you …' were the last four fading words I heard
from the railwayman. I could just about guess what the fifth one was.

* * *

'You're in a bit of a state,' Tina said after one of her luscious
'Hello' kisses.

'Are you really going to get engaged?' I said, trying to change the
subject.

'You're very sweaty,' she said, slipping her hands under my shirt.

'What do you expect after a kiss like that?' I murmured to her.

'Your clothes are covered in dust,' she continued with some
concern.

'Don't worry; I hope to be taking them off pretty soon,' I said,
trying to propel myself into the mood for love and romance. I held
her close.

'Your shirt's torn at the elbow. What have you been doing?' she
said, breaking away from me. 'And I'm sure you smell of booze. And
is that perfume?'

I decided to be brave and tell her the truth.

'Oh, yes, I fell off the train.'

'What?'

'When I arrived in Cambridge, I wasn't paying attention and I
got out on the wrong side. Fell onto the track.' I pulled her back
towards me.

'Do you expect me to believe that?'

'That's the total, God's honest truth. You can believe it or not.'

'You look like you've gone ten rounds with Montrose Maggie!'
she said unbuttoning my shirt.

'Ha! Um … no fear.'

'Your back's all scratched.'

'Gravel.'

'Gravel?'

'Track ballast. Crushed stones. Or whatever the aggregate is that they use on rail tracks. Come here you, we haven't got long.'

After the genuinely loving spell of our hour in bed, Tina suddenly became businesslike.

'You'd better get ready and go,' she said, getting up and wrapping a towel round herself.

'Oh, yes,' I said. 'I've got to be back here in two hours for your party.'

'Exactly. I want you looking nice and clean and presentable to meet the man who might be my fiancé soon. If he gets a move on and buys me a ring.'

I started getting dressed and flinched as I put my shirt on over the scratches on my back.

'I can't believe you would even suggest I'd sleep with Montrose Maggie.' I looked at myself in the mirror for other telltale signs.

'Well, careful if you do. She gave James a rather unpleasant infection.'

I exchanged a startled glance with my reflection that looked, if anything, even more scared than I did. 'When was that?'

'Oh, ages ago. I'm sure she's cleared up by now. Where are you staying tonight, by the way?' she asked.

'I haven't thought about it. I presume it'll be too late to go back to London after the party,' I said, making a mental note to myself that I might want to avoid the railway station for a while.

'Corinna's driving back tonight.'

'Who's Corinna?'

'You know. My friend from when I worked at Everett's. Blonde with glasses. Plump.'

'Oh, the fat, speccy one. She's quite sweet.'

'She's driving back whatever time. She doesn't drink, so she's always good for a lift. She lives in Swiss Cottage. That's near you, isn't it?'

'Quite near,' I said. And very near to Shady Sharon, whom I was supposed to phone today to discuss our future, I suddenly remembered.

'I think I spent an evening chatting up Corinna once. I think she quite fancied me,' I said for something to say, certainly with no thought that it may be true.

'Er, I think not,' said Tina wryly. 'I wouldn't be recommending her to you for a lift home if I thought that.'

'Spoilsport.'

'I probably shouldn't tell you this but she thinks you're a complete tosser. She thinks I was mad ever to go out with you. She thinks I'm certifiable to be seeing you today, before the party. Maybe I am!'

'You're just saying that to stop me chatting her up on the way home!' I suggested jokily.

Tina laughed. 'Do try. Be my guest. Corinna'll probably throw up at your first cheesy chat-up line.'

'They worked on you,' I protested.

'I fancied you, didn't I? Corinna thinks you're a twat. For a while, she was convinced you were homosexual.'

'Really? I'm rather flattered. Well, a lift home's a lift home, I suppose,' I conceded. Corinna thought I was gay. Cheeky cow. Cheeky blubber-arsed cow. Cheeky blubber-arsed, four-eyed cow. Never remotely fancied her.

I decided to phone Sharon.

* * *

'How was the lunch thingy?' Sharon's voice sounded genuinely interested down the crackly phone line.

'Dull,' I answered unenthusiastically, 'and tiring. So boring I nearly got on a train and came home.'

'Shame you didn't,' she answered with real disappointment.

I was feeling guilty enough already.

'I've been thinking, Sharon, about what you said this morning.' I paused to take a deep breath of courage.

I was too late; she interrupted. 'Oh, talking of which, I've told Nick. He was amazingly cool about it. He says he'll move his stuff out as soon as possible but it might not be this weekend.'

'I can't be your new boyfriend. I can't,' I blurted.

Silence from the other end of the phone.

'Not yet anyway.'

More silence. She was evidently surprised by my sudden announcement. So was I. I couldn't believe I'd done it.

'Oh,' she eventually stammered. 'Maybe I was taking too much for granted. I thought you felt the same way.' She was hurting and her hurting was hurting me.

But I was still not up to being totally shitty. I wasn't brave enough.

'No, I do feel the same way. It's just that I wasn't ready. I'm not ready. Let's give it a few days. A week or so. Who knows?'

'When are you coming back to London?' she asked in a small voice (which surely must have been put on for my benefit).

'Next week some time. I'll probably stay up here for a few days now. Think about things. Take stock. Weigh up the pros and cons. Try to assess just where I am. Who I am. What's happening and so on,' I burbled, hoping I didn't sound like someone talking bollocks.

'You're talking bollocks, Rory,' she said flatly, adding straight after, 'Is there someone else up there in Cambridge?'

'Absolutely not.' I was adamant.

'But me and Nick have split up,' she said pathetically.

'Well, that's good, isn't it? You said yourself there was nothing left in the relationship. It's irrelevant whether you and I are going out; the point is you're out of a bad thing.'

She didn't sound convinced. 'Can we meet up when you get back? Just for a coffee and a chat?'

'Of course. I'll call you as soon as I get back.'

The line went dead. Damn, that was harder than I thought. I felt decidedly low as I made my way back to Tina's for the party. I was far from being in the mood for small talk and chitchat with fiancés and fat girls who thought I was gay. It was going to be a long night, and suddenly the thought of snuggling up in bed with Shady Sharon seemed very appealing.

* * *

'So, what's Tina said about me, then? Come on, dish the dirt!' Corinna asked as she revved her little sports car and sped off into the early hours of the morning. She was much more attractive than I remembered. Not fat at all. Maybe the cuddly side of voluptuous, but a fine womanly figure. Her glasses made her look quirkily provocative and she had a full mouth that I'd somehow overlooked on our previous meetings. I was beginning to be quite irked by that fact that she didn't fancy me and thought I was a tosser and a poof.

'She hasn't said anything about you. Honest,' I said, nearly honestly. I noticed the speedometer was showing nearly a hundred. 'She said you drive too fast!'

'This is slow for me. Anyway there're no cars around.'

Just as well, I thought, as she seemed to be not too choosy which side of the road she drove on.

'Come on, come on! She must have said something worse than that. She must have slagged me off. She's dead jealous of me. 'Cause all her boyfriends fancy me more than her.'

This turn of conversation took me by surprise. 'What about James, the possible fiancé-to-be?'

'Oh, he's a tosser. A complete wanker. I reckon he's gay. I don't know why she didn't stick with you.' She winked at me and blew a kiss, which must have been the rudest kiss possible for one travelling by air. I was now completely off-guard and apprehensive about more than just Corinna's driving.

'Got any booze at your place?'

'Yes,' I answered, 'at least three bottles of wine, but—'

'Cool. Two for me and one for you!'

'But I thought you didn't drink?'

'I don't,' she said, 'not when I'm driving. I do when I'm fucking, though.'

I laughed, hoping that might encourage her to say, 'Only joking!' She didn't. She just fixed her eyes intently on mine.

My voice sounded strangely high-pitched and timid as I said, 'Hey, look, there's a road in front of the car.'

* * *

Corinna was a woman, of that there was no doubt. Part bouncy-castle, part strawberry and banana smoothie, maybe, but mainly woman. She was fun to be in bed with and patient and tolerant while I worked through my early fumblings up to adequate sex. We fell asleep cuddling each other.

Irritable knocking at my front door abruptly kidnapped me from a warm, pink, woman-scented planet. I put a towel round me and stepped over a wine bottle on the way to the hall, thinking that despite my recent experiences I was still no nearer to beginning to understand the female sex. I opened to door to the oppressive twin glares of sunrise and Shady Sharon.

'Oh, hello, I thought you were staying in Cambridge for a few days,' she said, in a tone that was somewhere between amusement and rage. A bit closer to rage, maybe.

'Then what are you doing here knocking on my front door?' was the logical reply to this statement, but my mind was preoccupied with other things, like the huge presence of Corinna in my bed. Maybe she would realise something tricky was afoot and get dressed and climb out of the back window and drive home. I realised she hadn't when she appeared behind me wearing only her glasses.

'Ooh, hello! Threesome time,' Corinna said with a raucous giggle as she disappeared down the hall towards the bathroom.

'I see you've got company,' Sharon went on, her tone of voice moving well into the rage-end of the amusement–rage continuum.

'Yeah, Corinna's an old mate. She gave me a lift home last night so I said she could crash here in my floor, er, on my bed ... er, on my floor. Me, that is. On the floor. Her in the bed.' It was not a convincing performance.

'I was going to pop a note through your door. To say that Nick should have moved all his stuff out of my flat by tomorrow and I'll be on my own. But I don't know why I'm wasting my time.'

'Look, Sharon, I did say, let's give it a few day–'

'Well, I'm so sorry. Obviously I'm just not loud, short-sighted, blonde or fat enough!' said the petite brunette as she turned to go, stopping only to kick over my dustbin, strewing the contents over the path. She looked back at me and pointed to the mess. 'Garbage, look! Garbage, that's what you are!'

Corinna joined me in the doorway and Sharon departed with an, 'And your fat tart!'

Before I had time to think the situation couldn't get any worse, the situation got worse. The sound of a large motorbike speeding past took my attention away from the detritus that was apparently now my personal life. The horn tooted and the driver waved at us ostentatiously. It was Michelle Seymour. Just my luck that she should be driving past at that moment. I wondered what she thought of the situation.

* * *

'I just thought, well, at least he's seems to have got over me!' Michelle looked tickled by the whole scene. She had phoned not long after Corinna had gone and we had met for a drink. It was the first time I'd had seen her properly since I'd gone round to kill her boyfriend a few years ago.

'You've got more women than you can cope with, obviously. Perhaps you've turned into a shit like most men do, eventually. What happened to the good, shy Catholic boy from Cornwall? Master of loyalty and honour?'

What indeed? I had nothing to say but her words troubled me. Michelle offered an answer to her own question.

'Perhaps you're still so hurt by JJ that you're punishing the rest of womankind.'

I didn't like the mention of JJ in this context. Michelle's comment cut into me and I snapped at her, 'I believe you shat on me long after JJ left my life.'

'So you're taking me *and* JJ out on all these other women?' She laughed and sipped her wine. She was annoying me now, even more so as she still looked confidently attractive. And I didn't want her to know I still thought that.

'So, I'm not going to get a look-in any more?' she pouted mockingly.

'You've got a nerve, really, after what happened,' I returned. 'I presume you're still with Opera Paul? Husband-to-be?'

'Oh no, me and Paul split up ages ago,' she said dismissively, flicking the long brown hair out of her eyes. 'How amazing to see you this morning!'

'Well, that is where I live.'

'I know but I was intrigued by that hilarious little scene.'

'Yes, that was a witchy coincidence, wasn't it? Very suspicious. You driving by at that precise moment.'

'I was going to see my brother. You know he lives round the corner from you.' She moved closer to me and spoke quietly: 'I don't suppose you've got any energy left for an old friend, have you?'

I could feel her warm breath on my face. She knew she was still very sexy. I knew she was. Did she know I knew? She kissed me. Yes, she knew.

* * *

Why didn't this feel like the best weekend of my life? As I thought about the last day and a half, a certain shame started leaking into my soul. I was beginning to fill up with emptiness. I had lied to and mistreated everybody I'd come into contact with. Sharon, Maggie, Tina, Corinna and Michelle (well, maybe not Maggie; it had been her idea). Poor Shaz. Poor little Shady Sharon. I'd treated her the worst. I'd led her on to think I wanted more than I did. I hadn't controlled the events of the weekend but I hadn't exactly been a helpless victim who'd bumbled into sleeping with every girl he met. There had been physical pleasure certainly (not as much as you'd expect), but that hadn't really made me feel better. Or even good. It felt as if it had been happening to someone else. Maybe that had been the problem. It wasn't me. It didn't happen to me. It happened to a role I was playing. The role of a 'real bloke'. Yes, that was the part I was playing, and not that convincingly.

I thought again of Shady Sharon. She'd kicked the boyfriend out and was now all alone. She was probably in her lovely Swiss Cottage flat crying her eyes out. I needed to say sorry. I'd call her. No, she'd slam the phone down on me. Maybe I'd just turn up. Yes, that's what I'd do. I'd go to her flat about eleven o'clock. That'd be too late to kick me out, surely. I'd take some flowers. No, that's too guilty. And corny. I'd take some booze. Champagne, that's it. I'd ring the doorbell, give her the pre-chilled bubbly as soon as she opened the door, put my hand against my heart and say, 'I'm sorry. Sharon, I'm sorry.'

That was perfect. All I needed to do was buy the fizz and have a shower.

Yes, a shower was a very good idea.

* * *

I was nervous as I approached Sharon's front door. It was about ten twenty-five in the evening and I could see lights on deep in the house. I rang the bell. It was hellishly loud. Perhaps I should have phoned first. No, she would have refused to speak to me. This was the right thing to do. I could hear doors opening and closing then nothing. Just the sound of time passing and of nerves tingling. Ah. Wait! Footsteps approached the door from the inside. The unmistakable slap-slappy steps of girl's slippers on marble tiles. I breathed deeply and coughed. My heart was pounding, but I felt very confident and before the door was fully open, I had started my speech: 'I'm sorry. Suzie, I'm sorry—'

'You cunt!' said Nick, standing in front of me, wet from the shower, a towel wrapped round his waist and flip-flops on his feet.

'Is … er, Suzie in?'

'She's gone to her parents for the weekend while I move my stuff out.' Ah, I obviously hadn't paid enough attention to their logistics.

'I'll have that, though,' he went on, grabbing the champagne and putting it on the shelf in the hall.

I'm caught now, I thought. But as I'd made the effort to come all that way, I decided to ask one final question.

'I suppose a fuck's out of the question?'

* * *

'The black eye, bloody nose and swollen lip were not sexually transmitted,' the doctor announced, ebullient with sarcasm. He held up a sheet of paper on a clipboard, lifted his glasses up onto his forehead and perused the results.

'Now, let's have a look,' he said to himself and my stomach tightened with apprehension and with the memory of a frightened boy and his father in a doctor's surgery a long time ago.

'More good news,' he suddenly chuckled. 'You haven't got AIDS. Or syphilis. Well done. But I'm afraid there're lots of things you have got. Quite a few ticks in quite a few boxes, I'm afraid. But that said, you haven't actually got ticks! Ha ha ha!' This was clearly the funniest joke he'd ever heard.

'Lice, yes, but no ticks. Ha!'

His tittering abated and he assumed a pompous, moralistic tone. 'I don't have to tell you about the hazards of promiscuous behaviour. It would be courteous to inform the girl you had liaisons with just in case she is unaware of her condition; you should, of course, refrain from further sexual relations with her until you are both clear and it goes without saying that you should not sleep with any other partner. Do I make myself clear?'

'Yes, doctor.'

Oh, dear. This was a bad one. What penance would Father McEvedy give me for this? More than three 'Hail Marys', I should think.

'If you'd like to pop out into reception and wait five minutes or so, my lovely assistant, Marijke, will give you the typed-up medical report and prescriptions for the not-inconsiderable-medicaments you require. Good day, sir. I hope never to see you again.'

Pompous git, I thought. I never want to see you again, either. He looked up and added keenly, 'Unless, of course, you want to see me privately. I do several sessions a week. Here's a card with my rates.'

Bastard. I left his room feeling like the most disgusting worm on the planet. One pathetic wanker.

'But I'm not a promiscuous person. I'm not a Casanova. I'm not a "lad". I'm a nice boy. And I'm a nice boy who's talking to himself,'

I muttered till the sight of the cool Marijke brought me back to reality. She was folding a printout of the doctor's report, which she placed in an envelope and handed to me without a word or a look in my direction.

'Thank you,' I paused. 'Hey, Marijke. Fancy going out for a drink some time?' I said optimistically.

'My God.' She shook her head. 'No way. I can't believe you're asking me!'

'I'm actually quite a nice person,' I persisted desperately.

'No. I can't. Against rules here. Not professional.' She explained, her near-fluency suddenly deserting her.

'Oh, I see. Fair enough,' and I made to go. Just catching her last words: 'Pathetic wanker.'

Chapter 39

Good Catholic Boy Gets Confirmation

'Lust,' I suddenly remembered. 'Yes, of course; lust!' I didn't know exactly what lust was at the time but I knew it was a bad thing that bad people did. Or had. Like a lot of the seven deadly sins it was a bit vague. But, at least now, I'd remembered all seven.

I was sitting in class revising my catechism prior to the 'big day'.

'And, then …' said Sister Stephen, 'are you listening, Rory?'

'Yes, Sister.'

'And then,' she went on, pausing to add to the excitement, 'you get to kiss the bishop's ring.'

A loud splutter of laughter from the back of the class made us all turn round to see Spike, the school bully and all-round naughty boy, wiping snot from the front of his shirt where it had landed after he'd try to repress the laughter and redirected it though his nose.

We all laughed too, though none of us were sure what was in any way funny about kissing the bishop's ring.

'Now, then, Michael Spizer, what was so funny about what I just said?'

'Nothing, Sister,' he said, red-faced but still juddering with stifled mirth.

The nun went on, 'Now, the bishop has a very big ring.'

A muted squeal from the back of the class.

'Michael!'

'Sorry, Sister.'

But the giggles were beginning to spread and we were all infected, though still ignorant of the reason for our frivolity. We were, by and large, still at a pre-double-entendre age but when Ann-Marie Wilson asked *her* question, Spike, and therefore all of us, was sent tumbling over the edge.

'Please, Sister,' the prim girl asked, 'does the bishop's ring have a jewel in it?'

Chaos.

'I don't know what's got into you children today. Michael Spizer, you can stand outside until you've cooled down. The rest of you can do catechism revision. Those of you getting confirmed could be asked a question by the bishop, which could be any question from the whole book!'

That was a big worry. I was one of the ones getting confirmed. The catechism had hundreds of questions in it. The rest of the class, parents, nuns, priests and the bishop himself would be there. I'd better get learning.

Confirmation is the first grown-up sacrament a Catholic can take. You have to be at least eleven or twelve. I know that doesn't sound too young but it is when compared to the three previous ones of baptism, penance and holy communion. At baptism you are a child of less than a year so you have no memory of it. The extravagant promises you make to God are done for you by your nominated adults, i.e. those nominated by other adults. Penance and holy communion are memorable only because the first makes you feel nervous and ashamed for the rest of your life, and the second means you have a big, slap-up breakfast and get to wear white trousers.

The big thing about confirmation is that you get an extra name. I chose 'Peter' because it's a saint's name and it's sufficiently non-nationalistic to balance out the Irishness of Patrick and Rory.

The idea is that now you're old enough to speak for and think for yourself (or at least think that you think for yourself), you can now confirm the promises you made (or someone else made on your behalf) at baptism. I suppose this is to stop you having a convenient get-out clause when you break one of your promises to God: 'Here, I never promised that! Someone else did! I couldn't speak then; it's not fair.'

The ceremony involves the laying on of hands, anointment with oil and kissing the bishop's ring.

Bishops' rings usually contain the gemstone amethyst, which is a beautiful, pale purple form of quartz. I have no idea why bishops should use this stone for their ring, but it is sometimes called 'monk-stone', and the story goes that medieval monks used to dip it into their wine because it was alleged to remove the wine's alcoholic properties. The word comes from the Greek *a-methystos*, which means 'non-alcoholic', and is etymologically connected to 'methylated', as in 'spirits' (bet you weren't expecting to learn *that* in a book largely about Catholicism).

The mythological origin concerns the Greek god of wine (Dionysus, or Bacchus, as the Romans called him). Dionysus had got involved in some row with a human (over a borrowed lawnmower or something) and swore that he would take his revenge by killing the next mortal he came across. (It's a bit of a non-specific revenge but obviously this didn't bother the divine wino.) To carry out this bloody revenge on the, presumably innocent, passer-by, the god created a bunch of ravenous tigers. Of course, the next passer-by happened to be a – wait for it – beautiful young maiden called Amethyst. ('Non-alcoholic' seems an odd name to give your daughter but that's a discussion for another time.) The scrummy maiden was on her way to pay tribute to Artemis (or Diana, if you're Roman), the goddess of hunting and chastity (interesting combination!). When Dionysus's tigers approached, Amethyst screamed for help. Artemis answered her call and saved her from the tigers by turning her into a block of quartz. (Obviously! How else do you save people from marauding tigers?) Dionysus was overwhelmed by the beauty of the crystalline statue of Amethyst and out of remorse for his actions, he wept. And being who he was, his tears were red wine and when his tears rained down on the statue it turned purply-red, the colour of Amethyst, in fact. (I love a happy ending.) In years gone by, wine goblets were actually carved out of amethyst so the drinker could drink wine all night and not get pissed. (What a waste! Why not just drink diet Coke?)

But I digress.

So, after the rites of confirmation, you emerge from the church to the congratulations of elders and betters and the proud owner of a new name, a soul full of the Holy Spirit and an assured place in the Army of Christ. But it's not that easy. You first have to endure the catechism test, with the bishop himself asking the questions.

Catechism is the bedrock of Catholicism. Every Catholic, as soon as they can read and write, is given a catechism book that contains about 370 questions and answers. You have to learn them off by heart so that at any time in your life if, say, a stranger were to jump out at you on the Moscow underground and ask, 'Why did God make you?', you would be able to say without hesitation, 'God made me to know him, love him and serve him in this life and to be happy with him forever in the next.'

Of course, it doesn't work like that in practice. For a start I'm unlikely ever to be in Moscow and, like most Catholics, I have wiped this stuff off my hard drive to make room for more practical stuff like birthdays, anniversaries, girls' phone numbers and Arsenal results. If a gun was put to my head and I was forced to recite my creed I could probably stutter out the basics: 'I believe in God, the Father Almighty, Creator of Heaven and Earth. I believe in Jesus Christ (bow head), his only son, Our Lord. He was conceived by the power of the Holy Spirit (eh?), and born of the Virgin Mary (eh?). He suffered under Pontius Pilate (boo!), was crucified, died and was buried. He descended into hell (that's no place for God, is it?). On the third day (third day of what?), he rose again (hoorah!). He ascended into heaven, and is seated at the right hand of the Father (left-handedist, or what?). He will come again to judge the living and the dead. I believe in the Holy Spirit, the Holy Catholic Church, the communion of saints (Southampton FC?), the forgiveness of sins, the resurrection of the body and life everlasting.' Phew.

But that's enough; no more questions, please!

* * *

'Now here's a question!' the bishop's voice made me jump. My nerves were beginning to jangle as his eye roved over us. 'It's time to find out, my dear children, if you're ready for the wonderful thing, this wonderful sacrament of confirmation that you're about to go through.'

I was petrified he would ask me one of the questions but equally petrified that he wouldn't. I knew all the answers and what if I never got to answer any? The bishop would never know how clever I was. And what if he asked someone who doesn't know anything, someone who hasn't even bothered revising the catechism? Like Dud Trevena or Billy Brookes?

I don't believe it. He's pointing to Billy Brookes. Oh, and what an easy question!

'What is the Third Commandment?'

'Er,' Billy begins to mumble. 'Thou shalt not kill?'

And he's got the answer wrong! Incredible, Billy Brookes got it wrong! He wasn't even close. 'Thou shalt not take the name of the Lord thy God in vain.' Everyone knows that!

But the bishop didn't say anything. He just smiled and carried on. This is just not on. I've swotted for weeks to learn all 370

answers and Billy Brookes probably spent ten minutes over breakfast this morning.

Now, he's asking Dud Trevena one. Another easy one.

'Who made you?'

That's the first question in the book. Everybody knows that. Even
Protestants would know that. Even Charlie Owens who once said the
f-word knows that. I bet even Kitchie George, the legendary tramp,
would know that.

Dud Trevena may have answered correctly and said, 'God made
me,' but his voice was so quiet and his Cornish accent so thick that it
was impossible to tell.

Make him repeat it louder, bishop, I urged mentally!

But again the bishop said nothing.

Make him say it again, bishop!

The bishop just smiled and nodded.

I reckon he's not even listening. The bishop's not listening! Or
maybe he's deaf? Or maybe he doesn't actually remember the right
answer himself?

I was beginning to lose interest in the whole palaver when he
suddenly pointed to me. My throat tightened.

I took a deep breath and swallowed hard. 'Now then,' he said epis-
copally, 'what's your name?'

My mind went blank. What *was* my name? Where did that come
in the catechism? Hang on; I don't think that's even *in* the catechism!
That's not fair!

'You,' he said, still pointing at me.

'Rory,' I plucked from somewhere in my jittering brain.

'And what name have you chosen for your confirmation name?'

Ah, I knew this. 'Peter.'

'Ah, yes,' he nodded, 'an excellent choice. Do you know what
"Peter" means?'

I knew this one would come up. I had looked it up in the dictionary the night before.

'Yes, your excellency, Peter comes from the Greek word—'

'That's right,' he interrupted, '"rock". And it's from the Greek, you know. *Petros.* "Thou art Peter and upon this rock I shall build my church and the gates of hell shall not prevail against me!" Well done, Peter,' he said smiling annoyingly at me. 'And what name have you chosen for your confirmation name?'

'Peter,' I said. Again.

'Another Peter, eh? Good choice.'

Chapter 40

Grown-up Boy Does His Laundry in Public

'Why is he living on his own in that cramped, grotty bed-sit? Hasn't he got a fabulous house in Tufnell Park and a lovely wife and two gorgeous children?' I imagined each passer-by thinking.

'Fancy cocking up such a good life!' I could see it in their eyes.

'Horrible man, abandoning his family like that!' they muttered as I struggled up Haverstock Hill with two bags of dirty washing.

'Off to do his own laundry in a shitty self-service laundrette. I thought these telly people had servants for that,' sneered a dustman underneath his loud, chirpy, 'Alright, Rory?'

At the entrance to Chalk Farm tube I noticed a busybody. Out of the corner of my eye, I could tell he was coming up behind me; his face almost split in two with an inane grin.

'Wakey, wakey, Rory,' he said, beginning a failed effort to be chummy and amusing. I turned on him with a vicious, 'Fuck off and mind your own business.' He reeled back on his heels, white with shock. He was a middle-aged man, neatly dressed with a kind, open face. He was holding something in his hand that he was offering to me. A shirt. An Arsenal replica shirt. Was he giving me a present? A total stranger was approaching me in the street to give me a present?

No. The shirt belonged to my son, Joe. We'd played football on the heath after school and he'd left it at the bed-sit for me to wash. It was the least I could do.

Or was it the most I could do? What *could* I do for my son? What *should* I do? I can't have been the worst father in the world, could I? Not the best, I know that. Do most fathers constantly assess how good or bad they are? Or do they just get on with it? Would I be assessing my paternal performance now if I weren't separated from my children? Was my father better or worse? I'd never thought about it. He was always there, unlike me. He was always present. How important was that? How nurturing? How important was my absence? How damaging? When would I find out? How would I find out?

The man's hands were shaking as he gave me the shirt and his words came stutteringly slowly. 'Sorry, but you dropped your shirt. It fell out of one of your bags. I didn't mean to intrude. You seemed miles away. You didn't seem to notice.'

I felt wretched. 'I'm so sorry. That's really kind. I *was* miles away, sorry.'

The man walked quickly away and I heard the news vendor say to him sympathetically, 'What an ignorant git. Not so funny in real life, is he?'

Hating myself, I continued on up the hill to the laundrette. The pain of the banal is what you never expect. I'd known several marriages split up, some of those of quite close friends, and you can only think of the big things: whose fault? Who will it affect more? Will the children be OK? How will the money be sorted out? What if one of them gets another partner or remarries? You don't think about the humiliation of walking to the laundrette with your dirty washing. Maybe there was no humiliation. Was it just me? Was it more vanity than shame that I was wandering through Hampstead thinking everyone was looking at me, smirking, nudging each other knowingly, muttering insults about the sad bastard living in a bed-sit having to go to the laundrette and then going over to have his breakfast among the tramps and builders in Brenda's café?

I hadn't been to the laundrette for over two weeks so both my bags were full and very heavy. There were no other customers there, which was good. No beady eyes, no furtive looks over the tops of newspapers, no judgemental glances. There was no sign of the owner, Phil the Bubble, either, but Mrs Kelly was there, loading a hefty pile of damp clothes into a tumble-drier.

On my first visit, Phil the Bubble had recognised me from a television programme and was delighted to see me in his shop. He never once asked why I was doing my washing in a public laundry, he didn't ask why I'd suddenly appeared in the area, he never asked about what I was up to at work and the only time love, marriage, wives, children, separation and money cropped up was in the dozens of Jewish jokes he'd trot out whenever I was in there. He never even mentioned the numerous items of Arsenal wear that occasionally showed up in my laundry. Phil was a Tottenham fan, unlike most of the North London Greeks I knew. The first time I went in there, he gave me a free service wash and had all my shirts ironed and put on hangers. Looking at them in the cramped wardrobe in my flat afterwards had given me a small glimmer of self-respect. If Phil the Bubble was in the shop when I called in, he'd dump my laundry on Mrs Kelly and take me up the road to a better-than-average coffee shop. I'd always buy the coffee and the cakes he loved, and he would tell me how much he was going to knock off my laundry bill. It was a peculiar friendship, unexpected, occasional and thoroughly welcome.

As the shop was empty, I greeted her more cheerily and loud than normal: 'Morning, Mrs Kelly.'

'Oh, hello there,' she said flatly. She looked less sprightly than usual and she read the concern on my face. 'Have you heard about Phil?'

I hadn't.

'He was killed. In Cyprus.'

This was nonsense, what was she saying?

'His boy made it.'

His son? Did he have a son? I felt the sickness welling up inside me. 'I don't understand,' was all I could manage.

'They were in a car crash. His son was trapped, see. Phil went in to get him. The boy got out. A miracle. Phil didn't.'

This was too much. I turned round and walked straight out. The café. No, I couldn't go there; it'd be full of 'Have you heard about, Phil?' I needed to get away.

St Thomas More church, like so many urban Catholic churches, is a modern building. A peculiar, rounded, red-brick building amid the leafy gentility of Swiss Cottage. I sat in the gloom, biting my nails and thinking of fathers and sons and sons and fathers. Alone in my retreat but for two bags of dirty laundry.

Chapter 41

Good Catholic Boy Retreats

I looked it up straight away: 'Retreat – the act of withdrawing or retiring in the face of opposition, difficulty or danger.' That didn't sound very promising. Quite unpleasant, really.

'Ooh, it'll be an amazing weekend. Do you the world of good,' I was assured by my mother.

'What's so good about a retreat?' my eleven-year-old self asked genuinely.

'A hundred boys from Catholic schools all round Devon and Cornwall,' she explained, 'having a weekend away in a beautiful setting and spending all the time in church or at prayer or having religious instruction!'

What's so good about a retreat? I reiterated inwardly.

'Retreat,' I read on. 'A temporary retirement from one's usual occupation for the purposes of religious exercises, contemplation and reflection.'

'Will I be retiring from my usual occupation?' I asked, not sure what that was.

'Well, it's a weekend so you won't be missing school. Well, except you have to go up on Friday so you will miss one day of school,' my mother explained.

Perfect. A day off school was a day off school, though perhaps not adequate recompense for two stuffy days of religious exercises, contemplation and reflection.

'What are religious exercises?' I asked my brother, Stephen.

'Press-ups in Latin,' he answered unhelpfully.

'It's to see if you want to become a priest,' my mother said keenly, as if selling the virtues of life imprisonment over execution.

'Why do I have to go away to find out if I want to be a priest? I know if I want to be a priest already. No,' I said glumly.

'Well,' she went on undeterred, 'you may well change your mind after a few days of contemplation and reflection.'

'What's contemplation and reflection?' I asked Stephen.

'Well, contemplation is when you look at something and think about it and reflection is the same but in the mirror.'

Thanks, brother. There was another definition in the dictionary: 'Retreat – a place where insane people or habitual inebriates are admitted to undergo proper supervision.' I couldn't tell if that sounded more exciting or if it was just a different wording for 'A hundred Catholic schoolboys doing religious exercises with old priests'.

The idea seemed to be that a load of prepubescent Catholic boys spent the weekend away from home at a convent where they would have Mass every day and receive lessons from priests on several different aspects of Catholicism, with the emphasis on the priesthood. There were to be communal meals and down-time, where we could visit local places of interest, play sports, in particular a Cornwall v. Devon football match, watch telly or read. Towards the end of the last day, a panel of priests would interview each pupil to ask what he thought of the weekend, how much closer to or further away from the church he felt and, most importantly, had it given him any desire to join the priesthood.

* * *

It was undoubtedly the worst weekend of my life.

It took place in the pleasant seaside town of Torquay. Torquay was named the Queen of the English Riviera by the Victorians, and was built close to beautiful beaches at the foot of seven green hills. It was also, apparently, the birthplace of Agatha Christie and Basil Fawlty. Though we didn't know this at the time. For us Cornish boys it was in Devon, therefore it was bad.

I was the youngest there and so I was the most sought-after target for, if not bullying, then general sarcasm and insult. Two rather plump boys from an exclusive school in Plymouth were the lucky winners, getting to me first and baptising me 'Garfunkel'. This was a word I'd never heard before, but it was evidently a very rude word for a young person or an idiot. It wasn't until much later that I learnt they called me this because of my frizzy hair and resemblance to the celebrated musical legend.

At nights, we were divided into 'dorms' of about twenty boys to a room. Fortunately the pig-faced Plymouth boys were in a different dorm so I was spared any lights-out aspersions. Still, to someone like me who had never been to boarding school this seemed like hell in pyjamas, but the rest of them seemed to love it. There were massive pillow fights and the conversation was distinctly irreligious. I was kept awake by several of the boys fidgeting constantly or playing with something under their bedclothes. The yells and giggles seem to go on all night. At the following morning's repulsive breakfast, the sotto voce sniggering continued and certain boys were singled out for a specific slander to do with nocturnal fumblings, the significance of which went completely over my head.

As the youngest there, I was also singled out to be the chief altar boy for the big Sunday service. At that stage in my life I had never served on the altar and I was far too nervous, or possibly shy (or even ashamed), to explain this to the priest. I didn't know when to stand, when to kneel; I didn't know when to offer water, when to offer wine and I had no idea whether I should ring the bell or not, or for how long.

'Ha, you were useless!' one of the Plymouth boys scoffed, giving me a shove. 'You rang the bell in the wrong place!'

'And you did it four times instead of three!' said the other. I was overcome with first shame, then rage.

'Fuck you and fuck your mother, you fat cunts. One day when you're in jail for kiddy-fiddling, I hope the biggest headcase in the prison kicks seventy-seven shades of shit out of you, you fucking Devonian hippos.'

Yes, these were the *exact* words that I didn't say that day. In my defence, I didn't know most of those words then and would certainly have been too polite, too well brought-up and too scared to use them even if I had. I think I opted instead for, 'Go away and leave me alone,' while going bright red and feeling nauseous.

On the afternoon of the last day came the personal interview with the panel of priests. There was a young chaplain with us in the waiting room so there was no chance for any seditious chitchat or 'non-Catholic' fun. We waited in a prim and tense silence for our names to be called. Waiting in line for something unpleasant; this seemed to be a recurring theme of growing up Catholic.

We were called alphabetically so the Russian roulette aspect of it was diminished. I came after Lyons, McBride and McFee. McFee came out red-faced and smirking and mimed a painfully sore backside in my direction. I knew he was joking but still the apprehension solidified inside me.

In the office, in an intimidating arrangement of furniture, three priests sat in a shallow semicircle facing one empty chair, which was soon filled by a very nervous version of me.

Two of the priests I'd seen before. One of them was the clearly biased cheat who'd refereed a Cornwall *v*. Devon football match the previous day. The other was the priest who had been the main celebrant at Mass that morning, who had grabbed the bell off me and put his foot on it to shut it up; the same one whose sleeve I'd poured wine over during the Eucharist. The third looked solemn and irritable. He wore one of those strange hats that foreign priests wear in fifties films set in Italy. (I probably should have known what it was called: a mitre, perhaps, or a zucchetto? Or was it a biretta? No, that's a handgun. Priests didn't wear those, well, maybe a few Italian ones, but not on their heads.) The hat, thick-framed glasses and the weighty crucifix round his neck made it clear that, in this room, anyway, he was the *capo di tutti capi.*

With exemplary sincerity and mature piety in my voice, I answered each of their questions with a whopping great lie.

In general, how was the weekend?

Great. It was a really good mix of serious stuff and fun.

How did you get on with the other boys?

Really well. It's nice to be with people who are the same age as me and share the same religious beliefs. It's also nice to meet boys from Devon.

Had you ever considered becoming a priest before you came here?

I cannot tell a lie, no, I hadn't. But having said that: yes, I have. When I was being confirmed, you know, being made a soldier of Christ, I did think about whether I had what it takes.

Has this weekend made you think any more about it? Or has it put you off?

Yes, definitely, it hasn't put me off.

What do you think you'd like most about being a priest?

Er ... well, that's an easy one. Er ... being a priest, for me, I would say, probably, er, the best thing above all the other things and, of course, there are quite a lot of good things about being a priest, very good things, I mean, would be ... er, God?

You mean being closer to God than if you were still part of the laity?

Exactly. Ha, I think that's what I was trying to say.

Good. A few quick general questions: can you name the seven sacraments?

Oh, yes. Definitely.

Well, go on then!

Oh, right … er. Baptism, penance, Eucharist, confirmation, matrimony … er, marriage.

That is matrimony!

Oh, yeah, 'course. Er, extreme unction and, er, that's seven, isn't it?

What about holy orders?

Which one's that?

BECOMING A PRIEST, THAT'S WHICH ONE!!!

Oh, sorry, I thought you meant the seven apart from that really most important one …

Were you on the Cornwall team or the Devon team yesterday?

Cornwall.

Ha, thrashed you, didn't they?

Yes, Father.

What lessons have you learnt this weekend?

* * *

I can't remember how I answered this last question but I'm pretty sure it wasn't like this.

1) I've learnt how much I hate sharing a dorm with twenty other boys.
2) I've learnt that some boys do something really disgusting under the bedclothes (something I will never do!).
3) I've learnt that even priests cheat at football.
4) I hate being an altar boy.
5) I never want to become a priest.
6) I'm never coming to Devon again.

7) I've learnt what real loneliness is and that I hate being away from home and despite what I thought about sharing a house with my parents, brothers and sister, I am really happy at home and can't wait to get back there.

8) I've learnt that I'd rather have gone to school on Friday and missed this weekend.

9) And I've learnt that there's an American pop singer called something like Simon Garfunkel and he's got frizzy hair.

No, after a weekend like that what I really needed was a proper retreat: 'The act of withdrawing or retiring in the face of opposition, difficulty or danger.'

Chapter 42

Grown-up Boy and Playtime

I had set my alarm for 8.15 a.m. It was the latest I could get away with. That would give me fifteen minutes to get ready and down to the school. Not much of a lie-in when you've been up drinking until 4 a.m., but at least I'd gone to bed numb and crashed out immediately. And there had been no dreams, thank God. No desperate odysseys of missed trains, lost luggage, plane crashes, children missing in war-torn forests; no holiday tidal waves; no barefoot teetering on the edge of giant crumbling cliffs; no death sentence in a court full of ghosts; no beautiful gifts, tantalisingly offered then snatched away; no childish delights from the past revisited for a second then lost for ever, and no taunting, smiling family snapshots. And no total and categorical sunlight.

For the four hours of sleep I'd had, my brain was, happily, a solid block of black stupor.

The clock had nearly run out of buzzes by the time I switched it off. I sat up in bed and breathed deeply, acting the part, unconvincingly, of someone who didn't feel like death. I had an appointment that was too important to miss. I had to be at my best. I stood up unsteadily and walked towards the tiny toilet and shower room.

'Ow, what the ... Oh, shit.' I had trodden on a wine glass and broken it and I was now bleeding copiously from the sole of my foot. I couldn't let this delay me. I had to be there by 8.30. There was no leeway in the timing. My clothes were spread out on the floor. Jeans, underpants and socks were one intertwined garment, just as I'd removed them the night before. My shirt was unwearably sodden with beer, and torn. I emptied a laundry bag onto the floor and found a T-shirt. It was spectacularly creased but clean. I struggled into my trainers, noticing the right sock was showing a dark, expanding red stain. Nothing I could do about that now. I'd have to set off a bit earlier to allow for limping.

The short dash downhill was painful, but the discomfort from the cut on my foot at least drowned out the nausea I felt throughout the rest of my body. The streets were full of real people, clean and sober people who were going about the daily business of getting to work and dropping off at school with an energy and optimism borne of self-confidence and self-esteem. My shabby shuffle along the pavement must have looked quite out of place.

I went past the haughty facade of the school. We'd lost sleep and had anxious dreams about getting the children into a good school. A free school. A local school. A Catholic school. We'd toyed with turning up at the end of Mass every Sunday to give the impression to the priest that we were regular Catholic church-goers and therefore suitable applicants for the good, free, local, Catholic school, but in the end it didn't matter. This was a good, Catholic school. It was very expensive and local to mother and children but not quite as local to father.

I hobbled past the high wall that flanked the side of the school and turned next left, where I came to the high wooden fence that enclosed the playground and the small playing field. I looked at my watch: 8.25, perfect.

Then a very unpleasant shock.

They'd fixed it. They'd fixed the hole in the fence. The bastards. I looked round in panic. What could I do?

Relief. My mistake. They'd re-creosoted the fence and it looked different, that was all. I was standing in the wrong place. I moved a few yards further on and there it was. A knot in the original tree had left a huge hole in one of the fence planks. I crouched down and levelled my eye to it. It gave a perfect view of the playground. A perfect view of the perfect girl. Only just standing out from the blue and red uniforms and the uniform blonde bobs was my little daughter. Her pretty heart-shaped face scrunched with laughter as she played a lively ball game with a few of her boisterous friends.

With things between me and her mother being at a particularly low ebb, I was getting increasingly nervous, if not paranoid, as all recently separated fathers do, about contact with my children, which to me, even at the best of times, seemed fleeting.

This was the high point of my day. She looked happy, which was the main thing. She wasn't standing alone in the corner of the yard worrying about her parents, wondering where Daddy was, fretting about the uncertainness of the future. Her distinctive laugh seemed to separate itself from the giggly rowdiness of the others and float directly over to me.

The circular view of my girl grew bleary with tears. I backed away from the spy-hole and took out my handkerchief to wipe my eyes. I shoved it back in my pocket, and when I looked again she'd gone. Her group of friends must have gone to the bit of the playground behind the music hut. I shuffled along to the end of the fence, grabbed the top of it and levered myself up on the corner of a low wall. Pain stabbed through my foot but there she was.

Oh my God. She was crying.

Had she seen me? Had somebody said something? But she was rubbing her knee, she had fallen over. One of her friends had an arm round her. She smiled again and pushed the friend away. They both laughed and skipped out of view again. I took out my hanky and once again wiped my eyes.

How long would this last? Stolen glimpses of my little golden girl. Getting up and beating my way through a hangover to get to school in time. Three mornings in a row now. The weather had held but autumn was on its way and if it was raining, the children would stay inside before school.

And the next question: what now? Do I go straight home and go back to bed? Do I try to work? Do I go to the pub? I looked at my watch. Just under two hours till morning break. I'd go and get a paper, sit in the café, have breakfast and come back to see my lovely girl at break.

I got down gingerly from the wall and limped off. Just as I turned the corner to the main road, I walked straight into a stern old lady and a police officer.

'That's him, constable. Looking through the fence at the little girls, he was.' I was stunned and helpless.

'This is a very serious allegation, sir,' said the policeman to me, with a pomposity beyond his years.

'Listen,' I began to explain but the old woman interrupted.

'He had his hanky in his hand. Beggars belief, these sick people.'

You think things can't get any worse, because you don't expect situations like this; ones that spring up out of nowhere and catch you completely unawares.

'I had my handkerchief out because I was crying,' I said, and took out my handkerchief because I was crying.

Chapter 43

Good Catholic Boy Serves in Mass Destruction

It was enough to make you cry.

'*Agnus Dei, qui tollis peccata mundi, miserere nobis.*'

Lamb of God, who takest away the sins of the world, have mercy on us.

Isn't that beautiful? As beautiful as the 'Hail, Holy Queen'. And in Latin.

'*Et da nobis pacem.*' And grant us peace.

Catholics in the sixties were learning Latin from the age of four, long before you had to do it in school. (Another good reason to feel separate and superior.) I remember the joy I felt at my father's pride as I sat on his knee after school one day and read the Latin Mass to him out of my prayer book. Or at least the first page. I can still remember the first line: '*Ad Deum, qui laetificat juventutem meam.*'

No idea what it meant, of course, but that was the point. The Latin Mass made us feel like participants in something truly mystical, unworldly – something almost religious! It means, 'To God, who gives joy to my youth'. I found this out years later. Imagine my disappointment.

Loving Latin, in particular the Latin Mass, was something I didn't realise I did. We would trudge with recalcitrant obedience every Sunday morning at ten o'clock to attend Mass and feel excluded by the thousand-year-old mumbo jumbo. Going to church was boring enough without a dead language chipping in with its own irrepressible yawns.

'Why isn't the Mass in English?' we whined to our parents.

'Because it's a Roman Catholic Mass and the Romans spoke Latin,' was the answer we were fobbed off with.

Then something terrible happened.

In 1962, Pope John XXIII abolished the Latin Mass. Except on special occasions, the 'Ordinary of the Mass' would be in the vernacular.

'Well, it's ridiculous that we have to celebrate the Mass in a foreign language. A dead one as well,' the elders exclaimed, nodding sagely.

I was shocked when I heard my first vernacular (English) Mass. It was no longer meaningless. It was just incomprehensible. I understood every word but couldn't quite catch what they were on about. The Ordinary of the Mass was suddenly ordinary: it was Latin that had made it exciting. It was as if the lights had been turned on in the theatre during a magic show and you could see the shoddiness of the stage and the drab innards of the tricks.

Now that Mass was in English, it was more difficult not to join in, and it was considered easier to be part of the rites and the prayer. All I could do was think how much I had enjoyed the mystical, mythical distance that Latin put between me and going to church. To this day, at Christmas, when I'm in church or in public and the crowd start singing 'Oh, Come All Ye Faithful', I can't resist banging in with '*Adeste fideles, laeti triumphantes*' and its thrillingly raucous crescendo of, '*VENITE, ADOREMUS, DOMINUM!*'

Belting!

So now Mass and church and Sundays and weekends were even more boring. What was to be done? Stop going to church? No, that would be unthinkable.

'You're old enough to be serving on the altar,' my mother informed me one Sunday morning when I was twelve.

Of course, that's it! That could be a hoot. My brother had been doing it for years; he could show me what to do, and my experience of serving on the altar at the retreat in Torquay would be but a distant memory, as would the two fat boys from Plymouth.

Within months I was a regular server at ten o'clock Mass. The service would fly by and Mass lost all its trepidation for me. There were also several perks.

You didn't have to put on your best clothes because you were covered up with your altar clothes: full-length cassock (black or red) and a crisp white cotton cotta (surplice).

One important lesson I learnt early on was to make sure I arrived at church before any of the other altar boys: HC, Plug and Pants. It was a first-come, first-served basis in the boys' vestry and, one Sunday, I was in first and put on HC's clobber. HC was the 'senior' server and usually wore the best cassock (the one that had all the buttons on it), and the cotta without the brown triangular iron stain on it.

'Er, you're wearing my robes,' HC said haughtily when he finally deigned to show up.

'I thought they belonged to the church,' I replied.

Oddly enough, that was the last word on the subject and as long as I turned up first to church, I would be wearing HC's gear. Plug was a foot taller than us and there was only one cassock that would fit him, while Pants was a bit of a maverick and insisted on wearing the one red cassock and putting his cotta on back to front to see if Father McEvedy would notice. He never did.

The first duty as altar boy was to get from the vestry – where you had changed your clothes – at the back of the church, to the sacristy at the side of the altar. This meant a walk down the aisle past what-ever members of the congregation had arrived.

Sometimes I'd thunder down the aisle, heavy-booted and author-itative, head down and businesslike, reminding the flock that I was a bit closer to the priest now than they were, and therefore closer to God. Other times, I'd affect a wafty sashay, the better to show off the flowing robes of the acolyte, my face slightly upturned for this, eyes to heaven and a reverent grimace fixed on my face. Occasionally, I'd do a slow meticulous two-step, my gaze sweeping from side to side and pew to pew as if I were a prison guard inspecting the inmates. This was made special if I got a frightened look from an old lady or a young child. When I got to the sacristy door, I'd open it, step in smartly and turn to face the congregation as I slowly shut the door with a withering, 'I'm allowed in here, you're not.' Yes, basically I was a bit of a prat.

Then it was time to light the candles. It was a point of pride for me to set them alight on the first attempt and not wiggle the long-handled taper around too much. This was another occasion when you were at the altar before Mass had begun and the congregation were filtering in. So there was time for one more, quick disdainful look at the common herd, before genuflecting in front of the tabernacle and returning to the sacristy.

When Father McEvedy arrived, it was time to help him on with his garments and try not to mention he really needed a bigger size. Pants and I used to make up rude fat jokes before he arrived and, as we helped him in the struggle with his robes, there were always barely suppressed sniggers as we contemplated mentioning that a new marquee-hire firm had just started operating in the area.

The priest would then give the appointed reader for the service the details of the epistle that was to be read. It was an extra bit of fun doing the reading and probably the last time I didn't feel sick before standing up in public and addressing a crowd of people. Reading the epistle also meant you could survey the congregation to see who was there, and who wasn't, and presented yet another occasion for a glare at noisy children, perhaps a sternish look at someone who coughed, and maybe an indulgent smile at a gurgling baby. (Thinking about it, perhaps I really *should* have gone into the priesthood.)

Most importantly, doing the reading meant you could scour the crowd for girls. Being an altar boy, in retrospect, was an unlikely way of attracting the opposite sex, but it seemed to work. Particularly as back then the only girls I knew would be girls who came to church.

At the misty age of twelve, the concept of 'girls' was not fully formed in my head or my body. But even so, from the altar, I'd be disappointed if the only girls in the congregation were the five O'Malley sisters. They were two sets of twins who all looked roughly similar and similarly rough, and a one-off called Oonagh whose different looks gave rise to whispers and nudges after Mass (whispers that were, again, meaningless to me). They were nice girls, I'm sure, but seeing only them was always a disappointment and I had no idea why. Just as I had no idea why the presence of Catherine Fielden in the flock was very much *not* a disappointment. The only physical difference I could observe between Catherine Fielden and any other girls in the parish was a painfully red face. *My* painfully red face. If I looked at any other girls and they looked at me, nothing happened. If I looked at Catherine Fielden and she looked at me, my face promptly changed colour.

The business-end of Mass was the offertory. It involved handing the priest water and wine, pouring them into various vessels, wiping the priest's hands with a cloth, ringing some bells and bowing devoutly at specific intervals. This was a nice moment because on the one hand it meant you had something concrete to do to stop you getting bored, and on the other, the congregation all had their eyes closed and heads bowed so you could have another good gawp at them.

After Mass there was just the extinguishing of the candles left to do, and a smug walk up the aisle to the vestry to get changed again.

Being an altar boy was fun while it lasted, but with each passing Sunday, I could feel that particular novelty wearing off rapidly.

Ita Missa est. Deo gratias.

It used to be.

Now: Mass has ended. Thank God.

It's just not the same, is it?

Chapter 44

Way to Go

He had only taken a few steps out of the crematorium when Jonesy, Wales's foremost painter and decorator, took out a cigarette and with exaggeratedly precise movements put it into his puckered lips. 'Ah, bliss. About time. It's a crematorium, for God's sake. One place you should be allowed to smoke.'

'It was hot in there, as well,' chipped in Danny.

'Hotter for some than others,' I pointed out.

'Frank wouldn't have minded people smoking at his send-off,' Jonesy went on. 'It's what he would have wanted. He loved a fag, did Frank.'

'Yes,' I agreed. 'You don't die of lung cancer inadvertently.'

Danny, still on a smoke-free promise from Rachel, his new 'girl-friend', was keen to change the subject.

'Anyway I'm glad that's over; I hate funerals. Whatever sort.'

'What sort of send-off are you going to have?' I inquired.

'I'm going to be cremated, definitely,' he replied instantly. 'No, actually, I think I'll go for the burial, on second thoughts. Just in case I'm not dead.'

Jonesy exhaled some cloudy death over us and asked, 'So, you'd rather wake up nailed into a coffin and suffocate, than be incinerated?'

'If I woke up alive in a coffin,' Danny answered, 'I'd bang on the lid and scream, "Let me out, I'm not dead!"'

'They might not believe you,' I suggested. 'They might say, "He's lying, leave him where he is. Get away from the coffin, it's a trap!"'

Jonesy continued, 'But if you're buried under six feet of earth when you wake up, you'd feel different, wouldn't you? You'd think, I wish I'd opted for the cremation.'

'What are you going for then, Jonesy?' Danny asked.

'I expect you'll find out in the next week or so,' Jonesy went on, returning to one of his favourite topics of conversation.

'Oh, here we go. I suppose you think it should be you today instead of Frank,' I said.

'Of course,' Jonesy said, closing his eyes and shaking his head gravely. 'Can you believe it, Frank Grennan popping his clogs?'

'Well, it was an occupational hazard for him,' I said.

'How d'you mean?'

'Well, he was a clog-popper by trade.'

Jonesy tutted. 'Now you're taking the piss. No, I mean, can you believe him croaking before me? Compared to me, he was in rude good health.'

'Compared to you, Jonesy, he still *is* in rude good health.' Strobo had joined us and had clearly decided he wasn't going to indulge Jonesy's pessimism.

'That's not nice. That's cold, that is!' Jonesy went on, failing to get any more pity. 'I'll tell you what, though, it makes you wonder. Perhaps I'm immortal. I've seen off Frank Grennan, Nobby, Peter the Heater. Perhaps I'm just meant to go on and on and on.'

'You do go on and on and on, Jonesy,' said Strobo.

Danny suddenly stuck his hand out and shouted 'Taxi!' and we were soon cramped in the vehicle headed back into town to the Maypole, Frank's old boozer.

The taxi driver looked in the mirror at me, Danny and Strobo, then turned to Jonesy next to him in the front. 'I remember you lot. You were working down the church hall on Christmas day, weren't you?'

'Indeed,' we assented.

'I was the taxi that took that dosser up to casualty. The one that got boiling soup all down the front of his trousers.'

We all murmured some sort of vague recollection. He then turned to Jonesy and said, 'And you were a mate of Richie Coles, weren't you? Colesy.'

'Colesy!' exclaimed Jonesy, 'there's another one. Forty-five and a heart attack.'

The driver added, 'That's right and fit as a fiddle. Never smoked, never drank, never did drugs and never went with dodgy birds.'

'How come you ever got to know him then, Jonesy?' smirked Strobo.

'It's a scary thought, though, death,' Danny said quietly.

'That is because,' I explained to Danny, 'you're a heathen non-believer, you see. You don't really think about the death and the after-life and all that.'

Danny thought about this and said, 'Well, the truth is, I suppose: if I die, I die.'

'What if you don't die?' asked Strobo in his whacky cyber-geek way.

'I'm sure I will,' Danny went on, not really thinking.

'Well, your dad died, didn't he?' I said helping out. 'And his dad did, and his granddad did. His great granddad did, etc, etc.'

'So, it runs in the family,' Strobo mused. 'Must be genetic.'

'My family too,' I added. 'All my ancestors ended up dying sooner or later. No, hang on. One noteworthy exception. My great, great, great, great uncle Jasper. Born in 1811. Still going strong.'

'You're kidding?' Danny asked.

'He remembers the coronation of William IV.'

The cabbie looked in his mirror with a sardonic frown.

'No?' asked a wide-eyed Danny.

'When he was nineteen he went on the first beer-and-sex package holiday in Ayia Napa.'

'Really?'

'Yeah. Club 1830 it was called.'

The driver raised his eyes briefly to heaven and pulled over and stopped the car as Danny was saying, 'You're taking the piss.'

'Right, here we are,' the driver said, adding, 'Thank God. I was getting fed up listening to that bollocks.'

At the packed bar of the Maypole we waited for our turn to be served. Jonesy was still reeling, less from the shock of the death of his close friends than from the shock that he was still alive.

'I'd forgotten about Colesy. All that exercise. Does you no good in the end. Forty-five, he was; forty-five.'

'Yeah, only sixty years younger than you, Jonesy,' said Strobo.

'Well, if it's any consolation,' Danny assured Jonesy, 'I'm sure he'll be going to heaven.'

'Yes,' nodded Jones, 'I'll probably see him there. Next week.'

'Do you think they'll let you in, Mr J?' I asked.

'Of course, especially if they take into account all my painting and decorating, to say nothing of my glittering and distinguished career as a movie extra.'

'Of course,' I said, ordering four pints of bitter.

'Don't forget,' the Welshman was orating, 'I was "drunk man in the pub" in *Turn of the Screw*.'

'Typecasting,' said Strobo, taking a sip of beer.

'And I was the first on the screen in the opening of *Alien Virus 2*. I was "dead man in car park".'

'More typecasting,' Strobo couldn't resist.

'And …' Jonesy waited till all he had all our attentions, 'Marlon Brando once told me to fuck off!'

The hushed silence didn't take long to degenerate into sniggering.

'He might be in heaven when you get there, Jonesy,' Danny said, and I added, 'Yeah, and he's going to say, "Hey, Jonesy, I thought I told you to fuck off".'

'That's not nice,' said Jonesy, pulling an unconvincing hurt face. 'I might do some painting and decorating while I'm there. Big place, heaven. Take a tidy few pots of paint for that job.'

'And,' I said, 'you'd have eternity to finish it, mate.'

'That's slightly more than you normally take for a job, isn't it, Jonesy?' said Strobo.

Chapter 45

Good Catholic Boy Meets Death, Marriage and Near-death

Now you might think that only a cynic, a world-weary pessimist or a native of the fantasy world of mother-in-law gags would couple the two concepts of death and marriage together. But having been an altar boy in a remote, provincial Catholic church forever unites them in my mind.

Marriage and death, weddings and funerals: so much in common. Both life-changing events, you can't deny that, and both, more often than not, requiring the solemnity of the Church. There are marked differences, of course, and in my experience these seem to be to do with the tone of the occasion: weddings are often sombre, strained and anxious, whereas funerals are often whacky, racy and relaxed.

The atmosphere of a wedding seems totally predicated on the massive number of tiny but vital details to do with timings, flowers, dresses, rings, speeches, food, drink, seating plans, place name-cards, weather, cars, inappropriate telegrams, the price of presents, drunken relatives, unwanted guests, unwanted family members, punch-ups and skeletons (of the cupboard variety). While a funeral, largely, I assume, because the most important person is not technically present, can be much more easy-going. It doesn't matter who you are, what you look like, what you bring, what you say, how much you eat or drink or how badly you behave because it'll either be 'just what so-and-so would have wanted' or 'so-and-so will never know', or you'll be excused because of the obvious grief you're feeling.

In general I prefer funerals by far but this is because I've never had to do a best-man speech at a funeral. As someone who deplores standing up in public and trying to be funny, especially for no money, such weddings are excruciating for me. Even if I'm not the best man, I feel such sympathetic anguish with the best man when speech time arrives that I can barely eat, drink or smile.

The last one I did was for a Catholic friend who was marrying a non-Catholic girl. The ceremony was fairly High Church Anglican and there were quite a few distinguished burghers, several worthies, citizens of an upright persuasion, society pillars and, of course, the vicar at the reception. Thankfully, there was sufficient of our mutual low-life friends (and Catholics) to balance this out, so my speech had a fighting chance of going quite well.

Several firsts in my speech-giving career were accomplished that day: I had actually written it out on cards (and legibly). I had actually practised it. And I had remained completely sober the entire day.

I was nearing the end of my speech. It had gone so well that I decided to do the flowers joke. This was down on my last card as: *Flowers joke: optional. Only include if crowd seem friendly.*

Well, they did seem friendly, and I included the joke, which purported to be about the shyness and naivety of the groom in his younger days.

In the story, the groom, whom we shall call 'P', sees a very attractive girl on the bus going home. He is struck at first sight and vows to get to meet her. However, she gets off the bus a few stops earlier than he, so he is left to continue home, downhearted. The next day he gets off at the same stop as her. Unfortunately his shyness kicks in immediately and, as she walks off homewards, he is left to wait glumly for the next bus.

This goes on, and he gets a bit closer to her every day. Smiles at her. Walks some of the way home with her, finds out where she lives, walks up to her front door then runs away and so on.

You can make this bit as long as you like, but the narrative ends when, almost a year from the first encounter, P finds the courage to go to the girl's door with a magnificent bunch of roses. He rings the bell, she opens the door and, despite quaking with fear, he manages to thrust the flowers at her saying, 'These are for you. I love you.'

The next thing P knows, she's invited him in and has told him to sit down for a moment while she goes upstairs. When she comes down a few minutes later, she is completely naked but for a pair of very high-heeled patent leather boots. Getting down to lie on the floor in front of him, she opens her legs very wide and says, 'This is for the roses!'

P replies, 'Haven't you got a vase?'

The joke caused mayhem. It certainly divided the audience. There were those who screamed with trouser-wetting laughter; those who shook their heads with an 'I can't believe he told that joke' grimace; those who didn't understand it but laughed anyway; those who did understand it and didn't laugh anyway and those who fixed me with an unwavering stare of contempt. The vicar, though, afterwards, shook my hand with hearty approbation and vouchsafed that he had contemplated telling the same joke himself.

Perhaps unsurprisingly, though, my two favourite weddings of all time were both mine: two very different and special days separated by eighteen years of ups, downs, ups, downs, ups, downs and ups-and-downs and downs-and-ups; but not necessarily in that order.

On reflection, there is generally too much emotion involved in weddings. Give me funerals any day.

But the main reason that the nuptial and the necrotic go together in my mind is that, as altar boys, we got paid for being Mass attendants on special occasions: holy days of obligation, saints' days, Christmas and Easter, weddings and funerals.

Now, by some quirk of Father McEvedy's psyche, he deemed that funerals were worth more than weddings: £5 for weddings and £10 for funerals. Christmas was equated to a wedding and earned us a fiver, while Easter, very much a death, led to the very satisfactory trousering of a tenner (thank you very much, Jesus, for dying on the cross for our sins).

One particular funeral even earned me a bit extra for an additional service. Father Mack was rambling on in his usual way, when it became clear that he'd forgotten the name of the dearly departed.

'And let us not forget, my dear brethren, that even though we are here to remember the dead, let us also remember the living. For as we are in life, we must remember that we are also in death and though we may be in death, life is all around us. For Jesus, in dying, brought us to life and when we die so do we live again with Christ and let's not forget that. Let us also not forget to remember those whose memory we are remembering today lest we forget what it was that we now remember ...' and so on.

The priest looked imploringly at me as his homily trod verbal water. I realised what was happening and was able to whisper 'Alan' quickly and surreptitiously enough for him to get through to the end with just a cough to punctuate the gap: 'So let us now remember Alan, your good servant. Alan, he was called and that was even his name. Alan as he was known to all his friends and those who knew him. Even those who did not know him knew him as Alan and that's how we shall remember him this day, O Lord. Alan, who has passed away to join you in everlasting blah blah blah ...'

After the requiem, the tenners were handed out to the three of us altar boys and, as we left the sacristy, McEvedy winked at me and stuffed a furtive fiver into my hand. God truly does work in mysterious ways.

One unusual Christmas, Mass could have been a disaster on many fronts. It involved a near-death. And Catherine Fielden. Again.

I had been chosen to be the main reader for the service. I had made sure to have no clandestine alcohol before Mass that Christmas, and my expected abstinence from food had been well over the obligatory hour. I was on top priggish form and was going to treat the drowsy and bleary congregation to a top-notch reading.

I stepped up to the lectern with my best frown in place. I surveyed the congregation with severity. Somebody coughed. I singled them out for a withering stare. It was Ed Davey, a tall, cadaverous man who'd had a mild stroke a few years before and walked with marked awkwardness. He was a gentle giant and was allowed to take the collection at the offertory, though he did it so slowly that the value of sterling had often changed by the time he'd finished. He was a sweet man, though, and a long-standing parish stalwart, though he looked as if he wasn't going to be long standing.

He coughed again with a painful splutter, but he wasn't going to put me off. A slightly longer stare. I took a theatrically deep breath. No smile, no trace of a smile, no hint of anything but the total gravity of the true acolyte. There is nothing worse than a spotty altar boy who smirks during an epistle. No smirks on my face. (Just spots.) I introduced a worldly sombreness to my best speaking voice and began.

'The first reading is taken from Isaiah, Chapter Nine.' I said this without even looking at the text. I hoped the congregation noticed. Father McEvedy nodded appreciatively in my direction. *He* had noticed.

With all my affectations in place, I looked down and intoned the words of the prophet. My mother would be pleased and the ladies of the parish would be thinking I'd make a lovely priest and, who knows, one day perhaps a bishop, and they'd be saying an extra rosary to that end.

'The people who walked in darkness have seen a great light; they that dwell in the land of the shadow of death, on them hath the light shined.'

I looked up just to check the flock was riveted to the resonance and deep wisdom that I was adding to Isaiah's frankly rather dull prose, but as my eyes were returning to the lines of Scripture, I suddenly caught a glimpse of a girl's thigh. Catherine Fielden was on the front row. Her legs were crossed and her skirt had ridden up, exposing several inches of flesh.

I should say at this point that this was several years on from the time when the sight of her would merely make my face go painfully red. As a typical fourteen-year-old, I was now all too aware of her, and the fact that she was wearing her kinky boots.

Back in the sixties, knee-length shiny leather boots were known as 'kinky boots'. For a young man, the word 'kinky' held the promise of who could say what unbridled pleasure; who could say what unfettered delights; who could say what sensual joy?

In actual fact, nobody could say. Because nobody knew what 'kinky' meant. None of my peers, anyway. Except for Callum Stevens. *He* might have known. There was a rumour that he'd been to bed with a girl. He'd been to bed with a girl on the upstairs of a bus, where I didn't even know there *were* beds. Apparently, he and this girl had *done* it; that is to say done *it*. This had caused untold excitement despite the fact that nobody knew what it was that they had done. Or rather nobody knew what the *it* was that they had done.

And so it came to pass that there before me on Christmas Eve, as I stood at the lectern doing the first reading, in front of a packed congregation, was Catherine Fielden's pale, firm left thigh, spilling out of a kinky boot and just reeking of *it*.

I looked from her thigh to her eyes and she was looking straight at me. My face turned painfully red, and this time even my ears joined in (I had hoped I was through that phase but obviously not). As best I could, I continued the lesson.

'The people who walked in darkness have seen a great light.' I realised I'd already read this bit. 'They that dwell in the land of the shadow of death, on them, hath the light shined … Er, I say again, unto thee. Once more.' Another glance at Catherine and I knew from the way she was looking at me that she knew. She knew it was she that was making me gibber. I quickly looked away again, but another furtive glance at her and I knew she knew that I knew.

I looked down at the words of the prophet. Isaiah's stuttering prose swam before my eyes. I didn't have a clue where I was.

'The people who walked in the darkness were no longer the people who walked in the darkness because a great light had shone upon them making them the people who walked in the light. Not darkness.'

A few frowns in the congregation now. Ed Davey rasped out another phlegm-rattling cough. And another. The congregation began to be more concerned with him than my rhetorical fumblings. Father McEvedy beamed podgily in my direction, nodding with beatific encouragement and clearly thinking of his Christmas dinner. I stabbed a finger at the page and hoped the text would stop swirling. 'Unto us a child is born; unto us a son is given; and he shall be called …' – I turned over two pages by mistake – '… Catherine.' I coughed and mumbled an, 'Excuse me', then continued: 'Counsellor! He shall be called Counsellor!'

The state of Ed Davey's bronchia seemed to be vying with me for the flock's attention as he let out an alarming repertoire of croaks. I ploughed on, 'He shall be called Almighty!'

Catherine Fielden lifted her skirt a little to scratch her leg.

'God Almighty!' I gasped and repeated '… he shall be called!'

Ed Davey gurgled and clutched his chest.

'God Almighty!' said the little old lady next to him. Then he collapsed.

'Jesus Christ!' said Father McEvedy.

My epistle was taken as read, as Mr Davey was helped to his feet and escorted out of the church. He had saved me from a potential nightmare and had given me every reason to believe, as I heard the ambulance approach, that a tenner would soon be winging its way towards me.

Chapter 46

Grown-up Boy Celebrates the Birth of Christ

There have been worse Christmases than this one.

In the trenches of the First World War, for example. Apart from the twenty-four-hour armistice for Christmas in 1914, and the football matches in no-man's-land. The haunting strains of 'Silent Night' played on a mouth organ, drifting across from the enemy position, as deadly in its poignancy as mustard gas.

No. Thinking about worse Christmases than this was not going to help. It would just add to the misery. Why not think of happier Christmases? The early Christmases of your childhood? Of your children?

No. That's not going to work, is it?

I had to concentrate; it was getting late. The coffee was ready and I poured a cup. Pull yourself together.

The children would be in bed by now and their mother wouldn't be up for much longer. I had about forty-five minutes to wrap the presents and take them round. And if I could get some sleep when I got back, I might be in a fit state to get up early enough and be round there before the children were up. Then they'd think I'd been there all night. Perhaps they'd think I was Father Christmas. Or did they already know he didn't exist? I couldn't remember. Should *I* tell them? That Father Christmas doesn't exist? Their friends might tell them that their father is Father Christmas. But at the time I felt that I didn't exist either.

Just get on with it. Paper, scissors, Sellotape, labels, ribbons. Right, go. My hands were shaking too much to cut straight but that didn't matter; I could always fold over where the join was and put some coloured sticky tape over it. I was useless at wrapping presents at the best of times. This was the worst of times.

I'd wandered round the West End of London the day before in a half-drunken haze, buying inappropriately expensive presents, being cursed by the people I bumbled into. And the pubs shut so early. Five o'clock they were calling time in Soho. I felt robbed of the last bit of companionship I was going to have this Christmas.

Buying drinks for strangers. Getting drinks off strangers.

Ah, now this was a lovely book. Perfect for my son; my little boy sleeping less than a mile from me in his mother's house.

I lined it up on the wrapping paper and cut as parallel to it as I could. Folded the paper over. Too much. Cut off the excess. Oh, shit, shit, shit! I'd cut through the front cover.

Shit, shit, shit!

I'd never find the end of the Sellotape like this.

Christmas. A time for families and children. But not for fathers who'd left the family home.

I had finished just one present. I would have to hurry. I took out its silvery cardboard label and began to write. 'To my lovely boy ...' I started with a tremulous scrawl, but that was as far as I got before a large tear splattered the ink and erased most of the words.

Shit, shit, shit! Perhaps it would be easier just to deliver the presents and not hang around tomorrow? Could I stand being there all day? Would the over-the-top presents and lavish treats disguise the despair I was feeling? Would my face muscles survive the strain of wearing a mask of jollity for that long?

And how long would these Christmases go on? How long would it be before we asked questions like, 'So who's having the children this Christmas?'

'How long for on each day?'

'Morning with Mum, afternoon with Dad?'

'Who had them last year?'

'And what about New Year?'

I loathed Christmas absolutely.

I used to rail against it, describing it as a vacuous week of tawdry self-indulgence, of forced jollity and excess.

An empty week of mindless self-gratification would be most welcome this year.

I started wrapping a gorgeously dressed doll for my little girl and managed to stab my finger with the scissors.

'To my darling daughter,' was as far as I got before a drop of blood ruined the label and the intricate wrapping I'd been at for five minutes.

Shit, shit, shit!

I got up from the floor where I was doing the presents and sat in the armchair. I took five minutes off wrapping for some deep breaths and the rest of my coffee, now stone cold.

I restarted my tremulous attempts at labelling my children's presents and reflected that the magic of Christmas had been briefly offered to me and then snatched away before I could properly enjoy it. After years of boozy, festive cynicism, having children had meant the seasonal joys were reawakened. I could sound excited again hearing carol singers at the door.

'Hey, listen, children, carol singers!' had replaced 'Carol singers! Quick, where's my air-rifle?'

I could enthusiastically point out to my children the Christmas trees in windows as we drove around town and enjoy their wide-eyed delight. I could stop carping, 'What sad pillocks, putting up their Christmas trees in November! How fucking chavvy is that?'

And I believed the excitement of waking up on Christmas morning with a stocking full of goodies at the end of your bed is easily matched by the excitement of trying to sneak upstairs and put out the stockings without waking your children up.

I could also, without embarrassment or inhibition, cry my eyes out at my son's school nativity play. My boy was starring as Joseph. No 'myrrh king' for him. It was the main part. The father of the Son of God (or was it the Son of Man? Certainly not the Son of Joseph). Dads with camcorders vied for the best viewpoint with sly nudges and crafty barges. In the scrimmage of the church hall, it was hard to keep the camera still but I did manage to capture a few frames of Jo walking on stage, seeing us, waving, climbing off the stage and walking over to sit on his mother's lap and take no further part in the proceedings.

Yes, the wonder of Christmas had revisited me briefly and then suddenly disappeared like Scrooge's mocking ghosts.

Shit, shit, shit!

I had dropped a present I was trying to put in the Woolworth's Santa's sack I had bought, grabbed it by the ribbon and ripped the entire wrapping off it.

I started to sob.

Deep breaths, deep breaths. Think of the future. One day, my children will be old enough to appreciate the total bollocks of Christmas. One day, they'll be all cool and cynical about Christmas and we'll agree to loathe it good-humouredly or adore it tongue-in-cheekily. And as we age together, I hope that presents will become less important. And parents too, as they made new friends. They'll have parties. They'll start saying things like, 'I'm thinking of going away for Christmas, Daddy. Is that alright?'

Of course it's alright. It's wonderful. I might even go down to Cornwall and spend one more Christmas with my ageing parents and see how much my formative Yuletides had changed. I might even accompany them to Mass.

These thoughts cheered me up as I put the badly wrapped presents in their gaudy Santa's sack.

'The people who walked in darkness have seen a great light.' The small neon bulb across the top of the mirror made me wince. My eyes were bleary with drink and tears. There were streaks of ink and splashes of blood on my face. Not a very convincing Santa, I thought, as I headed out to my sleigh to deliver magic to my sleeping children.

Chapter 47

Good Catholic Boy Goes on a Pilgrimage

'You may be interested to know,' said Bernard Davis from the front of the coach, 'that this ta-ta-ta-ta-ta-ta-ta …'

'Here we go,' whispered my brother Stephen, who was sitting next to me at the back of the coach as Davis changed his word from 'town' to 'village' to bypass his stammer.

'You may be interested to know that this … er, village, because it *is* more of a village than a ta-ta-ta-ta-ta …'

'Oops, that didn't work,' murmured Stephen.

'Ta-ta-ta-ta-ta-ta-own, St Neot, is named after Anietus who was a c-c-c-c-c-c-c …'

'-unt?' suggested Pants and we all cracked up in fits of giggles.

'C-c-c-eltic saint who preached round here around the time of the ninth century.'

Davis looked round the passengers on the coach, pleased to have finished the sentence, and pleased with himself as he passed on his knowledge to the rest of the coach. The smug ex-school teacher had taken it upon himself to stand up at various stages on the church outing and blather on about points of local interest. His self-satisfaction was so great that his pronounced speech impediment didn't hold him back, nor did his completely bald dome which, coupled with his pink roll-neck sweater, made him look, as Pants pointed out, like a six-foot prick.

The destination of this church pilgrimage was the shrine of St Blessed Cuthbert Mayne in Launceston, and the occasion certainly made for a better Sunday than most. It meant no Mass in the morning, a two-hour coach trip with lemonade, sandwiches and cakes, and reckless smutty sniggering in the back seat where me, my brother, Pants, Plug and Wicksy had ensconced ourselves just out of range of priest, nuns, parents and teachers.

'Jesus C-c-c-c-c-c,' Davis, the man-size member attempted to continue.

'Jesus Christ, spit it out, man,' Wicksy hissed, to our private amusement.

'Jesus C-c-c-c-c,' a pause, then, 'the son of God, appeared to St Neot in the guise of a fish.'

This was too much for us and we fell about laughing and posing daft questions to each other.

'How did he know it was Jesus? It could have been a fish.'

'Perhaps the fish said, "Don't eat me, I'm Jesus Christ."'

'No, coz then St Neot would have said, "Shit, a talking fish," and rung the Guinness Book of Records.'

'You, mean, "Shit, a blaspheming fish!"'

'Then he said to the man in the chippy, "'Ere, I asked for cod, not God!"'

Howls of mirth snort from the back of the coach.

This wasn't just any Launceston pilgrimage, like the previous seven I'd been forced to attend; this one was a very special occasion. It was also my last ever Launceston pilgrimage, but I wasn't to know that at the time, so this wasn't what made it special.

It was 1971, and I was fifteen years old. Last year, Cuthbert Mayne had been 'promoted'. Beatified in 1886, Cuthbert had hitherto only been 'Blessed Cuthbert Mayne' but in 1970 Pope Paul VI had canonised him so he was now St Cuthbert Mayne.

From all over Cornwall and Devon, coachloads of Catholics came to pay homage to him in Launceston, the old county town of Cornwall where he died.

Strangely, being away from the church on a Sunday gave us a rare sense of community. People who were normally just the congregation (yawn, yawn!) seemed more at ease, different, almost fun. We almost felt we belonged together and, needless to say, superior to the non-Catholics in the towns and villages we went through, who were busy going about their drab and secular Sunday.

And Cuthbert Mayne was a real historical fact. This also made it slightly easier to describe to our sceptical Protestant friends at school the next day. There were no dodgy apparitions to explain away. Launceston wasn't like Knock in Ireland, where fifteen people saw the Virgin Mary, St Joseph and St John the Evangelist hanging round the church bathed in celestial light for a couple of hours in the wilds of County Mayo. Or like Fatima and Lourdes, where simple shepherd children or an over-sensitive teenage girl saw visions of the Blessed Virgin Mary. There were no Weeping Madonnas, embarrassing statues that cried 'real' tears; no skulls that could cure leprosy; and no lameness-curing sandals that Jesus may have worn on his way to Calvary.

This was just history, and a grim history at that. In the sixteenth century, when the Protestant Elizabeth I was on the throne, the scholarly Mayne went to Oxford where, under the influence of some learned Catholic thinkers, he converted to Roman Catholicism and became a priest, working in the south-west of England. Elizabeth's soldiers tracked him down to Launceston in Cornwall where he was arrested, tried and, refusing to do a deal by recanting his faith, he was sentenced to be hanged, drawn and quartered.

The guide showing us round Launceston Castle did not spare us the details of what this bloody end entailed: 'A condemned man was roped to a wooden frame and dragged through the streets behind a horse to the place of execution. Then they were hanged by the neck but not killed. They were hanged until they were unconscious or, better still, just vaguely conscious, so they'd be aware of everything that happened next. Then they were drawn. Anyone know what that means?' A beady, threatening eye swept over us youngsters.

Pants put up his hand and said innocently, 'Someone with a pencil and paper did a sketch of them?' A few of us giggled at this but the guide was not amused.

'The victim was disembowelled, that is, had his abdomen cut open while he was still alive and had his intestines, stomach and liver pulled out and burned before his very eyes, and, at the same time, he was emasculated, that is, he had his genitals removed and they too were often burned. The body was then beheaded and quartered, that is, cut into four parts.' The guide smiled at the satisfactory silence engendered by his gruesome description.

'What if he still wasn't dead after that?' Pants asked.

* * *

On the coach home, Father McEvedy unfortunately decided to mingle with the boys at the back of the coach. This killed the day stone dead, as he had clearly decided we hadn't yet sufficiently appreciated what a huge thing dying for your beliefs is.

'Before being brought to the place of execution,' he informed us, with furtive glances at the brochure we'd all been given, 'Mayne was, apparently, offered his life in return for a renunciation of his religion and an acknowledgment of the supremacy of Queen Elizabeth I as Head of the Church. And do you know what he did?'

'Did he decline both offers and kiss a copy of the Bible?' asked Plug, also referring to the brochure.

'That's right,' the priest went on, 'and he declared that, "The Queen neither ever was, nor is, nor ever shall be, the head of the Church of England."'

Father McEvedy smiled ruefully. 'Isn't it amazing,' he continued, 'that a man could be brave enough to stand up to the huge authority of the Church, as it was then, and the State and the Monarchy and invite his destruction because of his religious beliefs?'

'Like Latimer and Ridley did, you mean?' asked Plug.

A thunderous look paled the priest's normally ruddy face.

Chapter 48

Goodbye to Sinner Boy

Can I do it? I wonder. Can I just turn up at Holy Joe's one Saturday evening and go to confession? The fact is I want to. The amazing fact is I want to.

The priests don't know me there. The only experience of confession I've ever had is with Father McEvedy, and my current list of sins would probably overwhelm him.

'Pray, Father, give me your blessing. It is seven hundred and eighty-three weeks since my last confession …'

The imaginary Father McEvedy sounds very much like the real one. I can sense warm stale-tea breath as he goes through the confessional liturgy in a soft Irish mumble, tut-tutting from the other side of the grille.

'My sins are' – I clear my throat and take a deep breath – 'lies. I have told lies. I have told so many lies that there's no way I could possibly say how many. I started counting them up to give you an exact figure and when I got to three thousand and six, I … no, forgive me, Father, that is a lie as well. I didn't start counting them up. I was just trying to sound good. I have lied to my family and my loved ones. I have lied to get myself out of trouble and I have lied to get others intro trouble. I missed a relative's funeral saying that I was very ill in bed but I was in fact on a stag weekend in Torquay. It's funny, though, as I did end up very ill in bed, though I realise it's still a sin.'

'That's not funny, my child,' says the imaginary priest, 'it's sad.'

I am disconcerted by this, but continue: 'I have wilfully missed Mass, Father, and been blasphemous on stage. It was a sketch about young men arguing about the bill after a meal in a restaurant. Thing was, it was set at the Last Supper and I played Christ. And Christ said a very rude word. At the end of the sketch he said, "This is the last bloody supper I come to."'

'Predictable,' was what I'm sure the imaginary priest tutted.

'Anyway, er, what else? Oh, I have treated people with disrespect. Everyone I've met, I think. I have insulted them and been arrogant to them. I have despised my fellow man even though I realise I am no better than them and in many ways I am worse.

'One night when I had over-indulged with strong drink, I met a girl who invited me back to her place and I intended to have a sin of the flesh with her but I didn't, Father. I didn't on this occasion, anyway. When I got back to her flat she showed me her bedroom that contained about three hundred cats. Not real cats. Soft toys, I mean. You know, sort of teddy-bear cats. And she started to introduce me to them by name, one by one. I said she was obviously a head-case and should be locked up. I said it in a friendly way, though. But she burst into tears and I went downstairs to get some more wine to calm her down and promised when I got back we'd make love. But when I went down stairs I climbed out of the lavatory window round the back and legged it. Apparently, about half an hour later, she tried to commit suicide. If she'd been successful, it would have been me who'd helped murder her, wouldn't it, Father?

'And I have, you know, er … played with myself. Paid homage to Onan, you know. Spilled my seed on the ground. Lots of grounds, in fact. Even White Hart Lane, ha! Well, that's full of wankers. Sorry, Father, just my little joke.'

'Very little,' says the imaginary priest.

'And once after another drinking session, I took a taxi all the way home. I took a taxi. I stole a taxi, I mean. The door was wide open, the

engine was running and the keys were inside. The cabbie was reliev-
ing himself in a nearby public convenience. I didn't take any of his
money although it was there in an open cash box for all to see. I may
have done him a favour by moving his cab from a dangerously public
place. He eventually turned up outside my house and asked me what
the taxi was doing there. I said it had suddenly arrived there at about
two in the morning and some bloke had got out and run away. When
he asked me if I recognised the man I told him the name and address
of someone who had once pissed me off, cheesed me off, excuse me,
Father, by copping off with a girl I fancied. Apparently, the cabbie went
round and beat him up. That was me beating him up, Father, in effect,
wasn't it?' I laughed, self-deprecatingly. 'It was all quite funny, really.'

'Not,' said the priest. 'If anything, my child, it's sad.'

'Then one day, I noticed that the girl in the flat opposite had
installed the frosted glass in her shower room the wrong way round
so that at night when her light was on and she was in the shower you
could see everything … not *you*, I mean, *I* could see everything. It
was massively bushy, Father. I had lots of sins of thought, Father. And
I daresay Onan got paid some homage.'

'I feel your sadness, child,' he interjects again, beginning to put
me off my stride. I carry on.

'I have stolen from people. I have stolen not just goods from
people. I've stolen love and time and energy. I have stolen from the
government. Is that a sin? No, it can't be, can it?

'I have disobeyed people. Most people, in fact. And I've lost track
of how many times I've taken the name of the Lord in vain, how many
times I've used abusive and violent language. And physical violence,
or threat thereof.

'I think I raped somebody once but it was inadvertent. I didn't
think I was raping her at the time. And she didn't think I was till about
three days later when I called her by her sister's name when we were
in bed. That was supposed to be a joke, Father. But I'm sure I've forced
myself upon unwilling women.'

'Oh, dear,' says the priest letting out a very long, lingering sigh of either contempt or boredom. Probably both.

'I'm lazy at work,' I continue, getting into my stride now. 'I hate my work; that's why I'm lazy about it. I know it's no excuse. I've let people down. Hundreds of times. I have attempted to kill people and wished people dead. I have been gluttonous and drunk. Once I threw a scalding-hot Cup-a-Soup at next door's cat when I found it crapping in our window box.

'I have broken the laws of the land by dabbling with banned substances. Usually cannabis. Once, when I had the munchies after eating a hash-cake, I ate four goldfish in a tank in a doctor's waiting room. I took coke on a few occasions, though strictly speaking it wasn't cocaine as it came from Walking Dead Dave and his stuff is mainly crushed caffeine tablets and Polyfilla.

'I have lost my temper and caused actual harm to people and damage to objects. I once lost my temper and put my foot through my mate's television screen when Noel Edmonds won a Bafta.

'I went with a girl of loose virtue and caught an anti-social disease. Then I knowingly slept with another girl and passed the infection on to her. And to two other girls but I didn't know then that I'd got a dose, as it were, Father.

'I have ridiculed the Pope during the televised Easter Address. Worse, I did it in front of others to cause deliberate offence. But I did end up knowing how to say "Christ is risen" in fifteen different languages. I don't know if that makes it any better, Doctor. I mean, Father.

'Oh, and there was this girl. JJ. She was the only girl I—'

'I think we've heard enough about her, thank you very much,' the priest interrupts with surprising vehemence.

'Oh, right, well, er, the thing is, I suppose, since I left home, left school, left the Church, my life's had no structure, no timetable. It's been chaotic. I'm self-employed for work, so there are hardly any external rules at all. I'm too weak, lazy or frightened to impose a routine on my life. In short, I'm a lazy, selfish, drunken, overweight waste of space, with a gaping emptiness in my soul that I try to fill with self-indulgence and cheap thrills. I hate myself and have nothing to live for. I'm basically just a cunt, Father, pardon my French.'

There is a long pause. Have I offended him? Are my sins too massive for him to cope with?

When he does eventually speak, it is with unexpected tenderness: 'Thank you for your confession, child. You told me so much. Not by what you told me but by what you didn't tell me. What you told me was garbage. Silly macho stories that you hoped might impress me, while hoping still to give the impression you were confessing. You were half confessing, half not-confessing. You were trying to be funny and that's what I find most sad. Being funny is your way of protecting yourself. That's why I had to say, "That's not funny, it's sad." You don't offend me by your stories; I just hear the sadness of a child lost in the dark and whistling to pretend he's not frightened. What you are "confessing" to me is that you're wearing a mask. That's easy. That's not a confession. What you should do is take the mask off and show your face. That's a confession.'

The imaginary priest is full of wisdom. I feel a lump in my throat and pricking in my eyes.

'What should I do, Father?'

The reply is not what I'm expecting, even from an imaginary priest.

'Grow up, and get a fucking life.'

Chapter 49

Goodbye to Grown-up Boy

Suicide.

Is it really born of total, abject misery?

Is it sometimes an angry gesture to punish those who have hurt you?

Once again I was on the Hornsey Lane bridge over Archway Road. Suicide Bridge. I recalled a time, about eleven years ago, when I stood on this very spot having spent a wild night of anger and revenge seeking out Michelle and Opera Paul to punish them. I recall thinking that that moment was the lowest point in my life.

It would have been hard to imagine or predict a worse time in my life.

And yet here it was.

How could I have thought what happened with Michelle and Paul was remotely painful? That now seemed a laughable aberration. A rather embarrassing adolescent romp. That was nothing compared to this. Splitting up with my wife, being separated from my children, uncertain of our future and living in a squalid bed-sit in Hampstead.

And within days of all that, this.

For reasons I won't go into I found myself out of the television company I'd co-founded. The company had been the last thing I had. The remaining security. Now that had gone too; with spookily bad timing.

Where was I now? Oh yes, suicide bridge. How did I end up here? I felt I was reliving the worst day of my life, only worse. I leant over the parapet and gazed down at the A1, busy with evening traffic. A sudden pang of vertigo made me recoil instinctively and step backwards into the road behind. A horn blared and brakes screeched.

'Watch where you're going, you pisshead!' yelled the driver.

I could hear my mother's voice: 'Your guardian angel must have been looking after you.' I clung to the railings of the bridge; lungs panting, heart pounding. Of course it's a sin. A mortal sin. It was the same as murder. The fact that it was you being murdered was irrelevant; it was you doing the murdering.

Angels and sin.

Would the Church ever leave me alone?

And then, again, as if on cue, there it was, squatting massively in front of me: St Joseph's Roman Catholic Church, Highgate. Sturdily forbidding, not quite at the top of Highgate Hill but nevertheless dwarfing the surrounding land, an upright finger of authority and menace.

* * *

I walked the four miles from the company's office to Hampstead. I had to keep moving. Taxis, buses or the underground were out of the question. That would mean seeing people. Talking to people. Worse, people seeing me and looking at me. Would they know? Could they tell?

Ironically, for someone so unwanted, I felt like a wanted man. I scuttled through the streets like a fugitive, a guilty man, a criminal. I kept my head down and collar up, expecting any moment that a car would pull up beside me and a man get out and arrest me.

Why was I going to Hampstead? I couldn't go to my shitty bedsit. Hampstead is a nice place, but for me then it was just the place where I didn't live with my children. I couldn't go back there, I had to keep moving.

Nor could I go and see Mary and the children. I was uncertain of how sympathetic she would be and it would be too painful for me, and probably for them, to let the children see me like this.

I got to Hampstead and carried on walking; a further two miles to Highgate.

And suddenly I was in church again.

Away from the nearby rush-hour traffic, there was only coolness, serenity and placid harmony. I made my way down the aisle and went and sat in the front pew as the late afternoon sun illuminated the stained-glass windows with almost unbearable beauty.

Agnus Dei, qui tollis peccata mundi, miserere nobis. 'Lamb of God, who takest away the sins of the world, have mercy on us.'

I thought of Opera Paul and Michelle, I thought of JJ, of my wedding in this church, my children's baptisms, in this church, and I cried. The interior of the building was resplendent in the levelling rays of golden, western light.

It was a strange place to be experiencing hell. But as life continues ruthlessly intruding into your life, you get to redefine Hell. Hells are relative and personal. Outsiders can't really know what it's like. There are unquestionably massive hells, total hells: the Nazi death camps, war, torture, disease, the loss of a loved one, the loss of a child. Nothing in my life could match those, of course, but numerous shards of hell had cut into my life that gave absolute pain. Girlfriend one, Philippa, leaving me. Then others; finding out that JJ had got married to someone without telling me. More girlfriends leaving me for other men; the shock of Willow James's death; the tragic accident that led to the death of one of my best friends; my separation from wife and children; the abhorrence of being left on my own, which led to disconsolate, pointless all-night binges with faceless drunkards; not being allowed to see my children; the excruciating awkwardness of parent–teacher meetings; harrowing post-separation birthday parties; the torture of saying goodbye at the end of contact weekends; the bleak pizzas and burgers after school on the occasional weeknight; a silly and unsatisfactory one-night stand that had gone appallingly wrong and ended up with me in a 'clinic' with a sobbing girl I hardly knew.

And now this.

My heart and mind and lungs were racing as I thought back over what had happened in the last few hours. My life had changed so much. The certainty of family, of work, of career had gone in a few days.

What was left for me now?

What was waiting round the corner?

What else was going to give me an unpleasant shock?

A sudden hand on my shoulder.

I jumped and turned round viciously: 'What the …?'

'Relax, relax, my friend.' It was the calm and measured voice of Father Henry, one of the priests who had officiated at my marriage to Mary and baptised my children. I doubted if he would remember me. To him I would have probably looked like one of those sad middle-aged lapsed Catholics who were going through a bad time and come into the church for a bit of peace and quiet; a tormented soul, a wretch fallen again from the right path and seeking sanctuary from whatever demons lurked beyond the walls of this holy fortress. He must find at least one in his church every day. At least he wouldn't recognise me.

'Hello, Rory, how are you?' His good cheer was out of place in the gloom. 'Hope the children are well.'

'Yes, er, thank you, Father,' I stuttered.

'Ah well, I can see you need a bit of time to yourself; a bit of time for reflection. I'll leave you be. Here.' Before he went he held out his hand to me. He was holding a white envelope. I assumed it was a prayer card or a religious pamphlet, or a flyer for some forthcoming parish events. I shook my head. 'No, it's alright, thank you, Father.'

He laughed. 'It's yours. You dropped it on the way in. It looks personal.' I took it and, as he walked away, he said, 'Be patient, child, you never know what's waiting round the corner. Good things can happen, too.' And he left chuckling to himself.

I looked at the envelope. It was part of the huge pile of post that I was handed at the office. I'd stuck most of the stuff straight in the bin but this envelope was marked 'personal'.

It contained a card. A simple floral design and inside, it was blank for a personal message, which read:

Rory, I wonder if you ever think about me, and that fabulous time we had all those years ago? I often think of you. I wonder what you're up to. Are you still spotting birds? Are you married? I'm getting divorced. Shall we meet up? (address and number are below.) Perhaps you won't have time for me. Perhaps you won't even remember me. Anyway, I thought I'd say 'hello'. Hello! All my love, JJ xxx

Chapter 50

Goodbye to the Good Catholic Boy

I woke up suddenly. The pale green hands on my bedside alarm clock showed 3.15 a.m. A car drove past, its headlights making shadows sweep across the bedroom walls. I turned over and pulled the quilt over me, hoping not to return to my dream of a misty graveyard where hooded figures loomed over me, mumbling curses in Latin, and gnarled fingers stabbed at me.

Wait, what was that? A sound downstairs. A creak of wood as a hand was placed on the banister. Footsteps getting closer. Someone was coming up the stairs to my bedroom. Someone holding an axe. Move, why didn't I move!? Why didn't I just get out? Hide under the bed! Scream! Why didn't I scream? My bed was now only feet from the axe-man. The blade glinted momentarily in the moonlight. I ran my fingers along it. This would do the job nicely. I barged the bedroom door open, stepped in and raised the axe. My bed was empty. I got in and put the axe under my pillow and waited for me to return …

I woke up suddenly. I peered into the gloom and, as my eyes adjusted, disapproving priests and tutting nuns changed back into clothes hanging on doors.

There was no going back to sleep now. I'd just lie there and wait for the worst day of my life to arrive.

Slowly the ashen light seeped into the room through the crack in the curtains and settled dustily on familiar, mundane objects. The room brightened pink then gold. It was going to be a sunny day. Oh no, I wanted rain today. I wanted greyness. I wanted darkness. Please God, not a sunny day. Not bright, inescapable, implacable sunlight.

Ah well, why not? The hiding was over.

'I'm not coming to church today,' I shouted from my bed, down the stairs, trying to sound matter-of-fact.

There.

I'd said it. I'd finally said it.

It had taken just under two seconds.

And the previous sixteen years, as well, I suppose. But I'd said it. Three years later than I'd originally planned, but now it was over.

Relief was drowned out immediately by the onrush of fear; the fear that had held me back for so long. What would my mother and father say? What would my brothers and sister say? The priest, the nuns, the teachers? How would my mother explain my absence from the church, from the altar? Wasn't I serving today? Wasn't I reading?

Perhaps it was really ill-mannered of me to do it so abruptly. Should I have given a week's notice?

'Er, look, Mum and Dad, I'm going through an existential crisis that may result in a total abandonment of my faith – an apostasy. So, can you call Father McEvedy and say I won't be going to church any more, serving on the altar again or doing the reading ever? Starting from next week, though, just so he'll have time to organise a stand-in?'

I wasn't convincing myself. Perhaps I should change my mind. I could say, 'No, only joking!' and leap out of bed and get dressed.

No, I couldn't unsay it. I couldn't go back on my word. My word to myself.

I owed it to myself.

For years I'd done it just for others. Not for God, not for me, but for parents and priests and nuns and fellow parishioners. Now, I was doing something for myself.

Was I being selfish?

No, I was being realistic. Was I being cowardly? No, I was being brave. This wasn't easy. This was an upheaval. This was a revolution. I was standing up to my parents, to my upbringing, to most of my education. I was standing up to God. A non-existent God, to my new way of thinking, but a God all the same.

Perhaps I should just try it out for a few weeks.

Yes, I'd tell my parents that I was seeing what life as an agnostic was like for a month or so and if I didn't like it, I'd return to the Holy Roman Catholic Church of St Peter. And I probably wouldn't like it, so I'd be back on the altar by Pentecost.

How long is that away? Well, today is Passion Sunday, so that means … what? Oh, no, today is Passion Sunday! The first Sunday of Passiontide!

Two weeks before Easter, Lent turns into a subsection known as Passiontide, which includes Passion Sunday, Palm Sunday and Easter Sunday. The axis on which the Catholic Church revolves. We were less than a fortnight away from the day that marked Jesus Christ's awful death on the cross to save us all from our sins, and I was about to spit in his face and walk arrogantly away. I was worse than one of the Roman soldiers, nailing his twitching, frightened hand to the rough wooden cross. Perhaps I should have waited until after Our Lady's Day, get the procession out of the way? Summer's a very slack time in the RC Church, feast days and saints' days are fairly thin on the ground. Maybe.

No, it's too late now. You've said it. You've said, 'I'm not coming to church today.'

I awaited the angry whirlwind.

'What?' my mother shouted back.

She hadn't heard. Or was she giving me a chance to change my mind, to rethink what I'd just said? She was testing me. Challenging me to see if I'd have the gall to say it twice. Or maybe she didn't hear me.

'What did you say? I didn't hear you.' She sounded annoyed.

This annoyed me.

'I said, "I'm not coming to church today."'

I'd made it through the first fifteen seconds.

'Don't be ridiculous!' was the dismissive reply. 'We're leaving in twenty minutes.'

There was to be no debate. Mum then also lobbed a small guilt-bomb up the stairs: 'Don't forget it's Passion Sunday today.'

I ducked. That was close. I came out fighting.

'I hadn't forgotten. I'm still not going to Mass.'

'Twenty minutes, I said. You won't have time for breakfast with this carry-on.'

She walked away from the foot of the stairs. I could hear serious adult exchanges punctuated by my brothers' sniggering. It was my father's turn.

'Come on, love. Stop messing about and get ready. We don't want to be late. I don't want to end up having to do the reading instead of you. Neither will the congregation.' My father's gentleness and humour made me feel worse. The whole affair seemed suddenly personal. It was between me and my father. I was upsetting him and no one else in the world. Was it worth it? Why didn't I just go and get it over with? After all, that's what I'd been doing for years. It was just an hour of boredom and irritation.

My vacillation was interrupted by my mother's forceful footsteps up the stairs.

'What the hell's brought this nonsense on?'

'I'm fed up with it. I don't want to do it any more.' I was still lying in bed, face turned to the window, avoiding my mother's eyes by watching the languid, snowy M-shapes of gulls wheeling against the blue spring sky.

'I've never heard anything more ridiculous,' she tutted. I awaited a further barrage of guilt.

'You're supposed to be serving today. What if Father McEvedy can't get another altar boy?' Answering this question didn't seem to be the main problem but I wasn't up to discussing the subject, so as usual in these episodes, I took up the tried and tested Sword of Sarcasm.

'It'll probably be the end of Roman Catholicism on Earth and the rivers will turn to Guinness and lobsters will rain down from the clouds and—'

'Don't you dare speak to me like that! What am I supposed to say to Father McEvedy?'

Before I could think of a suitably petulant reply to this, my father shouted from the bottom of the stairs: 'Come on, love. Leave him. It's quarter to!'

'You haven't heard the last of this,' Mum said and was gone. I heard muted anger from below. Snappy, muffled comments. Laughter followed by sharp recrimination. Doors banged. Car engine started. Car doors slammed. Wheels and gravel and car speeding off and … it was over.

It was over.

I was alone in the house.

But something else. I was also alone in the world. Though this wasn't absolutely clear to me at the time.

I smiled with anticipation. A new life had begun, I thought.

Though I had forgotten that an old life had died.

No more prayers, confession, Mass, Benediction, rosaries, processions, abstinences, the boring sermons, the meaningless liturgy, the dressing-in-best clothes, the irksome visits from priests, the yawning, the eerie feeling that your mind was not your own and that every thought you had had to be examined by a committee, that your every action had be assessed and processed in advance. I was free from so much.

Or so I thought. Had I also inadvertently 'freed' myself from certainty, safety, comfort, shelter, steadiness, confidence and hope?

I jumped out of bed and wondered if there was still time to get to church.

No, it was over. I was alone in the house, silent but for the gulls' laughter tumbling from the sky.

Or was it crying?

Chapter 51

Goodbye to Jonesy

'So *did* you commit suicide then?' Strobo asked. His wide, constantly blinking eyes made it seem that to him everything in the world was consistently unbelievable or always a total surprise.

'Yes, I did,' I admitted.

'You look well on it.'

'No, sorry,' I corrected myself. 'I didn't commit suicide.'

'And Tori, who you live with now; she's JJ?'

'Yes,' I explained, 'JJ was a silly nickname she had when she was younger.'

'Oh that's neat,' blinked Strobo, 'so you all lived happily ever after.'

'Yes, we all lived happily ever after,' I said, adding, 'for ever and ever, Amen.'

'Unlike Jonesy.' The blunt interruption came from Danny who'd just joined us outside the church.

Yes, there we all were in our best suits again, outside yet another church. But Jonesy, Wales's foremost painter and decorator and occasional film extra, wasn't with us on this occasion. He was 'detained' in church.

'It's a bit rude leaving before the end, isn't it?' Danny went on.

'It's what Jonesy would have expected,' Strobo pointed out. 'He'd be out here with us' – he paused – 'if circumstances had been different.'

'"The next time I'm in church will be for my funeral" were his words,' Danny reminded us as he took out a cigarette and lit up. Strobo and I exchanged shocked looks.

'You're smoking again!' I exclaimed.

'It's for Jonesy,' Danny said unconvincingly.

'Rachel's blown you out finally then?' asked Strobo.

'She didn't blow me at all,' Danny replied.

'So she's out the window for good, then?'

''Fraid so,' Danny admitted. 'At least I can have a snout again. Though it does seem strange to be leaving a church early for a fag and not have Taff the Splash with us.'

'I'm surprised it was a church service, though,' Strobo observed. 'I thought it would be something a bit more pagan for Jonesy. Something more "new-agey".'

'Rituals are very important,' I said. 'It makes it more part of history and tradition. Makes it more solemn and formal.'

'You sound like you're going back to the faith,' scoffed Danny.

'But I think there's something important about marking birth, marriage and death in a ritualistic way. Not particularly in a Catholic way.'

Strobo pointed an inquisitorial finger in my direction and asked, 'Well, tell us this, pray: do you have any regrets that you were brought up a Catholic?'

I didn't like questions like that. Questions about me addressed directly to me. My least favourite sort. It was also a difficult question and one that I struggled to find a smart-arse way to avoid answering. The inclusion of the word 'regrets' was my escape route. What's the point of regret? It's a waste of emotion. You can't go back and change what you did or didn't do, so what's the point of regretting it? I was happy to be where I was then in my life so how could I regret anything?

'Hey, today I'm happy with my life. How can I regret anything that's contributed to that? How can I wish undone anything that has led me here today? To happiness?'

'Mmm.' Strobo frowned. 'I'm sure you've avoided answering my question. Let me put it this way: are you a better person for having been brought up a Catholic?'

'One hundred per cent,' I said emphatically, as much to convince myself as my two companions. 'Listen, it may not be to do exclusively with Catholicism. My parents are good people who brought me up well. They were Catholics and it played an important part in their upbringing and their world view so it's hard for me to separate, in my upbringing, what was Catholic and what was parental. Their faith made them in part what they were and this had a bearing on me. I am more a product of my parents than of the Catholic Church. If I hadn't been brought up a Catholic I believe I would be a worse person than I am now.'

'Fuck me, what a monster that would be!' Danny smirked in between drags.

'But, hey, why are we talking about me? This is Jonesy's day!'

They agreed and moments of awkward silence passed till Danny said, 'If he was here with us now, we wouldn't be here. We'd be across the road in the boozer.'

We nodded and Strobo asked, 'How come so many churches are built so close to pubs?'

'It's a Catholic thing,' I assured him. '"People are thirsting after faith," my father used to say.'

'Do you think,' Strobo started hesitantly, 'that it's because of … er, alcohol, that Jonesy … er, that we're here today?'

A pause for reflection.

'Could be,' said Danny.

And I said in a below-average Welsh accent, 'It'll be me next. I know I've got to pay for my sins sooner or later; do your worst, God!'

Danny and Strobo smiled ruefully and Danny recalled Wizzer's do. 'Four years ago it was and Jonesy was in tears. Inconsolable, he was.'

Then it was Danny's turn to do a Welsh accent, even worse than mine, though I say it myself. 'Why Wizzer, of all people? It's not fair, it should have been me! Another one of my drinking buddies I'll never see again.'

'And now Jonesy himself has succumbed,' Strobo added, not attempting a Welsh accent.

'He'll stop drinking and smoking, though, won't he?' I thought out loud.

'It's an extreme way of doing it,' Danny suggested, 'and I'll tell you something: he's going to lose weight now.'

'Right, enough of this talk,' said Strobo decisively. 'Pub?'

'Good idea,' said Danny, lighting up what must have been his third in as many minutes.

'You're back on those things with a vengeance,' I said.

'I'm smoking to forget.'

'So how far did your non-smoking get you?' Strobo asked, keen for the graphic details.

'I'd rather not go there,' Danny said resolutely.

'So did you go there, then?' Strobo insisted.

'I'm trying to forget Rachel,' Danny said firmly. 'I don't want to talk about her. Let's go to the pub.'

'Green Dragon?' I suggested.

'I said I don't want to talk about her!'

We laughed and Strobo said, 'Well, come on, we can't go to the pub without saying a proper goodbye to Jonesy.'

We agreed and at that very moment the main doors of the church swung open and there he was.

Jonesy.

And his new bride.

'Ah, what a lovely couple,' I said only slightly mockingly.

'Yes, she has,' said Danny, going in a different direction.

'Let that be a warning to us all,' Strobo said portentously. 'Don't go speed-dating when you've had two bottles of wine and a spliff.'

'Ah, yes,' I said. 'Proverbs; chapter 3, verse 18?'

Danny shook his head. 'Fancy Jonesy marrying a vegetarian.'

'A PE teacher, as well,' Strobo added.

'She'll lick him into shape,' said Danny.

What a deeply unpleasant image, I thought to myself, as we went over to congratulate Wales's foremost painter and decorator and occasional bit-part actor on his new life.

Acknowledgements

The author would like to give special thanks to Ali Nightingale and Andrew Goodfellow at Ebury; Gordon Wise and Jacquie Drewe at Curtis Brown; Mari Roberts; Belinda Jones; Jonathon Simpson at JPSPC-Repair and all my family and friends who have directly or indirectly, deliberately or accidentally, knowingly or unwittingly contirubuted to this book. Thanks for your patience and good humour.